# History *and* Hope

# History and Hope

## The Alliance Party of Northern Ireland

Brian Eggins

First published 2015

The History Press Ireland
50 City Quay
Dublin 2
Ireland
www.thehistorypress.ie

British Library Cataloguing in Publication Data.
A catalogue record for this book is available from the British Library.

ISBN 978 1 84588 864 0

Typesetting and origination by The History Press

Printed and bound in Great Britain by TJ International Ltd.

# Contents

# Glossary

| | |
|---|---|
| AIA | Anglo-Irish Agreement |
| APPG | All Party Parliamentary Group |
| AV | Alternate Vote |
| CEDAW | Convention on the Elimination of all Forms of Discrimination against Women |
| CSI | Cohesion, Sharing and Integration |
| DDPs | District Policing Partnerships |
| DUP | Democratic Unionist Party |
| ELDR | European Liberal Democrat and Reform Party |
| FAIT | Families Against Intimidation and Terror |
| ICIR | Independent Commission for Information Retrieval |
| IICD | Independent International Commission on Decommissioning |
| IIMC | Independent International Monitoring Commission |
| IMB | International Monitoring Body |
| IRA | Irish Republican Army |
| ISE | Irish School of Ecumenics |
| LGBT | Lesbian, gay, bisexual people and transgender people |
| LGBTQ | Lesbian, Gay, Bisexual, Transgender and Questioning |
| LVF | Loyalist Volunteer Force |
| MLA | Member of the Legislative Assembly |
| NICIE | Northern Ireland Council for Integrated Education |
| NICRA | Northern Ireland Civil Rights Association |
| NILP | Northern Ireland Labour Party |
| NIO | Northern Ireland Office |
| NIWC | Northern Ireland Women's Coalition |
| OFMDFM | Office of First Minister and Deputy First Minister |

| OTRs | 'On the Runs' |
| PD | People's Democracy |
| PR | Proportional Representation |
| PSNI | Police Service of Northern Ireland |
| PUP | Progressive Unionist Party |
| RIC | Royal Irish Constabulary |
| RUC | Royal Ulster Constabulary |
| SDLP | Social Democratic and Labour Party |
| SOPG | Strategic Operational Planning Group |
| STEM | Science, Technology, Engineering and Mathematics |
| STV | Single Transferable Vote |
| TUC | Trades Union Council |
| TUV | Traditional Unionist Voice |
| UCUNF | Ulster Conservatives and Unionists New Force |
| UDP | Ulster Democratic Party |
| UKUP | UK Unionist Party |
| ULP | Ulster Liberal Party |
| UPNI | Unionist Party of Northern Ireland |
| UUP | Ulster Unionist Party |
| UUUC | Ulster Unionist United Coalition |
| UUUM | United Ulster Unionist Movement |
| UVF | Ulster Volunteer Force |
| UWC | Ulster Workers' Council |
| VUP | Vanguard Unionist Party |

# Chronology of the Alliance Party

1969 'Ulster at the crossroads' speech by Terence O'Neill
     New Ulster Movement established
1970 Formation of Alliance Party
1972 Phelim O'Neill becomes party leader
     Involvement in talks at Darlington
1973 Oliver Napier becomes party leader
     First elections: local government 13.3%, sixty-three seats
     Assembly elections: 9.3%, eight seats out of seventy-eight
     Sunningdale talks about the Council of Ireland
     Power-sharing Executive set up with Oliver Napier and Bob Cooper
     as Alliance ministers
1974 February Westminster elections: Alliance 3.2% from three seats contested
     Ivor Canavan First Alliance Mayor of Derry
     UWC strike and fall of executive
     October Westminster elections: Alliance 6.4% from five seats contested
1975 Convention elections: 9.8%, eight seats out of seventy-eight
1976 The Peace People
     Bob Cooper Fair Employment Agency
     Bertie McConnell is elected Mayor of North Down
1977 Local government elections: best result – 14.4%, seventy seats
1978 Lord Henry Dunleath's Bill passed to set up integrated education
     David Cook is elected Lord Mayor of Belfast City
1979 Westminster elections: Alliance 11.9% (more than DUP)
     First European elections: Oliver Napier gets 6.8%
1980 Atkins talks

1981    Hunger strikes in Maze prison. Hunger striker Bobby Sands wins
by-election for Fermanagh/South Tyrone
Local government elections: Alliance 8.9%, thirty-eight seats

1982    Prior 'Rolling devolution'
Assembly elections: Alliance 9.3%, best Assembly result, ten seats
out of seventy-eight. SDLP and Sinn Féin refuse to take their seats,
as there is no 'Irish dimension'
John Cushnahan is chair of Education Committee

1983    General election

1984    New Ireland Forum – Alliance decline to attend
European elections: David Cook 5.0%
John Cushnahan becomes party leader

1985    Anglo-Irish Agreement – supported by Alliance
Local government elections: Alliance 7.1%, thirty-four seats

1986    Alliance withdraws from Assembly, which then folds

1987    Successful High Court actions by Alliance members against
Castlereagh, Belfast and Lisburn Councils, to resume normal business
Westminster general election: Alliance 10%
John Alderdice becomes party leader

1988    Alliance document 'Governing with Consent'
'Secret' Talks at Duisburg – UUP, DUP, SDLP, and APNI
Forum for Peace and Reconciliation Alliance attends

1989    Local government elections: Alliance 6.9%, thirty-eight seats
European elections: John Alderdice 5.2%

1990    Brooke/Mayhew talks

1992    Westminster General election: Alliance 8.7%

1993    Local government elections: Alliance 8%, forty-four seats
Downing Street Declaration

1994    Framework Document and peace negotiations
European elections: Mary Clarke-Glass 4.1%
First IRA ceasefire

1996    Election for Negotiating Forum: Alliance 6.5%, seven seats

1997    Westminster general election, Labour wins. Alliance 8.0%
Local government elections 6.6%, forty-one seats

1998    Good Friday Agreement signed
Referendum on Good Friday Agreement: 71% yes votes in north,
94% yes in south
Assembly elections: Alliance 6.5%, six seats
Lord Alderdice resigns from party leadership

Seán Neeson becomes party leader

Lord Alderdice becomes Speaker of new Assembly

1999   David Alderdice is Lord Mayor of Belfast

European elections: Seán Neeson 2.1%

2001   Local government elections: Alliance 5.3%, twenty-eight seats

Westminster general election, Alliance does not stand in North Down, South Antrim and Upper Bann. Alliance vote is 3.6% from ten contested

Three Alliance MLAs temporarily redesignate to 'Unionist' to ensure re-election of Trimble and Mallon as First and Deputy First Ministers

David Ford becomes party leader

2002   Betty Campbell is elected Mayor of Lisburn, newly designated a city

2003   Alliance launches policy paper on Community Relations, 'Building a United Community'

Assembly elections: Alliance 3.7%, six seats out of one-hundred-and-eight

Anne Wilson is Mayor of North Down and Jim Briar is Mayor of Ards

2004   European elections: John Gilliland independent with Alliance support 6.6%

Tom Ekin is elected Lord Mayor of Belfast

2005   Local government elections: Alliance 5.0%, thirty seats

Westminster elections: Alliance 3.9% from twelve contested

John Matthews is Mayor of Larne

2006   Lynne Frazer is elected Mayor of Newtownabbey

Eileen Bell is Speaker of Assembly

2007   St Andrews Agreement

Assembly elections: Alliance 5.2%, seven seats out of one-hundred-and-eight

2009   European Elections: Ian Parsley 5.5%

Naomi Long is elected Lord Mayor of Belfast

2010   Naomi Long wins first Westminster seat in East Belfast: overall Alliance vote 6.3%

Fortieth Anniversary celebration of founding of Alliance Party

David Ford becomes Minister of Policing and Justice

2011   Local government elections: 7.7%, forty-four seats

Assembly elections 7.7%, eight seats out of one-hundred-and-eight

Dr Stephen Farry becomes Minister for Employment and Learning

Death of Sir Oliver Napier

2012   Flags protests

2013   Haass talks

2014   European elections: Anna Lo 7.1% – best Alliance performance

Elections to new local government councils: 6.7%, thirty-two seats

# Preface and acknowledgements

From the history of the troubles in Ireland in 1970 came a new political party expressing the hope of a less sectarian, reconciled and shared society. The aim of this book is to describe the origins, development and history of the Alliance Party of Northern Ireland up to 2014. Its successes and failures are charted; analyses and criticisms are made. The book describes and discusses the principles, some of the policies and the organisation of the party. Broad-brush portraits are given of the six party leaders and eight deputy leaders. The attitudes and involvement of party members towards religion and identity are presented. There is an analysis of the contribution of the party towards reconciliation. The opinions and analyses are entirely my own, unless otherwise stated. Included are some anecdotes of members' experiences particularly during election campaigns.

The idea for this book originated with my MPhil dissertation, 'The Contribution of the Alliance Party to Reconciliation', submitted as a part of the Irish School of Ecumenics (ISE) Course in Reconciliation Studies. The MPhil award was made through Trinity College Dublin in 2003. I took this course on retirement as Emeritus Reader in chemistry at the University of Ulster at Jordanstown, having previously taken an ISE course in Ecumenics in 1990–1992.

I came to Northern Ireland in 1972 to take up a post as chemistry lecturer at the new Ulster Polytechnic in Jordanstown. I had heard about the Alliance Party and quickly became a member, having had previous history of involvement with the Liberal Party in England. I was soon a member of the local Jordanstown branch of the Alliance Party and committee and attended annual conferences, initially in the Ulster Hall in 1973. I was an observer at the count for the new STV elections for local government in Newtownabbey and for the new power sharing Assembly in South Antrim in 1973. I subsequently served as chair of the Newtownabbey Alliance Party Association, later of the South Belfast Association and then of the South Down Association. During this time I was frequently involved as an election agent for Alliance Party candidates, was a regular member of the Party Council and from time to time a member of the Party Executive Committee. At one time I was convenor of the Policy Committee and sometime member of education, environmental and law reform groups.

The book was effectively co-authored with Alliance Party member Dr Mary Gethins, whose insights, sociological analysis and detailed editing was an invaluable complement to my own scientific, rather factual approach. She also made major contributions to sections on policing and education, derived from her extensive study of policing in Northern Ireland as she had written *Catholic Police Officers in Northern Ireland – Voices out of Silence* (published by Manchester University Press) and based on her PhD thesis for Aberdeen University. Her experience as senior lecturer at St Mary's College, Queen's University of Belfast, a Staff Tutor in the Open University at Cambridge and Manchester, a visiting lecturer at the University of East Anglia as well as her experience as Director of Open Learning at the University of Limerick and as Assistant Director of Education, Royal Borough of Kingston upon Thames also contributed to her sociological and educational insights.

Alliance Party founder member Denis Loretto also gave great help, firstly by supplying a copy of his article 'Alliance, Liberals and the SDP 1971–1985', a personal memoir, presented to the Liberal Democrat Party in England. Denis has subsequently assisted generously by meticulously checking and editing all the chapters. He has contributed to and corrected many factual events and political opinions, especially regarding the formation of the party in which he was actively involved and discussion of the Anglo-Irish Agreement (AIA).

Retired solicitor Jim Hendron, another founder member, has also provided valuable insights into the party's beginnings and development as well as some legal advice about the content.

During research for the thesis, I carried out interviews with a number of key Alliance Party people, particularly Sir Oliver Napier, Jim Hendron, Addie Morrow, Eileen Bell, Seamus Close, Philip McGarry and Patricia Mallon. I also interviewed Revd Timothy Kinahan, son of former Convention member and party president, Charles Kinahan. Great use was made of Alan Leonard's MA thesis, *The Alliance Party of Northern Ireland and Power Sharing in a Divided Society* (Dublin: University College Dublin, 1999). In 2003 I carried out a fairly limited survey of members' opinions about attitudes and backgrounds, particularly religious backgrounds. This was addressed to candidates for election, council members and other people participating in the Reconciliation Studies Course. Access was also obtained to surveys by Richard Rose (1968), Moxon-Browne (1978), David J. Smith (1986), Evans and Duffy (1992), Erwan Bodilis (1993), Alliance Party (1998), Gillian Robinson (1998), Evans and Tonge (2001).

Later I met and interviewed Sir Oliver Napier, who then sent some correspondence, about the foundation of the party. There were further discussions and information from Jim Hendron about the early days of the party. Great use was made of the Cain website and especially of Nicholas Whyte's web pages ARK, containing details and comments about all the Northern Ireland elections, local government, Assembly, Westminster and European, since 1973. Nicholas Whyte also read drafts of the manuscript and provided helpful comments and suggestions. Access was available to a large range of Alliance Party documents and reports as well as documents from the New Ulster Movement.

A major relevant survey was carried out by Jocelyn Evans and Jonathan Tonge of Liverpool University (2001), which included extensive comments. The authors sent me a full copy.

Further background material was obtained from archived copies of *Alliance News* and many party documents. Although reference to the party in political books was somewhat meagre, considerable information and comments were obtained from Paul Bew and Gordon Gillespie, *Northern Ireland 1968 – 1999 – A Chronology of the Troubles* (1999), John Whyte, *Interpreting Northern Ireland* (1990), Sydney Elliot and William D. Flackes, *Northern Ireland: Political Directory* (2001) and other books listed in the bibliography.

I also want to thank former party leader Lord John Alderdice; historian Lord Paul Bew; former chief executive of the party Gerry Lynch; former party leader John Cushnahan; party archivist Hugh Thompson; former general secretary Alan Leonard; former party leader Councillor Seán Neeson; Stewart Dickson, MLA; party leader David Ford, MLA; Dr Stephen Farry, MLA; Gordon Kennedy; Patricia Mallon; Dr Michael Healy; Mary Smyth-Farr, as well as staff at Alliance Party Headquarters, especially Debbie Spence, for their help and encouragement.

I thank Joe Leichty and Sr Cecelia Clegg for their guidance in writing my MPhil Dissertation.

Finally many thanks to my wife, Chrissie, for her love and support during the preparation of this book.

*Brian Eggins, 2015*

# Introduction:
# A sea of troubles

## NORTHERN IRELAND

Northern Ireland has been called 'A Place Apart'.[1] It is a place of approximately 1.7 million people, whose very existence was and still is continually disputed.

Geographically it is part of the island of Ireland. But politically it is part of the United Kingdom of Great Britain and Northern Ireland, which currently includes England, Scotland and Wales as well as Northern Ireland. It is variously also known as 'Ulster', 'The North', 'The North of Ireland', or 'The Six Counties'.

Historically Ulster was one of the four provinces of Ireland (the others being Leinster, Connacht and Munster), consisting of the counties of Antrim, Armagh, Derry/Londonderry, Down, Fermanagh, Tyrone (the six counties), together with Cavan, Donegal and Monaghan, but since the partition of 1921 the latter three counties were excluded as being 'too Catholic'. Even now for sporting events including rugby football and Gaelic sports, 'Ulster' consists of the original nine counties.

It is an extremely attractive part of the world with the Mourne Mountains in the south east, the Fermanagh Lakes in the south west and the beautiful Antrim coast leading to the Giant's Causeway in the north, which is geologically linked to Fingal's Cave on the island of Staffa in Scotland. The main city is Belfast, with its beautiful City Hall building and the Titanic Centre, 'celebrating' the tragic sinking of the *Titanic* passenger liner on its maiden voyage to America in 1912. In the north west is the maiden city of Derry/Londonderry, with its historic city walls. It was the European City of Culture in 2013. Like Belfast, Armagh city has both Catholic and Anglican cathedrals.

## THE TROUBLES

So what were the euphemistically named 'Troubles'? Are the differences due to religion, or politics or ethnicity? Was it a war or just criminal terrorist activity? Is the Irish Republican Army (IRA) a group of 'freedom fighters' or are they terrorists? What of the 'loyalist' paramilitary groups, allegedly defending their bit of territory – but against whom? Was the Ulster Volunteer Force was set up in 1913 to fight the British for the right to remain British?

When did the Troubles begin? There are many myths about the Irish situation, particularly about some of the details of the differences.

Some British people say that there has always been 'trouble' with Ireland since it was colonised by the English 800 years ago, bringing enduring State oppression of the Irish. Their island was invaded, their land was confiscated and the colonists tried to stamp out their religion. The first English colonisation was by Norman King Henry II in 1169, but it was the religious reformation of the sixteenth century that played a significant part in creating a lasting socio-political cleavage in Irish society that has led to the formation of two communities. Christianity is said to have come to Ireland through St Patrick in 431, and developed its own Celtic traditions. After the Synod of Whitby in about 664, the Roman tradition was imposed on the whole Church, though remnants of the Celtic tradition lingered in practice.

Following the Reformation led by Luther, Calvin and Zwingli in the sixteenth century, new Protestant churches developed. From England, first Henry VIII, then Elizabeth I tried to impose the new Protestant faith on Ireland. Later, James I, who was also James VI of Scotland, encouraged mainly Scottish Presbyterians to settle in Ulster. This settlement is termed the 'Plantation of Ulster' and began in 1609. In 1649 Oliver Cromwell, now 'Lord Protector of the Commonwealth of England', having replaced King Charles I who was executed, invaded Ireland. His soldiers' massacres of Irish Catholics, especially at Drogheda and Wexford, allegedly in retaliation for the killing of Protestants by Catholics in 1641, earned for his memory lasting detestation.

By 1767 the Irish population was 2.5 million and rose to over 4 million by 1781. It reached 5 million by 1800 and 7.5 million in 1831. By 1834 it is estimated that 81% of the population was Catholic, 10% was Anglican, and 9% was Presbyterian. 99% of Presbyterians and 45% of Anglicans lived in Ulster. About 5,000 Protestant families owned 95% of Irish land. This elite group was known as the 'Protestant Ascendancy' and were in part the result of the Penal Laws imposed by the ruling British on Irish Roman Catholics during the 1600s and 1700s in a bid to force people to accept the reformed Christian faith. The laws were very restrictive and have had a long-lasting effect on the daily life of Irish Catholics. The laws included:

- Restrictions on how children of Catholics were educated
- Banning Catholics from holding public office or serving in the army
- Expelling Catholic clergy from the country, or executing them
- Taking land and distributing it among British Lords
- Dividing inherited land equally between children, to reduce land size held by individual Catholics.
- Excluding Catholics from voting
- Ban on Catholics inheriting Protestant land

Another restriction during Penal Times was a ban on the celebration of Catholic Mass. Catholic priests and worshippers had to find hidden areas in the Irish countryside to celebrate Mass. Many of these places were marked with 'Mass Rocks'. The Mass Rock (*Carraig an Aifrinn* in Irish) was often-times a rock taken from a church ruin, and used as a place of worship for Roman Catholics.[4]

The Penal Laws also applied to anyone other than members of the Church of Ireland, which included Presbyterians and other non-conformists, to try and enforce uniformity to the established Church of Ireland's rules and traditions. The Church of Ireland was made the established Church in Ireland, as the Church of England still is in England. Eventually the Penal Laws fell into neglect after the Relief Acts of 1778 and 1782, especially after the failed uprising of the United Irishmen in 1798.

There had been an Irish Parliament, which met in Dublin, since 1297. This became the Reformation Parliament in 1536–1537, again meeting in Dublin. In 1541 King Henry VII was declared King of Ireland by the Irish Parliament.[5] The parliament was modelled on the English version and continued to meet from time to time without general restriction of membership, so some Catholics were included. Charles I convened Irish Parliaments in 1634 and 1640. Following the death of Oliver Cromwell in 1658 and the restoration of the British monarchy in 1660, Charles II called an Irish Parliament from 1661 to 1666. After the Williamite victories over Catholic James II in 1690 at the Battle of the Boyne on 1 July and at Aughrim on 12 July (*sic*) however, Catholics were excluded from this Parliament and in 1703 the Test Act was imposed on Protestant dissenters to encourage conformity to Anglican regulations. In 1782 Henry Grattan succeeded in obtaining what turned out to be short-lived independence for the Irish Parliament.

In 1791 Wolfe Tone and others of like mind formed the Society of United Irishmen in Belfast. The majority of members, particularly the leaders, were Presbyterians. In 1798 the countrywide rising was planned but was unsuccessful, due in part to sectarian divisions, and the ringleaders were executed. Grattan had retired from parliament in 1797.

Frightened by the possibility of insurrection and after much debate, dissension and bribery of Irish members, an Act of Legislative Union of Great Britain and Ireland was passed in 1800 and implemented in 1801. The Irish Parliament was abolished and Ireland was henceforth represented at Westminster. An Act of Union between England and Scotland had already been passed in 1707. The Union flag was then modified to add the Irish cross of St Patrick (a diagonal red cross on a white background) to the existing combination of the English vertical red cross of St George and the diagonal white cross of St Andrew on a blue background for Scotland, resulting in the current Union Jack of Great Britain and Northern Ireland.

Despite the relaxation in imposing the Penal Laws, there was still need for Catholic emancipation. Largely through the work of Daniel O'Connell and others, this was achieved in 1829. His major contribution to Irish history might be that his campaign highlighted the success of peaceful agitation in bringing about change rather than resorting to violence. In the United Kingdom Parliament there was much reform of the electoral system through the Reform Act of 1832. The franchise was extended to the merchant classes and 'rotten boroughs' were abolished.

Disaster struck in Ireland with the failure of the potato crop owing to blight, which resulted in a terrible famine that lasted from 1845 to 1849.[6] About 1 million people died through starvation and disease and 1.5 million emigrated, mainly to America.[7] Although the potato crop failed, the country was still producing more than enough grain crops to feed the population, but this was being exported. As a consequence of these exports and a number of other factors such as land acquisition, absentee landlords and the effect of the 1690 Penal Laws, the Great Famine today is viewed by a number of historical academics as a form of direct or indirect genocide. Others regard it as a mixture of cruel neglect and free market fundamentalism. What is not in dispute is that it decimated the population of Ireland, particularly the mainly Catholic peasantry. The famine soured the already strained relations between many of the Irish and the British Crown, making Irish republicanism an increasingly acceptable vehicle for achieving change.

With the first Vatican Council of 1870 and through the influence of conservative Cardinal Cullen, Roman Catholicism became very strong in

Ireland. Many new churches were built. The resurgent Church's dogma on the Sylabus of Errors (1864) and Papal Infallibility (1871) were understandably unattractive to Protestants. The encyclical 'Apostolicae Curae' in 1896 denied the validity of the Anglican priesthood. The Ne Temere papal decree of 1907 required non-Catholics married to Catholics to agree to educate their children in the Catholic faith, and often the non-Catholic partner was required to convert before the marriage.[8]

There were moves towards Irish Home Rule, with William Gladstone's failed bills of 1866 and 1893, then Asquith's bill in 1912 promising self-determination. Protestants however, concentrated very much in the north east, became very fearful of domination by a powerful Roman Catholic Church. They found support in Westminster; for example, the Quaker MP John Bright coined the phrase, 'Home Rule is Rome Rule'.[9]

So in 1912 Ulster Protestants, encouraged by Sir Edward Carson, signed the Ulster Covenant against Home Rule and pledged to resort to violent means if necessary to resist its imposition. They imported arms from Germany and in 1913 set up the Ulster Volunteer Force (UVF) with the intention of fighting Britain in order to stay British.

Debate on Home Rule was put on hold with the outbreak of the First World War. Many Irishmen, including the UVF, whose 80,000 members formed the 36th Ulster Division, joined the British Army to fight against Germany. 32,000 died, many at the Battle of the Somme in 1916.[10] Only in recent decades have northern Unionists acknowledged that many thousands of Irishmen from the south, notably in the 16th Irish Division, also fought and died, including 45% of casualties at the Battle of the Somme. Altogether 210,000 Irishmen fought for the British in the Great War and about 27,400 died.[11]

Meanwhile in Dublin a group of the Irish Republican Brotherhood led an uprising on 24 April 1916 (Easter Monday) and proclaimed a Republic outside the GPO. This was forcefully put down by the British Army and was at first widely unpopular among the Irish people. However, the subsequent execution of most of its leaders changed all that. The Easter Rising has been regarded ever since as a seminal event in the rise of Irish republicanism. After the First World War, Eamon De Valera set up the rival Dáil Éireann in Dublin in 1919. The Anglo-Irish War followed from 1919 to 1920 from which the term 'Troubles' was coined. Michael Collins was the leader of the Irish delegation who strove to obtain the best terms from the British Government, but he was out-manoeuvred by Prime Minister Lloyd George and his team, mindful of Ulster Unionist opposition. The result was the partition of Ireland. The Government of Ireland Act in 1920 established two parliaments, one in the north at Stormont, in Belfast, and one in the south in Dublin. Many in the new Irish Free State refused to accept partition and fought the partitionists in the Irish Civil War from 1922 to 1923,[12] during which Michael Collins was killed.

Sir James Craig (Lord Craigavon) became the first prime minister of Northern Ireland. He called it, 'a Protestant Parliament for a Protestant People'.[13] Historians and other commentators generally agree that systematic discrimination against Catholics was a distinguishing feature of the fifty years of Unionist hegemony which followed. Richard Rose was probably the first to highlight sustained, widespread discrimination in Northern Ireland, especially in public appointments and resource allocation. Perhaps surprisingly, under the Unionist regime before direct rule there were more poor Protestants than poor Catholics. Rose explains:

The notorious discrimination against Catholics in both central and local government was not a device to further the material interests of Protestant working people, but a political strategy which allowed the Unionist leadership to represent Catholics in general as a continuing threat to the Union, which only Protestant unity could fend off.[14]

Discrimination led to continuing violence by the now designated Irish Republican Army (IRA) with 232 people killed in 1922, including two MPs. From 1956 to 1962 there was a sustained IRA campaign, which included attacks on army barracks in Britain when twelve republicans and six policemen were killed. The Unionist government had set up the Royal Ulster Constabulary (RUC) in 1922, including the almost exclusively Protestant 'B Specials' who particularly targeted suspected 'republicans'. There was a Special Powers Act that allowed internment without trial and was much dreaded by Catholics, who were often all considered to be enemies of the State.[15]

The entirely Catholic Nationalist Party was rather disorganised, feeling impotent in the face of a solid Unionist phalanx, and refused to participate in the Stormont Parliament, even as an opposition until 1965. Nationalists justifiably complained about discrimination in the distribution of jobs and housing and voting rights. In the 1921 elections forty Unionists, six Nationalists and six Republicans were returned. These proportions changed very little over forty years, so that in 1965 there were thirty-six Unionists, nine Nationalists, and three Anti-partition members. Labour won three seats in 1925 and two in 1965. The Liberal Party had one seat. Thirteen MPs were elected to Westminster. All but two were Unionists who consistently supported the Conservative Party.[16]

Nationalist complaints of blatant discrimination in jobs endured, though largely ignored by both Stormont and Westminster. Catholics could not get jobs in local government or Protestant-owned companies, except at the most menial level. Housing was prioritised for Protestants. Electoral areas were arranged ('gerrymandered') so that Protestant minorities could elect councillors and MPs over Catholic majorities, especially in Derry. The discrimination in civil rights, justice and religion continued.

## DIVISIONS

So what are the causes of evident social divisions? Is it politics or religion – or both? Politics is about secular (temporal) power. Religion is about spiritual power. When inappropriately mixed the two make an inflammable, often explosive, combination. Jesus kept them apart when he said, 'Then give to Caesar what is Caesar's, and to God what is God's.'[17] Too often people lack the wisdom to discern the difference. Marva Down comments that, 'When dialectical truths are not held in tension, one side or the other side is easily sacralised'.[18] Sometimes political power is stated as a 'divine right' and sometimes spiritual power includes secular power, as in the Vatican State.

Anthony Gettins gave a detailed analysis of the problem in his book, *A Presence That Disturbs*:

> The first time someone separates people by drawing a real or symbolic line between them, the first time someone makes a moral judgement in choosing between people, at that moment the world has become divided where previously it was not. This act of division leads to dominance and destruction, inclusion and exclusions, hierarchy and privilege.
> Sometimes people manage to live in peaceful coexistence though not in true harmony. Differences can harden into disagreements and people come to blows or worse.[19]

The typical characterisation of Northern Ireland is of a province largely split into two communities who do not trust each other. Life is about 'us' and 'them'. So are the divisions and were the Troubles a religious conflict, or a political conflict, or an ethnic conflict? In summary one might say that it

is rooted in fear of the Roman Catholic Church by Protestants and fear of
British political domination by Catholics.

Andrew Marr, on the BBC Radio 4 *Today* programme on 14 June 2010,
discussing the problem of identity, remarked, 'People who feel powerless seize
on to identity politics'. The two communities in Northern Ireland clearly
exemplify the operation of 'identity politics'. Many of the Protestant minority
on the island of Ireland were afraid of being dominated by the Catholic majority
in a united Ireland scenario, so, since partition, those in the north-eastern part
have developed, supported and depended upon the almost exclusively Protestant
Ulster Unionist political party with its British identity to uphold and defend their
cause. Conversely, the Catholic minority in the six counties of Northern Ireland
for half a century felt powerless in the face of this Unionist domination and so
looked to a Catholic Irish-Nationalist identity for their politics.

So how were people to deal with this irreconcilable political and social
dichotomy? From time to time the IRA tried to make Northern Ireland ungov-
ernable by attacks with guns and bombs. For many years most Catholics just
kept their heads down and tried to get on with life. Their Nationalist politicians
saw no point in trying to play an active part in government, even as opposition.
The Protestant Unionists were fiercely defensive and tried to keep the lid on.
Indeed Stormont Prime Minster Basil Brooke (Lord Brookeborough), advised
his people, 'Not to have a Catholic about the place'.[20]

There were some, however, who thought differently, particularly some
members of the Liberal Party as well as some Unionists who supported the
next Prime Minster, Terence O'Neill, in his attempts to show sensitivity
towards the demands of an increasingly large minority population and the
demands of the growing Civil Rights Movement.

At this point in time Oliver Napier, a Catholic solicitor and member of
the Liberal Party, had a dream. He wondered if it would be possible to form
a non-sectarian cross-community political party. He and others realised
that violence would never bring about a stable, peaceful society and civil
rights marches were unlikely to bring about the seachange required. There
needed to be new political thinking. Initially Napier and Protestant Unionist
Bob Cooper set up what we would now call a think tank – the New Ulster
Movement, from which the Alliance Party was formed in 1970.

As current leader, David Ford, told the Alliance Party Conference in
February 2010:

Just forty years ago this year, a group of people had a dream. They came
up with the ludicrous idea that politics in Northern Ireland should not

be dominated by division, but should be about co-operation, partnership and reconciliation. The sceptics had a field day.

How could such a bunch of do-gooders have any prospect of success? The notion of overcoming tribal politics was preposterous. Commentators generally predicted that a party founded on such principles could not survive a single election.[21]

The commentators were wrong. Forty years and many elections later David Ford was elected Minister of Policing and Justice – the first since John Taylor in the old Stormont Parliament of 1972. The Alliance Party have, too, their first elected Westminster MP, Naomi Long, who previously served as Lord Mayor of Belfast. Alliance has a second minister, Dr Stephen Farry, Minister of Employment and Learning, elected by the d'Hondt method following a successful Assembly election in 2011.

The chapters which follow chronicle the mixed fortunes of the Alliance Party in the forty-five years which have elapsed since its founding fathers set out with optimism and determination to change Stormont politics and community relations in Northern Ireland.

# 1

# Perchance to dream: The founding of the Alliance Party 1969–1972

## INTRODUCTION

This chapter shows how Oliver Napier and others developed the new Alliance Party through the vehicle of the New Ulster Movement against the background of the Civil Rights movement, continuing violence from both Loyalist and Republican paramilitary groups and the prime minister of the day Terence O'Neill's attempts to provide a package of five reforms, thereby going some distance towards meeting increasing demands from the large minority.

## WHAT DREAMS MAY COME MUST GIVE US PAUSE?

There were those who dreamt of a united Ireland and were prepared to fight and die for it. There were those for whom such a vision was a nightmare and who were prepared to fight to prevent it. There were even some who thought an independent 'Ulster' might be preferable. There were others with more modest dreams, who just longed for a fair society. Among these was an expanded force of university-educated Catholics, together with some Protestants who could see the injustices of the Unionist-dominated society and who wanted change. Some members of this mixed group, together with English students attending Queen's University, formed the Civil Rights Association in February 1967 and held protest marches across the province.

In 1963 Captain Terence O'Neill had taken over as prime minister of the Stormont Government from the more hard-line anti-Catholic

Lord Brookeborough. Perhaps O'Neill had a dream too that reform was needed, which led to a meeting with Irish Taoiseach Seán Lemass. The meeting was opposed by firebrand preacher Revd Ian Paisley who is said to have called Lemass a 'Fenian papist murderer'.[22]

Catholics suffered systemic discrimination in terms of jobs, housing and electoral representation in Northern Ireland. In fact, many Protestant working people were not much better off, but they felt the Unionist government in the 'Protestant Parliament' at Stormont was looking after them. In the 1950s Ian Paisley came to the fore, vehemently opposed to all things Catholic, and opposed to anyone supporting Catholics.

Even after the defeat of the IRA in its 1956–1962 campaign, there was much fear among Protestants. Paisley whipped up this fear, and in 1965 the Ulster Volunteer Force (UVF), originally formed around 1913 to oppose the Home Rule movement, was revived. Perhaps they feared a fresh IRA campaign in the fiftieth anniversary year of the Easter Rising of 1916? In 1966 UVF members, including Gusty Spence who was subsequently convicted and jailed, murdered two innocent Catholics.

## THE CIVIL RIGHTS MOVEMENT

Since the 1944 Education Act, free secondary education had become more widely available in Great Britain (but not in Northern Ireland until 1947). More Catholics in particular were obtaining educational qualifications and moving into the professions, though the Civil Service continued to be mainly Protestant, especially in the higher echelons. The situation is demonstrated in an anecdote which describes the Minister of Agriculture's response when accused of employing Catholics in his ministry: 'I have 109 officials and so far as I know, four of them are Roman Catholic, three of whom were civil servants turned over to me, whom I had to take on when we began'.[23]

The Northern Ireland Civil Rights Association (NICRA) was formed in February 1967, as mentioned earlier, supported by both Catholics and some moderate Protestants. This association was largely student led and coincided with student civil rights movements across Europe, particularly in Paris and Prague, as well as in the USA, where they were protesting against the Vietnam War. The Association was campaigning for universal franchise for local government elections, the redrawing of electoral boundaries, the introduction of laws to end discrimination in employment, a points system for public housing and repeal of the Special Powers Act.

The Special Powers Act was introduced in 1922 by the Unionist government in an attempt to establish law and order. It contained draconian measures such as empowering the Home Affairs Minister to take whatever measures he deemed necessary for that end. A summary non-jury court could sentence offenders to up to a year's hard labour in prison or even a whipping. Actions could include the forbidding of inquests, closing licensed premises, banning assembly and marches in public areas, closing of roads, taking possession of arms, ammunition and explosives, seizure of land and destruction of buildings, and even spreading by word of mouth any opinions which might cause disaffection. There were provisions for stop and search and confiscation of motor vehicles, arrest and imprisonments on remand without a warrant. Originally the order was for one year, but in 1928 it was extended for five years and then in 1933 was made permanent following opposition from Nationalist MPs. The act was repealed in 1973 following direct rule. The full details are described in the CAIN WEB.[24]

The NICRA also demanded the disbanding of the Ulster Special Constabulary (the B-specials) who were almost entirely Protestant and alleged to be riddled with members of Loyalist paramilitary groups.

As in other parts of the world, the civil rights movement was vigorously repressed. Paisley and his colleagues often led the opposition, and the RUC as well as the B-specials often used violence against the protestors. Significant NICRA marches took place in Dungannon on 24 August 1968 and on 5 October in Londonderry. Home Affairs Minister William Craig officially banned this latter march. Over 2,000 people assembled and were viciously attacked by the RUC. Eleven policemen and seventy-seven civilians were injured. The following day students met in protest at Queen's University in Belfast and formed a more militant group, People's Democracy (PD), at which meeting Bernadette Devlin emerged as a leader along with Michael Farrell.

Following a meeting with British Prime Minister Harold Wilson and Home Secretary James Callaghan on 4 November, Terence O'Neill announced a package of five reforms on 22 November 1968, which were intended to meet the main points of the Catholic grievances. The five points were: a new system for allocation of houses by local government; an ombudsman to investigate complaints; a development commission to take over powers of Londonderry Corporation; the Special Powers Act to be abolished 'as soon as it is safe to do so' and the end of company vote – but there was no decision to enfranchise non-ratepayers. This innovation led to dissension in the Stormont cabinet, with William Craig calling for tough action against the NICRA, who were in any case not satisfied with O'Neill's package.

## ULSTER AT THE CROSSROADS

On 9 December 1968 Prime Minister Terence O'Neill appealed to the
people in a radio broadcast over the heads of his cabinet critics, with his
famous 'Ulster at the crossroads' speech.

> Ulster stands at the cross roads. I believe … the time has come for the
> people as a whole to speak in a clear voice. For more than five years
> I have tried to heal some of the deep divisions in our community …
> What kind of Ulster do you want?[25]

He apparently received overwhelming public support, especially from
Catholic leaders, including Cardinal Conway and Nationalist Eddie McAteer.
The Unionists as a whole supported O'Neill, with four abstentions. But two
ministers resigned, unconvinced by Terence O'Neill's policies. So O'Neill
called an Ulster general election for 24 February (known as the 'Crossroads
Election'). He himself defeated Paisley (standing as a Protestant Unionist)
and Michael Farrell (People's Democracy) in the Bannside constituency.
Independent John Hume won Foyle from Eddie McAteer. Nationalists
lost three seats to civil rights candidates. Republican Labour won two seats
in Belfast for Gerry Fitt and Paddy Devlin. The Northern Ireland Labour
Party (NILP) also won a seat. Of thirty-nine Unionist MPs, twenty-seven
supported O'Neill, ten were against him and two were undecided.

On 17 April Bernadette Devlin won the Mid-Ulster seat at Westminster in
a by-election. Finally, on 23 April, the government agreed to universal suffrage
in Northern Ireland elections – the same day the 21-year-old psychology
student, Bernadette Devlin, made her maiden speech to an astounded House
of Commons.

It is often forgotten that O'Neill had actually won the 'Crossroads' election
on 24 February 1969 in that twenty-seven out of the thirty-nine Unionists
elected supported his reform programme. They were, though, a mixture of
Official and Unofficial Unionists and the divisions at the grass roots were
serious. Despite having 'won' the election O'Neill had failed to unite the
Unionist Party, so in April he resigned and was replaced by James Chichester-
Clark. Violence continued when Loyalist gangs attacked and burned Catholic
homes in West Belfast. On 14 August 1969 British troops were brought in to
help the RUC. Initially Catholics, who were hard pressed by the Loyalists
in Belfast, welcomed them. The honeymoon did not last long. Once the
army called a curfew to search for weapons there were serious riots and the

Catholic people turned against the army. Many of them turned to the newly formed Provisional IRA for support.

## THE NEW ULSTER MOVEMENT

Meanwhile another group had a different sort of dream. A new political grouping emerged in January 1969 called the New Ulster Movement, which aimed to develop cross-community politics with moderate and non-sectarian policies involving both Catholics and Protestants. Its inaugural meeting was held on 5 February. As Denis Loretto recalled:

> Chaos was at hand and it was up to the Northern Irish people themselves to put aside their sterile divisions and build the solution. The root problem was sectarianism. A combination of absolute equality and involvement for Protestants and Catholics and respect for the rule of law was paramount.[26,27]

Catholic solicitor Oliver Napier together with Ronnie Boyle invited a number of Liberal Party members, including Tony Cinnamond and Denis Haslem, to this inaugural meeting. As we shall see, it was always Napier's intention that the NUM should be the launching pad for a new liberal non-sectarian party.

Sir Oliver commented that:

> We did our best to hide the fact that a group within the Liberal Party was handling it, which would be the kiss of death. We kept [Revd] Albert McElroy informed at every step but asked him not to attend. I wanted to tell Sheelagh Murnaghan, but Albert advised against. He said he would – it would come better from him as Sheelagh was suspicious of me because she thought I was 'too political'.[28]

The Liberals who helped found the NUM were promptly expelled from the Liberal Party. In the subsequent Stormont election, Liberal leader Sheelagh Murnaghan, who had held a seat for the Liberals since 1961 under the anachronistic university franchise, was only able to muster 15% of the vote in North Down.

It was very hard going to develop this new vision in the face of continuing violence and to produce credible documents that would form the basis of constitutional reform of the Stormont Parliament over many years to come.

During 1969 the NUM built an active organisation with about 7,000 members, drawn from all sections of the community. It issued many influential papers[29,30] and was the first organisation to call for a Community Relations Commission and a central Housing Executive. Its more radical members, however, were becoming dissatisfied with a movement. They wanted a new political party.

A key new member was another (Catholic) solicitor, Jim Hendron. In a very personal account[31] he recalled how he and his wife Máire joined the Bloomfield Branch of NUM in September 1969. He quickly proposed that the NUM should set up a special committee to lead to the formation of a new non-sectarian political party. His resolution was easily carried.

The NUM's first chairperson was personnel manager Brian Walker, followed by Dr Stanley Worrall, former headmaster of Methodist College Belfast.

1970 was the year in which NUM changed its role, owing to the formation of the fledgling Alliance Party. From being an electioneering organisation it became an 'ideas' organisation and one which sought to influence and shape political thinking and action in Ulster – and between Ulster and its two neighbours, Great Britain and the Republic of Ireland. A series of six sub-committees were set up which included:

I  The Political Sub-committee, which aimed to penetrate all the known political groups, which made up, or impinged on, the Northern Ireland problem. These included the Unionist Party, through its moderate wing, into the middle area held by the NILP, the Liberal Party and the Alliance Party, into the Social Democratic and Labour Party (SDLP) and Nationalist Parties, and out onto the Republican and Provisional wing of the IRA. In addition they talked with all kinds of fringe political groups, including the Northern Ireland Civil Rights Association, the Catholic Minority Rights Group, and the Movement for Peace in Ireland Group. Only two groups refused to meet them: the Orange Order and the Political Alliance recently formed by Mr Desmond Boal. The NUM was invited in September to join the London talks initiated by Home Secretary Reginald Maudling.

II  The Political Publications Sub-committee, which continued to produce documents such as John Whyte's *The Reform of Stormont*,[32] which proposed power sharing, and urged closure of Stormont. In 1971 *The Way Forward*[33] and a *Commentary on the programme of reforms for Northern Ireland*[34] emerged. The following year *Two Irelands or One*[35] and *Violence in Northern Ireland*[36] came out. The last publication was probably *Tribalism and Christianity*, published in 1973.[37]

III The Law and Order Sub-committee called for a renewal of the ban on
   all parades and marches and a ban on all gun clubs and the handing-in of
   all licensed guns. Members continued to try to find a way of helping to
   regain the acceptance of the RUC as a civilian police force in all parts of
   our province and amongst all sections of our people. The RUC was a very
   largely Protestant force, though there was no ban on Catholics joining,
   and was perceived by Nationalists as the military arm of the Unionist
   Party. The power which could be exercised by the Minister of Home
   Affairs over decisions by the Inspectors General lent support to this view.
   It was many years before even the moderate SDLP accepted the police
   and not until after the Patton Report resulted in a major restructuring
   of the RUC into the Police Service of Northern Ireland (PSNI) in 2001.
   Only in 2007 did Sinn Féin come to accept the service. The Catholic
   membership of the RUC, 'peaked at 22% in 1923 and declined to below
   8% by the year 2000. Since the formation of the PSNI this has increased
   to about 30%.'[38]

## THE NORTHERN IRELAND LABOUR PARTY (NILP) AND THE ULSTER LIBERAL PARTY (ULP)

The political history of Northern Ireland was dominated by unionism
challenged to some extent by nationalism. There have been other more
centrist political groups. The NILP was founded in 1924 as a centre-left
social democratic party, attracting those who shared the values of the sister
Labour Party in Britain. These values were: a fair deal, concern for the poor
and those unemployed or lacking opportunities, balance, duty to others.[39]
Significantly, in the Northern Ireland context, it crossed the ethno-national
and ethno-religious divisions to focus on issues rather than political structures.
As McGarry and O'Leary said:

> ... a reasonable facsimile of the British Labour Party ... for a significant
> part of its history [it] never made significant inroads into the Nationalist
> or Unionist vote and disintegrated in the wake of the polarisation of
> the late 1960s.[40]

In its early days it managed to remain neutral on partition and attracted a
considerable degree of support from both Catholics and Protestants until the
formation of the Republic of Ireland in 1949. This disturbed the Unionists

and in the election which followed there was a reduction in the Labour vote from 18.5% in 1948 to 7.1%, although the Irish Declaration was only one possible cause, however significant, for this decline.

A vast majority of Protestant workers supported the Ulster Unionists, because membership of the Orange Order enhanced their employment prospects over non-members, hence the predominantly Belfast trade unions not being supportive of the Labour Party.

As early as 1913 the British Labour Party gave the Irish Labour Party exclusive organising rights in Ireland. In the Northern Ireland general election of 1925 the NILP secured three seats in North, East and West Belfast after which the Unionist government dropped proportional representation – because it returned too many opponents. The only NILP candidate to be elected to Westminster was Jack Beattie (party leader 1929–1933 and 1942–1943), who was returned in 1945, but lost it in 1950 and regained the seat in 1951 under the Irish Labour Party banner. By 1949 the NILP abandoned its neutrality on the constitutional question and voted in favour of the Union with Great Britain, causing Catholic members to fall away. An earlier attempt to adopt this policy split the party when Harry Midgley (party leader 1933–1938) formed his own Unionist Commonwealth Labour Party and won a seat in 1945.

The NILP fortunes revived in the late 1950s when four of its candidates were elected to Stormont (Tom Boyd for Cromac, Billy Boyd for Woodvale, Vivian Simpson for Old Park and David Bleakley for Victoria) and the NILP became the official opposition. Following the civil upheaval of the late 1960s, the Prime Minister Brian Faulkner appointed David Bleakley to a Cabinet post as Minister of Community Relations in 1971. Direct rule was imposed in 1972 and the Northern Ireland devolved government of half a century's duration had gone because Faulkner refused to give up Stormont's control of security matters. In the 1973 referendum on the border the NILP declared its colours clearly over the constitutional question by campaigning for Northern Ireland to remain in the UK. A comprehensive, balanced book about the NILP was written by Aaron Edwards,[41] published in 2009 and favourably reviewed by Jon Tonge in 2012.[42]

The British Liberal Party developed during the latter half of the nineteenth century. It drew on values and inspiration from renowned philosophers and economists, including Hobbes, Locke, Adam Smith, Tom Paine, and J.S. Mill. By the First World War it had placed much significant legislation on the statute books. These included the Irish Church Act (1869) which disestablished the Anglican Church in Ireland, the Education Act (1870), the Reform Act (1884), the Old Age Pensions Act (1908), and the Home Rule Act (1914) – intended to extend access to primary education and the franchise, to relieve penury in old age and to allow a measure of self-determination to Ireland.

There was an active Northern Ireland Liberal Association before the First World War, when the Liberal Party was in power in Westminster. They made gains in the 1925 Stormont elections. But these were reversed when the Unionist Party abolished proportional representation in favour of single member seats, in order to reduce opposition in the Northern Ireland Parliament from Independent Unionists, the NILP and the ULP.[43]

The party was re-launched in May 1928[44] under the dynamic leadership of Revd Albert McElroy, a non-subscribing Presbyterian clergyman and formerly an NILP activist. The party re-emerged as the ULP, after a dormant period following disastrous 1929 election results.

The party's most successful office holder was the only female barrister practising in the province at the time – Sheelagh Murnaghan. She held one of the four Queen's University seats from 1961 to 1969, during which time she energetically pushed a Liberal agenda in Stormont. Her efforts were rewarded by Secretary of State William Whitelaw when he appointed her to his Advisory Commission where she continued to press the ULP's programme of reform, not least in relation to human rights, seeking equal rights treatment for Catholics within the existing state, rather than favouring unification of the island. An open letter to electors of South Belfast in 1959[45] reflected English Liberal aims of full employment, profit-sharing and co-ownership in industry, electoral reform and greater economic integration with Europe.

Her electoral success allowed her to challenge entrenched positions within the Chamber and promoted the formation of Liberal Associations across the province.[46] Described as 'both a courageous and a colourful political operator',[47] her debating skills were negated by Prime Minister Brookborough's and then Prime Minister O'Neill's denial of a free vote on the abolition of capital punishment, even though several Unionist back-benchers spoke in favour of her bill. Eventually, the government introduced similar legislation which was passed, the death penalty being retained only for the murder of police officers or prison warders.

She was infuriated by the introduction of internment without trial and concerned, as were her QUB constituents and NICRA members, by the government's continuing use of the Special Powers Act. This guaranteed her on-going and growing dissent. Even after her political career ended when she contested the North Down seat in 1969 and South Belfast in 1973, she continued to write for the *Northern Radical* (the ULP's monthly newspaper). Her reforming efforts along with those of the new Alliance Party members were

rewarded by Whitelaw's White Paper on Northern Ireland (1973) that established a Commission for Human Rights, a Fair Employment Agency and a PR/
STV electoral system. She later chaired the national insurance and industrial
tribunal and continued to press the case for education of itinerants' children.

By this time much of the ULP middle-class and liberal Unionist support
had gone to the Alliance Party, which succeeded in winning eight seats in the
seventy-eight-member Assembly in 1973. The Alliance Party has taken over
the task of the strenuous advocacy by the ULP for reform, long overdue in a
Western democracy, now carried on in the twenty-first century by tackling
new difficulties to be resolved under consociational arrangements. Similar
liberal values must continue to apply.

The efforts made by earlier centrist parties, both NILP and ULP, must be
acknowledged and celebrated. How the Alliance Party has been rising to the
challenge in its later contemporary context is the subject of this book.

## FOUNDING OF THE ALLIANCE PARTY

Sir Oliver Napier described in a personal letter how he came to consider
setting up a new party:

> As I was driving back from the Lisnaskea by-election in February 1969,
> I thought through the politics of non-sectarianism in Northern Ireland
> and came to the following conclusions;
> To put up Liberal candidates in elections where there was no organi-
> sation in the constituency was stupid in the extreme. Albert called it
> 'showing the flag'. It certainly was not a pattern for electoral success.
> That there were non-sectarian people supporting other parties other
> than the Liberal Party – Labour – some Unionists – some Nationalists.
> The Liberal Party was splintering them further.
> To launch a new party out of the blue was a recipe of disaster.[48]

He said:

> You have to be more subtle than that and organise your party before
> announcing it. That is what we did in NUM: [we] formed the basics of
> a party based on organisations in each constituency.
> It all worked a dream. No one suspected a Liberal Party foundation
> and we set up organisations in almost all Northern Ireland constituencies.

And so NUM was formed. As the Northern Ireland situation continued to deteriorate through 1969 Oliver Napier was joined by Bob Cooper and their close colleagues were increasingly aware that the current political structure was not going to work. The time had come for the next stage in moving towards a new political party. Without any publicity a group was formed late in 1969 consisting of some NUM members plus representatives of the 'Parliamentary Associations' which had formed around unofficial pro-O'Neill candidates in the February 1969 election. This group included Oliver Napier, Bob Cooper, NUM Chairman Brian Walker, Basil Glass, Tony Cinnamond, Denis Loretto, Robin Glendinning, Kate Condy, Tony Cowdy and some of those supporting Terence O'Neill, including John Hunter of Coleraine, Hubert Nesbitt, who was agent for Independent Unionist MP, Bertie McConnell and John Kane, a coal merchant from Larne. The group also included Cecil Hull, Alex Lyon, and Sydney Stewart. In October Jim Hendron was invited by Oliver Napier to meet Bob Cooper and to join this now sixteen-person group.

Behind the scenes the group worked on the logistics of forming a political party from the ground up. Denis Loretto said, 'I was proud to be a member of "The Group" and had no doubt that launch was now only a matter of timing'.[49]

The two by-elections on 16 April 1970 gave them the signal. Ian Paisley made his entrance into elective politics, and moderate Unionism had no answer, as he took O'Neill's former seat, Bannside, and Paisley's deputy, William Beattie, won a seat in South Antrim. An unknown candidate, David Corkey, standing as an Independent backed by NUM activists, gained over 25% of the vote and was just behind the Official Unionist candidate.

Denis Loretto recalls:

In a hectic weekend we wrote a declaration of intent containing the founding principles of the party plus all the supporting documentation for a press launch on Tuesday 21st April. The name of the party was one of the more contentious issues. In the end Alliance was chosen because it was new, avoided any partisan flavour and would fit into a newspaper headline unabridged![50]

They rejected not only the Unionist and Nationalist parties, 'for whom the clock stopped in 1920' but also the Labour and Liberal parties, though they did acknowledge that these parties had made some attempt to cut across sectarian divisions.

In drafting the founding principles they emphasised the healing of community divisions. A key issue in Northern Ireland was always the British link, which had to be addressed unequivocally as the Liberals vacillated on this issue. The Alliance Party founders knew that the majority of Catholics were prepared to settle for true equality and cultural freedom within a province largely running its own affairs within the United Kingdom. All that has happened since – up to and including the Good Friday Agreement – has borne this out.

The Alliance Party has always been totally in favour of a devolved Northern Ireland Assembly, whereas some people in the NUM were content with direct rule from Westminster. So much so that Alliance was always prepared to participate in talks and negotiations aimed at establishing a power-sharing devolved Assembly, even when other political parties refused to take part.

Alliance was totally committed to supporting law and order. On the economy they did not wish to take any 'doctrinaire' view, as with the left–right approach that pervaded politics in the British Labour and Conservative Parties.

The party launch on 21 April 1970 brought a positive response from NUM members and others of like mind. The leadership rapidly got on with building a province-wide organisation with over 10,000 card-carrying members. Some feelers had been put out to civil rights activists, including John Hume, but they kept their distance.

## JOHN HUME AND THE SDLP

In March 1970 the Independent MP for Foyle, John Hume, was invited to speak at a meeting of the Bloomfield branch of NUM in the Glenmachan Hotel. One-hundred-and-fifty people came, compared with the usual forty to fifty.

Jim Hendron, who was then chair of this branch, recalls:

> John Hume spoke about his background and work to achieve civil rights and fair play for every section of society in his Derry constituency. His main concerns were to alleviate poverty and to create employment. He spoke for well over half an hour and received a six-minute standing ovation.[51]

Later Jim Hendron was authorised to invite Hume to join their group of sixteen. He said:

I pressed John to join us and I begged him not to forego his status as an Independent to become in effect a Nationalist. John did not commit himself. He wished me and the Group well and he particularly asked me to keep in touch with him.

On 20 April, the day prior to the launch of the Alliance Party, Jim phoned John Hume to tell him about the new party, still hoping he might agree to become involved. He recalls:

He [John] asked me the name of the Party, which I declined to give him, saying it was embargoed until the following morning. He then asked me if any of the terms 'social', 'democratic' or 'labour' were included in the name. He went on to explain that he and five other Stormont MPs, including Republican Labour Gerry Fitt, former Northern Ireland Labour Paddy Devlin and Nationalist Austin Currie, were also working on the launch of a new Party.

It was a great disappointment to Alliance that this group got together with Nationalist members later the same year – on 21 August 1970 – to form the Social Democratic and Labour Party (SDLP). It had a constructive intent and its advocacy of a United Ireland was only by consent. Clearly the SDLP would get major backing from Catholics, but it would never be able to attract cross-community support and would always feel the danger of being outbid by the forces of militant Republicanism, which is exactly what happened eventually.

Oliver Napier commented:

Of course John Hume wanted a basically Nationalist party with strong socialist policies, not a cross community party such as Alliance. From his point of view he was very successful. But his SDLP was always looking towards the Republic of Ireland. He did not support sharing without an 'Irish dimension'.[52]

Subsequent events illustrated this, as the SDLP's insistence on a Council of Ireland was a major factor in the collapse of the 1973/1974 power-sharing executive and Assembly. In 1982, the SDLP declined to take their places in the Prior Assembly as there was no provision for an 'Irish Dimension'.

John Hume claimed in his book of 1996 that: 'The important issue for our party is human rights, not religion, and our objective is a continuous [*sic*] respect for rights and traditions of Catholics and Protestants alike. We are both non-sectarian and anti-sectarian.'[53]

These words may express his ideal personal view, but in practice the SDLP is clearly a Nationalist Party[54] looking for a united Ireland by peaceful means. It follows that their voter appeal is largely to the Catholic population. Furthermore the SDLP insists on promoting the Nationalist side in the Assembly and its voting patterns. It is disingenuous for SDLP to claim to be 'non-sectarian'.

## DEVELOPMENT OF THE ALLIANCE PARTY

Earlier in 1970 there was a Westminster general election within two months of the Alliance Party launch. Given the orientation of Alliance towards devolved government the decision was made to hold fire and not to expose the fledgling party to a contest for which they would be unprepared. Liberal candidates stood in two of the twelve seats and were bottom of the poll in both. Paisley continued his advance by winning the North Antrim seat.

The first general meeting of the Alliance Party was held in Portrush in 4 July 1970, attended by ninety association committee members, at which the Acting Executive Committee which had headed the party's initial organisation was established as a formal Executive Committee with Oliver Napier and Bob Cooper as joint political chairpersons, together with Kate Condy (Mid Down), Anthony Cowdy (Windsor), Robin Glendinning (Mid and East Tyrone), Jim Hendron (Bloomfield), John Hunter, (North Derry), John Kane (Larne), Denis Loretto (Mid Down), Hubert Nesbitt (Bangor).

Provision was also made for an Alliance Party Council formed from delegates of the constituency associations. The first Council meeting was then held in October 1970 at which the following were elected:

Chair: Basil Glass
Vice-chair: Oliver Napier
Joint chairs of the Political Committee: Oliver Napier and Bob Cooper
Treasurers: Hubert Nesbitt and Ronnie Boyle
General secretary: Grace Wilson until 1972, when she was replaced by
Bob Cooper
Publicity secretary: Anthony Cowdy
There were fourteen other members

A new constitution was approved. There was no formal overall leader at this point as there was no parliamentary party and the party leader would be the leader of the parliamentary party.

An editorial board for the *Alliance Bulletin* was set up consisting of:

Editor: Anthony Cowdy
Production editor: G.A. Tully
Production assistant: Wendy Austin, who became chair of Queen's University Alliance in 1972
Staff included David Ford, Will Glendinning, G. Nesbitt, and S. Wilson

Alliance leaders were soon involved in talks with British Government ministers. In October 1971 Basil Glass, Oliver Napier and Bob Cooper were in talks with Home Secretary Reginald Maudling.

## CONTINUING VIOLENCE

Against the background of continuing unrest with Republican no-go areas being matched by growing Loyalist militancy, Alliance spokesmen, particularly Oliver Napier and Bob Cooper, gained respect.

In April 1971 the party showed its strength by staging its first Annual Conference with nearly 2,000 members packing the Ulster Hall. The slogan was 'Towards Government' and that was their firm intent, though they had no illusions about how long it would take.

Denis Loretto recalls, 'We needed the impetus of high expectation to keep the adrenalin flowing in those crusading days'.[55]

Throughout 1971 escalating violence in the streets blocked further attempts at political progress. Despite hopeful signs of understanding emerging between the SDLP and the Unionist government now led by Brian Faulkner, the SDLP energies were absorbed by a demand for an enquiry into the deaths of two men shot by the army in Derry. They withdrew from Stormont and set up the strange 'Assembly of the Northern Irish People' at Dungiven in County Derry.

On 9 August the fateful step was taken to introduce internment without trial, supposedly to sweep up suspect IRA volunteers. Prime Minister Brian Faulkner had used internment in the 1950s when he was Minister of Home Affairs, with the collaboration of the Government of the Republic. He was keen to try it again though neither the army nor the RUC were in favour.

Even his Stormont Government were ambivalent about the use of internment. He went ahead and 350 men were taken into custody. The Alliance leadership was faced with its first major dilemma. While most Catholics would be incensed by this move, it was likely that the majority of Protestants would see it as a necessary measure to crush IRA violence which had caused most of the thirty deaths that year. At an emergency meeting of the party Executive they decided that an appalling error had been made that would increase rather than diminish violence and unrest. In any case the party's principles were clear – this was the antithesis of 'absolutely equal enforcement of the law'.

The NUM were much more ambivalent about internment. They advised the British Government that the Republic of Ireland must intern at the same time, that Protestant extremists must be interned as well as Catholics, and that there must be access to internees for lawyers and that there should be welfare workers to care for the women and children.[56]

Alliance immediately issued a statement totally condemning internment and warning of the inevitable consequences. On the same evening Alliance leaders travelled throughout the province and addressed hastily organised meetings of the party membership in an attempt to ward off any possible split on this emotive issue. In the event no members were lost. Not only had there been firm leadership but also the Protestant members asked their Catholic colleagues how they felt about the internment decision – and understood.

It was not long before their grim predictions came true. Between 9 August and the end of the year a further 143 people had been killed, including forty-six members of the security forces. On 30 January 1972 was the appalling Bloody Sunday, when soldiers of the Parachute Regiment shot thirteen unarmed civilians dead in Derry. It sent shock waves around the world and acted as a major recruiting focus for the Provisional IRA.

## PHELIM O'NEILL BECOMES THE FIRST PARTY LEADER

In January 1972 Basil Glass, Oliver Napier and Bob Cooper had talks with British Prime Minister Edward Heath at No. 10 Downing Street.

Shortly afterwards, in February 1972, Alliance acquired a parliamentary party when three Stormont MPs, Phelim O'Neill (Unionist), Bertie McConnell (Independent Unionist) and Tom Gormley (Independent Nationalist) left their former allegiances and joined the party. At the next Party Council Phelim O'Neill MP was elected as the first leader of the parliamentary party.

The new arrangements were short-lived, as Stormont was suspended on 24 March 1972 and replaced by direct rule from the UK Government at Westminster. The Conservative Secretary of State, William Whitelaw, together with several other Ministers of State, took over the administration of Northern Ireland on 26 March through the existing Northern Ireland civil service. This suspension was triggered by the refusal of Faulkner and his colleagues to accept the transfer of law and order powers to Westminster. Alliance had been ready to contest two local government by-elections as their first electoral test but the demise of the Stormont Government stopped them from taking place.

Alliance Party branches were expanding into such places as Shankill and Ardoyne, Andersonstown, South Derry and Portaferry. Bob Cooper, who was formerly a member of the Ulster Unionist Council and chair of Queen's University Belfast Young Unionists, took over from Grace Wilson as general secretary. In April 1972 seventeen aldermen and councillors on fifteen councils announced that they would be sitting from now on as Alliance party members. These members came from the Unionist Party, the Liberal Party, the SDLP and independents.

After brief ceasefires, violence continued unabated, including Bloody Friday in Belfast on 21 July when twenty-six IRA bombs killed eleven and injured 130 people. Ulster Vanguard, led by Bill Craig, former Minister of Home Affairs in Stormont, was formed as a symbol of Loyalist resistance and ideas for some form of independence for the province began to surface. Its membership included David Trimble and Reg Empey, both later to be leaders of the UUP.

## THE DARLINGTON AND SUNNINGDALE CONFERENCES

The British Government, under Prime Minister Edward Heath, decided to test the ground for the restoration of some form of devolution. In September 1972 he held a conference at Darlington to examine the options. As usual, several parties, including in this case the SDLP and Paisley's Democratic Unionist Party (DUP), refused to attend and only the Faulkner-led Official Unionists, Alliance and Northern Ireland Labour turned up. Not surprisingly there was no agreement, but the opportunity was taken by Alliance to put forward detailed proposals for an assembly and devolved government based on proportionality and without security powers in the initial stages. They also argued strongly that the link with Great Britain should not be broken without the support of a majority of Northern Ireland voters. In addition they said that there must be co-operation with the Republic of Ireland through an advisory Anglo-Irish Council involving Westminster MPs as well as members of the Northern Ireland Assembly. The ULP was not invited to the conference but nevertheless made a submission on similar lines, but with a Joint Council between Northern Ireland and the Republic only, rather than an Anglo-Irish Council.

Phelim O'Neill, Bob Cooper and William Whitelaw met regularly for lunch around this time. O'Neill and Cooper convinced Whitelaw that PR elections were needed. Whitelaw pushed it through against advice from his Cabinet colleagues.

In November 1972 a Green Paper was published by the British Government, which contained most of the ideas put forward at Darlington. The 'Irish Dimension' was clearly going to be the most contentious issue.

## CONCLUSION

A crisis was looming for Northern Ireland in the early 1960s. Although the IRA had been defeated by 1962 and a new prime minister was in post in 1963, other factors were at work. Fundamentalist preacher Ian Paisley was whipping up fear of the IRA and preaching vehement anti-Catholicism. Fear of the 50th Anniversary of the Easter Rising in 1966 promoted the revitalisation of the UVF in 1966, immediately followed by the Malvern Street murders of two innocent Catholics in 1966. Many Catholics with newly acquired confidence and energy were aware of the injustices and discrimination against themselves leading to the largely student-led Civil Rights Association formed in 1967. Terence O'Neill's offer of reforms was not enough for the Civil Rights movement but went too far for many of his Unionist colleagues. The Civil Rights marches merely angered the Unionist government and led to further repression. Republicans were provoked into more violence and the Loyalist extremes on the Unionist side retaliated with violence against the Catholic population. No progress was made in breaking down religious and community 'apartheid'. Indeed, it could be argued that the situation was in a downward spiral, with no solution in sight.

The New Ulster Movement had good new political ideas, but they needed others to put them into practice.

Despite escalating violence the new Alliance Party, based on firm principles, established itself with a solid organisational structure. It established associations and branches throughout Northern Ireland with over 10,000 members. Prior to any elections four Stormont MPs and one Westminster MP joined the party together with seventeen councillors. Party leaders were in regular negotiations with British Government ministers, aiming to establish a devolved Assembly with a power-sharing executive, based partly on the new thinking of the NUM, together with some of the half-formed proposals of O'Neill, Chichester-Clark and Faulkner. This led to new constitutional proposals, which would be then tested electorally.

The media largely ignored the emergence of the NUM and the Alliance Party. They were usually more concerned with the more dramatic and violent events and the more extreme political and paramilitary groups. This was always a problem for Alliance up until recent times.

The big question now was how would the new Alliance Party fare in elections? Would the initial enthusiasm be transferred into votes? Some thought that Alliance would overwhelm all the others parties and form a majority. Some opinion polls suggested 20% support for Alliance.

# 2

# 'To take up arms':
# The first elections 1973–1975

## INTRODUCTION

The first real electoral opportunities for the Alliance Party came in 1973, with elections to the twenty-six local councils, followed by elections to the proposed new Assembly. The Alliance Party's first attempts at electoral campaigning are described in this chapter. A novel voting method using the Single Transferable Vote (STV) and the effects of the system on the party's fortunes are discussed. The Assembly was set up with Alliance having two ministers, but this was quickly followed by Westminster elections, the Ulster Workers' Strike and hence the collapse of the Assembly. In 1975 there were more elections to a Constitutional Convention, which also ended in failure.

## ALLIANCE CAMPAIGNING FOR ELECTIONS

The fledgling Alliance Party had three (Stormont) MPs and seventeen councillors but none of them had been elected as Alliance Party candidates. So the first test of the Alliance Party at the ballot box was imminent. At first what the party lacked in experience and election campaigning know-how was made up for by lots of enthusiasm, energy and hard work. They began a campaign of doorstep canvassing. People who had connections with the Liberals in Great Britain were able to train canvassers in how to do it; 'faith, hope and door-knocking', as Liberal Eric Lubbock said when asked how he won the famous Orpington by-election in 1962. A *Canvasser's Handbook* was produced. The basic principles developed then still hold, referred to recently by former Chief Executive Gerry Lynch as 'PIG' – Persuade, Identify, and Get them out! First, one had to persuade people that voting for Alliance candidates was the right thing to do. This was never easy and is still not easy. Many people vote out of fear of the 'other side', or else they feel a loyalty to the group their family has always supported. The first step did not begin on the doorstep; the groundwork was laid by advertising, posters, leaflets, TV and radio broadcasts. Later, focus leaflets and local surveys were used, so that people would know what the Alliance Party was offering. Only then did doorstep canvassing begin. Enthusiasm was high among party members, as an opinion poll had suggested that there was about 20% support for the Alliance Party.

The aim on the doorstep in step two was to identify those intending to vote for the Alliance candidate while presenting a pleasant and courteous profile, whatever the response from the householder whose name would be obtained from the electoral roll. The aim was to cover as many households as possible in the time available, not to stop for discussion or argument on the doorstep. Most people appreciated being canvassed. It showed a concern for them personally. Rarely did one have a disagreeable experience, though non-committal responses were common. The canvasser needed to assess the degree of commitment to vote Alliance, and mark a canvass sheet accordingly as 'Yes', 'Possible' or 'No'.

On polling day step three was to call again to remind people to go and vote. This was sometimes difficult as people were often having their dinner or watching TV or said they would be out later. This 'knocking-up' was to be repeated several times if necessary. Sometimes the offer of a lift to the polling station helped. In the Glenville area of Whiteabbey, one of the local ladies, Alice McCarran, would organise lifts to the polling station, which was rather a long way to walk for the elderly. So a relay of cars was arranged. One had to be careful though that one was not giving lifts to those whose intention was to vote for an opposition candidate!

Canvassing was a relatively novel process in Northern Ireland at that time. Unionists went round waving the Union Jack (or other unmistakably Unionist flags) and speaking through a car-mounted public address system. Nationalist politicians had only had a token involvement in politics as they were invariably out-voted by the dominant Unionists. So for a new party it was most important to take a personal approach. I remember an instance where a person who normally voted for the SDLP was canvassed by Howard Johnston for the Alliance candidate, and as no one had bothered to call from the SDLP, she voted Alliance on that occasion.

It was said that the Liberals in Liverpool called on every house four times during a by-election campaign. Alliance rarely had the manpower for that degree of intense canvassing. They were sometimes very wary of canvassing in strongly Loyalist areas such as Monkstown, Rathcoole and the Shankill Road, and perhaps less so in Nationalist areas such as Bawnmore and Ballymurphy.

On one occasion when canvassing Hugh Thompson and John Campbell were shouted at in a posh area of Bangor, but when they finished a man came out and apologised. He was in the middle of a row with his wife!

Hugh Thompson and Phil McGarry were canvassing in the New Lodge Road. It went quite well until the last house where a man objected. He said they were in 'provo' territory. He threw stones at them and they had to run. But then some young people told them, 'It is not as "provo" as he thinks.'

## THE SINGLE TRANSFERABLE VOTING SYSTEM

Thomas Hare invented the Single Transferable Voting (STV) system in the nineteenth century.[57] It was used in both the Irish Free State (now the Republic of Ireland) and in Northern Ireland immediately after Partition in 1925 until 1929, when it was abandoned by the Unionist-dominated Stormont Government.[58]

For the first time since 1925 it was decided to introduce a form of Proportional Representation (PR) in elections for local government and Assemblies in Northern Ireland. Westminster elections continued to operate the traditional 'First Past the Post' system. PR was also used, and continues to be used, for all elections in the Republic of Ireland and in most other EU countries.

Various forms of PR were possible. In one system an elector would vote for the political party of one's choice and the seats would be allocated on the basis of the percentage of votes for each party. Then there is a list system, as used now for EU elections in Great Britain and also for the Forum elections in 1996. But these are rather impersonal. In the STV system one votes for the candidate of one's choice. Each electoral area is multi-member; thus several people are elected for the same area, usually between five and seven, though this rose to ten in one instance in 1982. Instead of putting an 'X' against just one candidate the candidates are numbered in order of preference. So if one's candidate of first preference is not elected, one's vote is transferred to the second choice and so on. To get elected a candidate has to obtain a certain 'quota' of votes, calculated as the total number of valid votes divided by the number of seats to be filled plus one, and then one is added on to that figure. A candidate whose votes reach or exceed the quota is 'deemed elected'. If an elected candidate obtains more votes than the quota then the excess votes are transferred to the voter's next choices. If no candidate reaches the quota, then the one(s) with the lowest vote(s) are eliminated and their votes redistributed to the second preference candidates. This procedure continues until candidates reach the quota, or until the remaining number of candidates equals the remaining number of seats still to be filled. Thus one's vote is never wasted, provided of course that one votes all the way down the ballot paper. Thus, one has a single vote, but it is transferable to second and third preferences and so on as far as one wished to go. It was the Alliance Party who persuaded then Secretary of State William Whitelaw to introduce this system in Northern Ireland.

The counting procedure is quite complex. It can last several days and involve a number of counts. The most celebrated (or notorious) example was in the 1982 Assembly election in South Antrim. There were twenty-six candidates and ten seats to fill. Counting continued for forty-two hours over three days. I was there as an observer for most of that time.

While the STV method of proportional representation has served centre minority parties well at times, the amount of cross-community vote transfers was never large. Horowitz argues that in a multi-seat constituency each tribe tends to transfer their votes between members of their own side.[59] A few will transfer to the middle, but very few across to the other community. He points out that in the Assembly elections of 1998, ninety out of the one hundred and eight MLAs were elected on first preference votes.

Horowitz suggests that an incentive is needed to encourage people to vote across the community,[60] such as the Alternate Vote (AV) system. In this system there is one seat per constituency, as in the classic Westminster system. One still marks one's ballot paper with preferences, 1, 2, 3, etc. In order to be elected, a candidate must receive or acquire 50+1% of the votes. As with STV, if the candidate is not elected on the first count, the candidate with the lowest vote is eliminated and her/his votes are redistributed according to the second preference. This procedure continues until a candidate has 50+1% of the votes or until there are only two candidates left, in which case the one with the highest vote wins. The voter knows that someone must be elected. If it is not his favoured candidate then it will be someone from another party, maybe from the other tribe. Thus he/she cannot put another of his own party as second choice, but must make the next best choice, which is likely to be a moderate or centre party candidate. An attempt to introduce this system across the UK for Westminster elections was unfortunately rejected in a referendum in 2010.

So how might Alliance Party candidates fare from an AV system? In general it does not sound as favourable as the STV system, where the quota needed to be elected is 16.67% in a five-seat constituency. In a by-election, for example, to replace one councillor, the voting system is nominally STV, but is in effect the same as AV. Alliance has had some surprising victories in by-elections. In twenty-seven by-election situations between 1973 and 1986, Alliance won five seats, two unopposed but three by the AV method. In February 1975 David Hilditch won a seat in Carrickfergus Area B with a first count of 37%, winning on the second count.[61] Louise Devlin won a seat in North Down in December 1976 in a straight fight with a Unionist, gaining 51% of votes.[62] In Derry City in February 1979, Arthur Barr obtained 31% and went on to win the seat.[63] Over most of these by-elections, even where the Alliance candidate did not win, the Alliance vote was usually increased compared with the original election.[64]

One can see that Alliance generally has done better in these by-elections with AV than in the original election with STV. Other factors need to be considered, though. In by-elections the turnout is usually much lower, and the party workers make a big effort to get out the Alliance vote. One cannot in fact draw any firm conclusion about the advantage of AV, except that Alliance fares quite well.

## LOCAL GOVERNMENT ELECTIONS 1973

The first opportunity for the Alliance Party to test its appeal to the people came on 30 May 1973 with local government elections for the twenty-six new council areas. The STV system was used.

With great enthusiasm the party put up a very large number of candidates – 238 – in all twenty-six council districts. These included twenty-three candidates in Belfast, sixteen in Derry and thirteen in Newry and Mourne. Some thought that perhaps the whole system would be changed with a large number of Alliance Party councillors elected.

This optimism proved to be misguided as the expectations were not realised. It has been observed that responses to questionnaires usually overestimate the support given to Alliance, while underestimating the support given to more extreme parties such as the DUP and later Sinn Féin. Alliance was a new party testing the electors' allegiance for the first time.

In the event Alliance obtained 94,474 votes (13.7%), second only to the UUP, and ahead of the SDLP. Alliance won sixty-three council seats out of a total of 526 (12.0%) in twenty electoral areas. The SDLP won eighty-three

(15.8%) seats with 92,600 votes (13.4%). The NILP, who had provided the main opposition in the old Stormont, obtained 17,422 votes (2.5%) for only four Council Seats (0.76%). Probably the reason for Alliance's modest yield of seats was that they put up too many candidates spread over too many electoral wards, whereas the SDLP concentrated their efforts in areas where they had the greatest support. The results are shown in Table 1, giving the local government electoral results for all elections from 1973 to 1997. Table 2 shows results from 2001 to 2014.

Table 1: Local Government Election Results for the Alliance Party

|  | 1973 | 1977 | 1981 | 1985 | 1989 | 1993 | 1997 |
|---|---|---|---|---|---|---|---|
| Antrim | 2 | 2 | 1 | 1 | 1 | 2 | 2 |
| Ards | 2 | 5 | 3 | 3 | 4 | 6 | 5 |
| Armagh | 1 | 1 | 0 | 0 | 0 | 0 | 0 |
| Ballymena | 1 | 1 | 0 | 0 | 1 | 1 | 1 |
| Ballymoney | 1 | 1 | 1 | 0 | 0 | 0 | 0 |
| Banbridge | 0 | 0 | 0 | 0 | 0 | 1 | 1 |
| Belfast | 8 | 13 | 7 | 8 | 6 | 5 | 6 |
| Carrick | 3 | 5 | 3 | 3 | 4 | 6 | 5 |
| Castlereagh | 5 | 7 | 4 | 3 | 4 | 5 | 4 |
| Coleraine | 3 | 2 | 1 | 2 | 2 | 2 | 3 |
| Cookstown | 0 | 0 | 0 | 0 | 0 | 0 | 0 |
| Craigavon | 4 | 3 | 1 | 0 | 2 | 2 | 1 |
| Derry | 4 | 2 | 0 | 0 | 0 | 0 | 0 |
| Dungannon | 0 | 0 | 0 | 0 | 0 | 0 | 0 |
| Down | 2 | 3 | 1 | 0 | 1 | 0 | 0 |
| Fermanagh | 0 | 0 | 0 | 0 | 0 | 0 | 0 |
| Larne | 3 | 4 | 3 | 2 | 2 | 2 | 1 |
| Limavady | 2 | 0 | 0 | 0 | 0 | 0 | 0 |
| Lisburn | 3 | 3 | 2 | 3 | 2 | 2 | 3 |
| Moyle | 0 | 0 | 0 | 0 | 0 | 0 | 0 |
| Magherafelt | 0 | 0 | 0 | 0 | 0 | 0 | 0 |
| Newry M | 4 | 3 | 0 | 0 | 0 | 0 | 0 |
| N'Abbey | 3 | 6 | 3 | 2 | 4 | 4 | 3 |
| N Down | 7 | 7 | 6 | 7 | 4 | 5 | 6 |
| Omagh | 3 | 3 | 2 | 0 | 0 | 1 | 1 |
| Strabane | 2 | 0 | 0 | 0 | 1 | 0 | 0 |
|  | **63** | **70** | **38** | **34** | **38** | **44** | **41** |

Table 2

| | 2001 | 2005 | 2011 | New Councils | 2014 |
|---|---|---|---|---|---|
| Antrim | 0 | 2 | 2 | Antrim & Newtownabbey | 4 |
| Ards | 4 | 3 | 3 | | |
| Armagh | 0 | 0 | 0 | | |
| Ballymena | 0 | 0 | 1 | | |
| Ballymoney 1 | 0 | 0 | 0 | | |
| Banbridge | 1 | 1 | 1 | Armagh & Banbridge | 0 |
| Belfast | 3 | 4 | 6 | Belfast | 8 |
| Carrick | 5 | 3 | 3 | E Antrim | 3 |
| Castlereagh | 4 | 4 | 4 | | |
| Coleraine | 0 | 0 | 0 | Causeway | 1 |
| Cookstown | 0 | 0 | 0 | Mid Ulster | 0 |
| Craigavon | 0 | 0 | 1 | | |
| Derry | 0 | 0 | 0 | Derry & Strabane | 0 |
| Dungannon | 0 | 0 | 0 | | |
| Down | 0 | 0 | 1 | | |
| Fermanagh | 0 | 0 | 0 | Fermanagh & Omagh | 0 |
| Larne | 2 | 2 | 2 | | |
| Limavady | 0 | 0 | 0 | | |
| Lisburn | 3 | 3 | 3 | Lisburn & Castlereagh | 7 |
| Moyle | 0 | 0 | 0 | | |
| Magherafelt | 0 | 0 | 0 | | |
| Newry M | 0 | 0 | 0 | Mournes & Down | 2 |
| N'Abbey | 1 | 2 | 5 | | |
| N Down | 5 | 6 | 6 | North Down & Ards | 7 |
| Omagh | 0 | 0 | 0 | | |
| Strabane | 0 | 0 | 0 | | |
| | **28** | **30** | **44** | | **32** |

Candidates' names are listed in alphabetical order on the ballot papers, so in the early elections those whose names were higher on the alphabet usually received more first-preference votes and thus were more likely to be elected, particularly in wards where Alliance had several candidates, who would at that time be mostly unknown to the electorate. An example of this effect was in the Jordanstown ward (Area C) of Newtownabbey. There were three Alliance Party candidates, Peter Johnston, George Jones and Claire Martin. Only Peter Johnston was elected in 1973, though he was the least committed to being a councillor. It later turned out that the best performing local councillor was Claire Martin, who was elected unopposed at a by-election. She had demonstrated notable success in relating to constituents. George Jones was also elected in 1977 and proved to be a very effective councillor. In time the party countered this effect by promoting particular candidates in particular areas and by asking for a first-preference vote for that person in those areas. This generally worked well, though sometimes the electorate was perverse and foiled these plans.

One can compare the percentage of votes obtained with the percentage of seats won to see the benefits and effectiveness of the PR system. Some examples of this analysis were recorded for the South and East Antrim areas. It was found that in Antrim Town Alliance won two out of fifteen seats (13.3%) with a first preference vote of 16.2%. In Carrickfergus they won three out of fifteen seats (20%) with 22.2% of the vote. In Lisburn they won four out of twenty-three seats (17.4%) with 18.1% of the vote. In Newtownabbey they won three out of twenty-one seats (14.3%) with 18.9% of the votes. The best results were: Antrim Area B, where they won one out of five (20%) with 12.1% of the first preference votes; Newtownabbey Area B, where they won one out of six seats (16.7%) with 13.1% of votes; and in Lisburn D, where they won two out of five seats (40%) with 24.8% of votes. The worst results were: Antrim A, where they won zero seats with 7.7% of votes and Lisburn A, where they won zero seats with 8.5% of votes.

The Alliance Party was particularly interested to see how well the transfer of votes worked, but they were not well organised enough to do this thoroughly in this election.

Overall Alliance won council seats in all but six council areas, with eight in Belfast, seven in North Down, five in Castlereagh and four each in Derry, Craigavon, and Newry and Mourne. Then they had three each in Carrick, Coleraine, Larne, Lisburn, Newtownabbey, and Omagh; with two each in Ards, Antrim, Down, Limavady and Strabane; and one each in Armagh, Ballymena and Ballymoney.

The trouble with elections in Northern Ireland is that there is only one issue for many people. Forget about the policies devised by Alliance to run the borough or the country. The only issue is The Border! In every election people tend to vote according to whether they are in favour of continuing the union with Great Britain or whether they wish to join an all-Ireland, thirty-two-county Republic, even in local government elections. An attempt was made to settle this issue with a border poll in March 1973 when 591,820 (98.9%) people voted in favour of keeping the union and 6,463 (1.08%) voted in favour of a united Ireland. However, as most Republicans and Nationalists boycotted the poll and refused to vote, the issue was not settled. The Alliance Party always said, and continues to say, that they go along with the wishes of the majority.

## ASSEMBLY ELECTIONS 1973

The next elections, in June 1973, were for the proposed new Assembly to replace the old Stormont Parliament. Following various discussions with some of the political parties, while no agreed conclusions were reached the British Government put forward a discussion paper, 'The Future of Northern Ireland', and then a government White Paper, 'Northern Ireland Constitutional Proposals'. Only the Alliance Party fully supported this paper. The SDLP gave it qualified support. Unionist leader Brian Faulkner fudged the key issue of power sharing to obtain the support of the Ulster Unionist Party (UUP). The DUP and Vanguard rejected it. However, it led to a Northern Ireland Constitution Bill and a Northern Ireland Assembly Bill, and so on 28 June 1973 elections were held for the proposed Assembly, just one month after the local government elections.

There was great controversy among Unionists for this election, because it was based on a government constitutional proposal for a new Assembly to involve a power-sharing executive, promoted in the White Paper (March 1973). The main principles of the Constitution Act were:

1.  Maintenance of the United Kingdom status of Northern Ireland, in accordance with the wishes of the vast majority expressed in the Border Referendum.
2.  The formation of a power-sharing executive, which should A have the support of the majority of the people, B should contain members adequately representative of the Catholic and Protestant sections of the community.
3.  Setting up a Council of Ireland composed of seven members from the power-sharing executive, and seven members from the Irish Government. It was to have 'executive and harmonising functions and a consultative role'. In addition there would be a Consultative Assembly to be made up of thirty members from Dáil Éireann and thirty members from the Northern Ireland Assembly, which was to have 'advisory and review functions' only.

Many Unionists were against the Constitutional power-sharing proposals (anti-white paper) and bitterly against the idea of a Council of Ireland, though a large group led by Brian Faulkner were 'pledged' to support them (pro-white paper). Of the others, Paisley's DUP was against as were Bill Craig's Vanguard Unionist Party (VUP). A rump of the Official Unionist Party led by Harry West was also against the proposals. Anne Dickson, a former Stormont MP, stood as an independent Unionist, who largely supported the proposals, though was not part of Faulkner's 'pledged Unionists'. She later became leader of UPNI as this group became known after Brian Faulkner's tragic death from a horse riding accident.

The Alliance Party and the NILP supported the proposals, but the SDLP gave only qualified support. The Workers Party (a new Republican party that had been formed from the now defunct Official IRA) also rejected it. In spite of opposition, the proposals went ahead and, crucially, all parties agreed to contest the elections to the new Assembly, which John Hume described as a 'negotiating table'.

At this stage Alliance had acquired two new members from the Unionist Party: Stratton Mills, Westminster MP for North Belfast, and Robin Baillie, Stormont MP for Newtownabbey. Neither of these people played any major part in Alliance, nor did they stand for re-election as Alliance candidates did.

The Alliance Party fielded thirty-five candidates in these elections, including some in each of the twelve electoral areas, which coincided with the Westminster Constituencies. These included four in South Belfast, four in North Antrim (Phelim O'Neill's' constituency), four in North Down (Bertie McConnell's' Constituency). In most cases the alphabetical effect worked. Thus in West Belfast, North Belfast, South Belfast, South Antrim, and North Down, the candidate highest in the alphabet was elected. The exceptions were East Belfast, where party leader Oliver Napier was elected over Kate Condy, and in North Antrim, where Dr Hugh Wilson was elected over Bill Kelly, J. Miller and Phelim O'Neill. Perhaps as a doctor Hugh Wilson was already better known.

This time Alliance Party candidates obtained 66,541 votes (9.2%) from which eight Assembly members were elected out of seventy-eight total seats (10.3%) which was a slightly better return on votes than the local government elections. Sir Oliver Napier suggested that the reason for the lower vote than in the local government election was that the SDLP had criticised Catholics for voting for the Alliance Party.[65] The SDLP obtained 22.1% to elect nineteen Assembly members (24.4%). The NILP had 2.6%, yielding one member (1.3%). None of the Alliance candidates was elected easily. The best result was in North Down where Lord Henry Dunleath obtained 4,482 votes

and former Stormont MP Bertie McConnell obtained 3,271 votes to defeat
UUP Andrew Donaldson by 233 votes. Both were elected on the thirteenth
and last count. Basil Glass was the first Alliance Assemblyman to be elected
standing in South Belfast. He was second to be elected on the twelfth count
with 5,148 votes (the quota was 7,532). Derek Crothers in South Antrim
with 5,975 votes (quota 8,338) was fourth elected on the thirteenth count.

It had been decided that Catholic Oliver Napier would stand in largely
Protestant East Belfast and Protestant Bob Cooper in largely Catholic West
Belfast. It just about worked. Oliver Napier obtained 4,941 votes and was elected
on the final (eighteenth) count (along with David Bleakley of the NILP who
defeated UUP Walter McFarland by 255 votes). Bob Cooper obtained 3,160
votes and was also elected on the final (twelfth) count. As already mentioned,
Hugh Wilson was elected for North Antrim with 2,876 votes on the last
(fifteenth) count, whereas former Stormont MP Phelim O'Neill with 1,701
votes was eliminated. John Ferguson was lucky to be elected for North Belfast
with 1,958 votes on the last (fifteenth) count, defeating UUP Cecil Walker
(later to become Unionist MP) by a mere eighty-eight votes. Unfortunately
in Derry Ivor Canavan was not elected, despite his success in the local government election and becoming Deputy Mayor and then Lord Mayor of Derry.
However, his brother Michael Canavan was elected for the SDLP. In Mid-Ulster
former Stormont MP Tom Gormley was defeated with 2,055 votes. No Alliance
candidates were elected for Armagh, Fermanagh-South Tyrone or Mid-Ulster.

The count in South Antrim was very interesting. Alliance observers were
beginning to get the hang of 'tallying' – watching as the counting proceeded to
see roughly what proportion of Pro-Alliance votes came from which ballot boxes.

There was a bit of a scare at the count in Mossley Primary School. Monica
Tomlin, daughter of Alliance Party candidate Joan Tomlin, did not have access
to the counting station and was sitting in a car outside. Shots were heard
(it was a fairly loyalist area). Joan asked if Monica could be allowed into the
building, if not into the counting area. Billy Snoddy (VUP) was against it,
but Revd Robert Bradford, a Methodist minister also standing for Vanguard,
was more sympathetic and fortunately his view prevailed with the Presiding
Officer, and Monica was allowed inside.

A detailed survey of the transfers in South Antrim was carried out for
these elections. The main conclusions were that the SDLP transferred very
precisely with 94% of their surplus votes coming to Alliance. Only 5% went
to any Unionists. The NILP votes were fickle, 2% was non-transferable; 50%
came to Alliance, and 20% to the SDLP, the remainder going to a variety
of Unionists. It was not clear where Independent Unionist Anne Dickson's

surplus vote went though Alliance gained 10%. Most went to pledged Unionists (42%) and non-pledged Unionists (32%). 10% were not transferable as voters had just plumped for her.

Unionist voters hardly distinguished between pledged (37%) and unpledged (45%) Unionists. The DUP and VUP received relatively few transfers from other Unionists, Alliance received even less and the NILP and the SDLP received negligible votes from Unionists.

Generally the DUP was disfavoured relative to the VUP by all parties (except the SDLP who ignored both). Alliance votes were transferred in all directions: SDLP 7%, NILP 3.5%, pledged Unionists 3.1%, unpledged Unionists 1%, VUP 0.7%, and DUP 0.3%. A clear distinction was made by Alliance voters between pledged and unpledged Unionists, 38% to 17%. 33% of Alliance votes became non-transferable, of which two thirds were originally first-preference Alliance votes and not just transfers from the SDLP or the NILP.

Of the 210 candidates in the 1973 Assembly election, only forty-two (20%) had been candidates in the last general election for the old Northern Ireland House of Commons in 1969; one had been a senator at the time the Senate was dissolved, and another had been a candidate in one of the last by-elections to the old House of Commons.[66]

The Assembly and Executive were elected by fair and democratic means, using an electoral system more truly representative than in the usual UK system. The number of seats gained was closely proportional to the number of first-preference votes cast for each party. Although no single party obtained an overall majority of seats, an overall majority of members (reflecting the overall majority of voters) were in favour of the principles of the Constitution Act, as set out in the White Paper published before the election.

The result of these elections was that of those elected in favour of the power-sharing Assembly there were twenty-two Unionists, nineteen SDLP, eight Alliance and one NILP, together with one independent Unionist (Anne Dickson), a total of fifty-one (65%). Opposing the power sharing were ten Unionists, eight DUP, eight VUP and one independent, a total of twenty-seven (35%). There were also a fair spread of 'Catholic' members (SDLP) and 'Protestant' members (Unionists). However, it should be noted that there was not a majority of Unionists of all persuasions in favour of the power-sharing executive. Although there were twenty-two Unionists in favour there were twenty-seven against. Overall there was a mandate to go ahead with the proposals and set up a power-sharing executive. This now included Alliance members Oliver Napier as Minister of Law Reform and Bob Cooper as (non-voting) Minister for Manpower Services.

## THE ASSEMBLY

The first meeting of the new Assembly was on 31 July 1973. A series of talks between the Secretary of State, William Whitelaw, with the UUP, Alliance and the SDLP, were held between 5 and 16 October to discuss the formation of the Executive, which was then formed on 21 November, with Brian Faulkner of the UUP as Chief Executive and Gerry Fitt of the SDLP as his deputy.

The issue of the 'Council of Ireland' had not been settled. So another conference was held at Sunningdale in England from 6 to 7 December with the British Prime Minister, Edward Heath, the Irish Taoiseach, Liam Cosgrave, and other ministers. There were six UUP, six SDLP and three Alliance delegates. Oliver Napier, leader of the Alliance, laid down the precondition that the Alliance Party would not agree to a Council of Ireland, 'Which in any way undermines Northern Ireland's position within the United Kingdom'.

The Republic of Ireland agreed to recognise the status of Northern Ireland but would not agree to delete Clauses 2 and 3 of their 1937 Constitution in which they claimed jurisdiction over all thirty-two counties of Ireland. They did agree on some cross-border co-operation on security, but the Republic was very slow to honour its obligations and would not agree to extradite wanted people, saying they would try them in the place where they were caught. A Council of Ireland was agreed which would allow co-operation on commerce, tourism, environmental matters and power supplies, in a bipartisan manner.[67]

Although the Council of Ireland was agreed, different parties had different perceptions of it. The Unionists considered it as an advisory body whereas the SDLP thought it was the route to a united Ireland. The DUP understood this SDLP angle and said, 'Dublin is only a Sunningdale away'.

After the meeting on 28 December Oliver Napier asked through a letter in the *Irish Times*, 'Do you really want a Council of Ireland? The Council of Ireland hangs by a thread … If you do nothing in the next few weeks, history will judge you and its judgment will be harsh and unforgiving.'[68] This prediction proved only too true!

## TWO WESTMINSTER ELECTIONS AND THE ULSTER WORKERS' STRIKE 1974

As already noted, the White Paper proposals did not have the support of a majority of Unionists of all persuasions in the Assembly. There had not been a referendum on the Constitutional proposals and twenty-seven Unionist

Assemblymen were against it, with only twenty-two in favour. So when the Assembly commenced, meeting on 31 July 1973, there was much disruption and even brawling and many objections, led largely by Ian Paisley, leader of the DUP. He led with slogans such as: 'No power sharing with Republicans' (intending that to include the SDLP), 'Home Rule is Rome Rule' and 'Sunningdale is the road to Dublin'. In these activities he was much supported by Bill Craig leader of the VUP. The new Speaker, Unionist Nat Minford, had a difficult time keeping order in the face of members' unbecoming behaviour. Despite this the Assembly continued to meet.

In Great Britain Edward's Heath's Conservative government was experiencing formidable economic problems. So when the British Government called a surprise general election, the anti-agreement Unionists put their differences aside and formed the Ulster Unionist United Coalition (UUUC) to fight the general election. Alliance appeared to be rather nonplussed by this decision and put up only three candidates who were in South Belfast, South Antrim and Armagh. Overall they obtained 22,660 votes (3.2%). This figure was, however, 12.2% in the seats contested. Of the eleven Unionists elected, all were from the UUUC against the power-sharing executive; only one seat went to the SDLP – Gerry Fitt in West Belfast. This election had effectively acted as a referendum against the power-sharing Executive and was followed by the Ulster Workers' Council strike.

On Tuesday 14 May 1974 there was a debate in the Northern Ireland Assembly on a motion condemning power-sharing and the Council of Ireland. The motion was defeated by forty-four votes to twenty-eight. But at 6 p.m., following the conclusion of the Assembly debate, Harry Murray (who after the strike finished, actually joined the Alliance Party for a while!) announced to a group of journalists that a general strike was to start the following day. The strike was organised by the so-called Ulster Workers' Council (UWC).

The strike began in the electricity industry, resulting in frequent power cuts. It was directed by Loyalist paramilitary groups such as the UDA and the UVF who set up barricades, controlled distribution of petrol and other essential supplies. It is alleged that there was much collusion by the predominantly Protestant RUC with these groups. The British Army seemed not to know how to deal with the situation. The new Labour government led by Prime Minster Harold Wilson was ill-equipped to cope.

At first the strike did not have overwhelming support. So on Tuesday 21 May 1974 (day 7 of the UWC strike), Len Murray, the then general secretary of the Trades Union Council (TUC), led a 'back-to-work' march. The march was supported by leading local Trade Union officials who attempted to lead workers back to the Belfast shipyard and factories in east Belfast. Only about 200 people joined the march, which was flanked by members of the RUC and British troops. A hostile crowd still managed to assault some of those marching.

Following this an updated list of those services which were to be allowed through roadblocks and the opening times permitted for shops were issued by the 'Ulster Army Council'. The Ulster Army Council was set up in 1973 by Andy Tyrie to coordinate the activities of the UDA and UVF during the UWC strike.[69]

Meanwhile the Executive brought to a conclusion its discussion on the Sunningdale Agreement on 22 May when Brian Faulkner, the Chief Executive, announced that the agreement should now be implemented in two phases. The first was to set up a Council of Ministers for consultation, co-operation, and co-ordination of action between the Northern Ireland Executive, and the Government of the Republic of Ireland in relation to social and economic matters. Further aspects, such as a Consultative Assembly, transfers of functions to the Council, appointment of a secretary general, would be part of a second phase following the testing of public opinion at a further Assembly election.

These proposals were rejected by leaders of the Ulster Workers' Council (UWC) and other Loyalist leaders. The British Government repeated their stance on not negotiating with the UWC. Then, on Friday 24 May 1974 (day ten of the UWC strike), talks were held at Chequers, the country home of the British prime minister, involving the British Prime Minister Harold Wilson, Brian Faulkner, Gerry Fitt, and Oliver Napier. A statement was issued after the talks stated that there would be no negotiations with those who operated outside constitutional politics.

Next day Harold Wilson made a broadcast on (BBC) television and radio at 10.15 p.m. The speech proved to be totally counterproductive. At one point in the speech Wilson referred to 'spongers' – meaning the UWC and its supporters. Most Unionists took the 'spongers' reference as a slight against themselves. Indeed some Protestants took to wearing small sponges in their lapels the following days as a gesture of support for the strike.

On Sunday 26 May the leaders of the UWC strike claimed that support was continuing to grow. The UWC also claimed that its system of permits was working well in maintaining 'essential services', particularly the supply of petrol. The British Army arrested more than thirty men in raids on Protestant areas of Belfast. Gerry Fitt, then Deputy Chief Executive, attended a meeting at the Northern Ireland Office (NIO). The SDLP met at 1 p.m. A meeting of Brian Faulkner's Unionist ministers also took place.

On Monday 27 May gas supplies to Belfast and other outlying districts were affected by a drop in pressure and a warning was issued that consumers should switch off their supply at the mains. The British Army took charge of twenty-one petrol stations throughout Northern Ireland. These petrol stations were to supply petrol to essential users who could obtain a permit from the Ministry of Commerce. The UWC retaliated by announcing that the British Army would have to undertake the supply of all essential services including basics such as bread and milk. A call was issued for workers to stop their assistance in the provision of essential services. The UWC also stated that the Ballylumford power station, County Antrim, would close at midnight.

On Tuesday 28 May, Chief Executive Brian Faulkner informed the Secretary of State, now Merlyn Rees, that he and his Unionist colleagues had concluded that negotiation or mediation must be considered, otherwise they would have to resign. The Alliance Party favoured mediation. The SDLP members were opposed to either negotiation or mediation. The Secretary of State declined to consider either proposal. Therefore Brian Faulkner and his Unionist Members resigned, effectively ending the Assembly and its power-sharing Executive.

Finally, on Wednesday 29 May 1974, the leaders of the UWC officially called off the strike and a return to work began across Northern Ireland. On Thursday 30 May 1974 the Northern Ireland Assembly was formally prorogued.

The illegal Loyalist paramilitary-led UWC strike had been allowed to bring down the power-sharing Executive and Assembly. Despite the Labour Party under Harold Wilson with Home Secretary James Callaghan having had experience of trying to deal with the early part of the Troubles 1968 to 1970, including bringing in the British Army, when the Conservatives surprisingly won the 1970 general election, new Secretary of State for Northern Ireland William Whitelaw was much more astute in dealing with the situation in that he talked to key participants, including members of the NUM and Alliance Party, before acting. However, when they lost to Labour in 1974, Labour Minister Merlyn Rees failed to deal with the UWC strike situation and then Prime Minister Harold Wilson showed total insensitivity in calling NI people (Unionists) 'spongers'. Following the collapse of the Assembly and Executive, the new Secretary of State, Roy Mason, dealt in a heavy-handed way with the security situation. Not until the Conservatives regained power in 1979 were new political initiatives attempted, with Tom King and then Jim Prior.

Another general election was called in October 1974. This time Alliance had six candidates. They were in North and South Belfast, North and South

Antrim, North Down, Fermanagh, and South Tyrone. This time Alliance obtained 44,644 votes (6.3%), which represented 16.8% in the seats contested. Again those elected were eleven Unionist anti-power-sharing candidates (UUUC) and one SDLP.

From then on it became party policy to try and field a candidate in all Constituencies at every Westminster election to obtain the best overall popular vote. So in 1979 Alliance fielded twelve candidates and obtained 82,892 votes (11.9%), but they gained no seats as voting was always by the UK first past the post system.

## CONSTITUTIONAL CONVENTION ELECTIONS 1975

Following the failure of the Assembly and Executive, the British Government published a White Paper in July 1974 which proposed setting up a Constitutional Convention to consider 'what provisions for the government of Northern Ireland would be likely to command the most widespread acceptance throughout the community there'.[70] If the recommendations produced commanded the support of the majority and widespread support in the community, a referendum would be held on these proposals. To facilitate this process, a new set of elections was called for 1 May 1975.

On this occasion the Alliance Party fielded twenty-four candidates, received 64,657 votes (9.8%) and again obtained eight seats. They lost the seat in North Belfast where they put up two candidates (John Ferguson who received 2,207 and James Robinson 518) but they obtained an extra seat in South Belfast where both Basil Glass and Jim Hendron were elected. Basil was second to be elected on the first count; Jim needed transfers. He had 2,499 votes and the SDLP had 2,500. He picked up NILP votes and some others. When the SDLP was eliminated he got 82% of their transfers! His brother Joe Hendron was standing in West Belfast for the SDLP and he had encouraged people to vote for Jim. After the election Basil and Jim obtained a tandem bicycle from Gilnahirk and rode round the streets. At the risk of being knocked over by a bus, they posed for a photograph which appeared on the front page of the *Belfast Telegraph* and of the *Sunday Times*.

In East Belfast Oliver Napier was second to be elected with 7,961 votes (the highest of any Alliance candidate) ahead of Kate Condy with 1,485 votes. Bob Cooper was again elected in West Belfast with 3,293 votes, ahead of Joe Hendron for the SDLP who had 2,840 votes. In South Antrim Charles

Kinahan took over the seat from Derek Crothers who did not stand again. He was fifth to be elected with 5,294 votes, while John Cousins obtained 3,228 votes. Hugh Wilson was again successful in North Antrim with 4,601 votes, coming fourth. Maurice McHenry got 1,311 votes for Alliance. In North Down Lord Dunleath and Bertie McConnell were again both elected. Lord Dunleath came in third with 4,616 votes, with Bertie McConnell coming sixth with 3,099 votes. Keith Jones also stood there and got 2,424 votes. In Derry Ivor Canavan again lost out with 2,889 votes to his brother Michael who took a seat for the SDLP. Bill Mathews took 1,889 votes in Derry. No other Alliance candidate was successful. Bill Barbour got 1,464 votes in Fermanagh-South Tyrone; in Armagh Brian English won 1,307 votes; in Mid Ulster Aidan Lagan won 1,826 votes and Douglas Cooper won 1,526; while in South Down Anthony Williamson won 1,612 votes and Denys Rowan-Hamilton 1,509.

Faulkner's pro-power sharing Unionists, now called the Unionist Party of Northern Ireland Local (UPNI), only obtained five seats with 50,591 votes, whereas the UUP/UUUC coalition obtained nineteen seats with 167,214 votes, twelve seats went to the DUP/UUUC with 97,073 votes and fourteen seats to the VUP/UUUC with 83,507 votes. There were two other Unionist seats. SDLP obtained seventeen seats with 156,049 votes (two seats fewer than in 1973 even with a larger vote) and NILP held their one seat with 9,102 votes. Republican Clubs (formerly the Official IRA) obtained 14,514 votes but no seats. Thus the anti-agreement Unionists now had forty-seven of the seventy-eight seats, while the pro-agreement parties had thirty-one seats.

The report produced by the Convention inevitably reflected the UUUC policy and was generally ignored. The elections also revealed the weakness of Faulkner's own position within Unionism, as his UPNI won only five seats.

The most important political effect of the Convention was the disintegration of Vanguard. At one point in the proceedings, in September 1975, William Craig, Vanguard's leader, floated the idea of a voluntary coalition between the Unionists and the SDLP. This was too much for the majority of his party to take, and they broke away under deputy leader Ernest Baird to form the United Ulster Unionist Movement (UUUM), subsequently the UUUP. Craig and his new deputy leader, David Trimble, folded the remnants of Vanguard into the UUP shortly afterwards.

Nothing conclusive emerged from the Constitutional Convention and little more political progress was made until 1982.

## CONCLUSION

The Alliance Party achieved much success in its first elections, though perhaps not as much as some enthusiasts hoped for. The format of a voluntary coalition in the power-sharing Assembly was probably a better model than the enforced power sharing adopted after the Belfast Agreement in 1998. Unfortunately there were Unionist/Loyalists who were not prepared to work with Nationalists/Republicans in the Assembly. The survival of the Assembly was always going to be a delicate matter with so many Unionists opposed to it, particularly over the issue of a Council of Ireland – an over-ambitious demand by the SDLP, as Oliver Napier had warned. An early general election acted as a de facto referendum and was followed by the Ulster Workers' Strike, which brought about its demise. The experiences of the years covered by this chapter show that the Alliance Party was now well established, electorally as well as organisationally. They now had sixty-three local government councillors, and had eight Assemblymen with two ministers in the short-lived Assembly, but were battling against enormous odds in trying to find common ground against intransigent opposition from the other parties, whose perceptions were still along historically tribal lines.

# 3

# 'Towards government?'
# Consolidation and successes 1976–1986

## INTRODUCTION

This chapter will show how the Alliance Party achieved considerable successes in the period following the demise of the Constitutional Convention in 1975, both electorally and otherwise.

## PROMOTION FOR BOB COOPER 1976 –
## FAIR EMPLOYMENT AGENCY

One of the major complaints of the civil rights movement was discrimination in employment. For example, in East Belfast at the Harland and Wolff ship-building yards almost the entire workforce was from the 'Protestant' community. William James Pirrie, chairman of Harland and Wolff in 1895 instituted an unwritten but strictly enforced policy that the firm would never knowingly employ a Roman Catholic, though some were employed after 1923.[71] Although the 1947 Education Act enabled many more Catholics to obtain third-level educational qualifications, no longer inhibited by financial constraints, their job opportunities were not enhanced in Unionist-dominated public/private sectors. In 1976 a Fair Employment Agency was set up. Despite relatively modest electoral achievements, the quality and fairness of many leading Alliance Party members meant that they were selected to carry out prominent cross-community tasks in Northern Ireland. Thus Bob Cooper, who as a Protestant had twice won Assembly seats in largely Catholic West Belfast, was appointed as Chief

Executive of the Fair Employment Agency[72] and subsequently in 1990 he continued to head the Fair Employment Commission.[73] He received a knighthood in 1998 for his achievements.

## LOCAL GOVERNMENT ELECTIONS 1977 AND FIRST NON-UNIONIST LORD MAYOR OF BELFAST 1978

A sad incident in 1976 led to the formation of the Peace People. In 1976, at 2 p.m. on 10 August, soldiers in Land Rovers were chasing a car down Finaghy Road North, driven by a young republican, Danny Lennon, with a passenger on board. The car was speeding when the pursuing soldiers opened fire. Danny Lennon was shot dead. Anne Maguire (née Corrigan) was wheeling a pram along containing six-weeks-old Andrew. Alongside, on her bicycle, was Anne's daughter Joanne, aged 8½, and her toddler son John, aged 2½. A few yards further along was another son, 7-year-old Mark.

Suddenly, the car containing the dead Danny Lennon and his comrade crashed through the family group into the railings of St John the Baptist school. Joanne and Andrew were killed instantly. John, medically dead, was pronounced clinically dead in hospital the following day. Anne was severely injured, and was unconscious for days. Her mind shattered, and haunted by images of the three children she never saw again, she took her own life forty-one months later.

The neighbourhood had had enough. The children's aunt was Mairead Corrigan. She and another local woman, Betty Williams, were so incensed by the continuing senseless loss of life because of the Troubles that they formed a women's peace movement, the Peace People, which attracted huge numbers of people to go on marches for peace, including many Alliance Party members and supporters. They were joined by journalist Ciarán McKeown. They marched in East and West Belfast, including the Protestant Shankill and the Catholic Falls roads, Ballymena and Larne. The culmination was in Drogheda where they met a group from the Republic who had travelled north to the new bridge over the river Boyne on Sunday 4 December. Joan Baez was there to sing. Nothing in all the years of violence did more to focus attention on Ulster. The result was a considerable decrease in violence. Both women received the Nobel Peace Prize. Unfortunately, owing to internal disputes, the movement went into decline and Betty Williams emigrated to the USA. However, Mairead Corrigan married Jackie Maguire, the dead children's father, and continues to campaign for peace worldwide.

Many people, including many Alliance Party supporters, joined together for peace marches. The effect was that at the next local government elections in 1977, the Alliance Party received their highest ever percentage vote (80,011 votes, 14.4%), resulting in seventy council seats compared with sixty-three in 1973.

The most spectacular gains were a doubling from three to six councillors in Newtownabbey. Jack Eliot (Area B) and John Drysdale (Area D Glengormley) held their seats along with Claire Martin in Area C (Jordanstown, Carnmoney). She had won the seat in an uncontested by-election. George Jones won an extra seat in Area C. Jim Rooney won an extra seat in Area D which he continued to hold till he retired in 2001, to be replaced by Tom Campbell who had held a seat in North Belfast from 1985 to 1997. Pat McCrudden won a seat in Area A (Ballyclare).

In Belfast City the number of councillors increased from eight to thirteen again, nearly doubling the representation. In fact only three Alliance candidates failed to be elected in Belfast, compared with thirteen unelected in 1973. In Area A (Lagan Bank) Basil Glass topped the poll with 2,580 votes and Denis Loretto also gained a seat. In Area B (East Belfast) Oliver Napier joined Michael Brown for an extra seat. In Area C (Balmoral) David Cook topped the poll. Muriel Prichard held her seat there and Bill Jeffrey won another seat. In Area F (Lower Falls) Protestant Will Glendinning won a seat with difficulty in a Catholic area; he continued to hold it till he retired after the demise of the Prior Assembly in 1986. John Cushnahan and Ossie Jamieson won seats in Area H (North Belfast) compared with one seat won by John Ferguson in 1973. Mary McKeown continued to hold a seat in Area G (Upper Falls) with a very low vote of 320. Sam Egerton took over a seat from J. Robinson in Area E, and Dan McGuinness took over from P.D. Corrie in Area D.

Although Alliance did not quite hold the balance of power, in 1978 David Cook became the first non-Unionist Lord Mayor of Belfast, due to a dispute among the Unionists.

However, there were some losses in 1977. Two seats were lost in Limavady, two in Strabane and two in Derry. The Omagh representation held at three in 1973 and 1977 with Paddy Bogan winning three times. Dr Aidan Lagan topped the poll in West Tyrone in 1977 and held the seat in 1981.

## EDUCATION IN NORTHERN IRELAND

Education has been a major problem and the cause of many disagreements from the beginning of the Northern Ireland state, though from Reformation times in England as well as Ireland, both Church and State have recognised education to be a crucial element in the socialisation process. It has been said of Northern Ireland that 'Historically schooling has been shaped more by clerics than by educationalists'.[74]

Not surprisingly both Catholic and Protestant Churches continue to exercise considerable influence on the management of schools in the province. There are currently two parallel systems: Controlled Schools and Voluntary Sector Schools. Controlled Schools are owned and run by the State, but are in fact Protestant in that pupil populations are almost exclusively drawn from Protestant families and taught by Protestant teachers. Voluntary Sector Schools mainly are owned and governed by the Catholic Church, although there are some voluntary grammar (selective secondary level) schools attended by Protestant pupils. Both categories cater for children until the statutory leaving age of 16 years and grammar schools (controlled and voluntary) provide education until pupils have completed A Level examinations.

Many parents find the dual system totally acceptable as a means of passing on to the next generation their cultural (especially religious) heritage, including dearly held parental values. However, growing numbers of parents and educationalists early in the Troubles began to question the wisdom of a segregated education system, some taking the view that it was the major cause of deep cultural cleavage, others that it reinforced division. By the mid-1980s pressure on government brought recommendations in the Astin Report of 1979 to add grant maintained integrated schools to the already established main categories of 'controlled', 'maintained' and voluntary grammar schools.

The Alliance Party figured prominently as a pressure group demanding integrated schools. There were several articles on the subject in *Alliance News* in 1973.[75] One in *Alliance News* 1974 described a de facto integrated school in Sion Mills, which had 90%, support across the community.[76] A movement was set up called 'All Children Together'[77] to work for this aim. Many Alliance Party members were involved, in particular Cecilia Linehan and Muriel Prichard.[78] There was considerable objection to this movement from both the Protestant and the Catholic Churches.

Lord Henry Dunleath was a local councillor for North Down who was elected to the Assembly in 1973 and the Convention in 1975. He put a bill through the House of Lords to facilitate the establishment of integrated schools in 1977.[79] As a result Lagan College, the first integrated secondary school in Northern Ireland, was established in 1981.[80] Integrated education is popular among some sections of the general public and the demand outstrips the supply. 700 applicants annually do not succeed in getting places in integrated schools.

According to a declaration of ethos by the Northern Ireland Council for Integrated Education (NICIE): 'The integrated school provides a learning environment where children and young people from Catholic and Protestant backgrounds, as well as those of other faiths and none, can learn with and about each other.'[81]

Since devolution of education to the Stormont Assembly with its own Minister of Education there has been an impasse relating to the selection procedure for allocation to post-primary education at age eleven plus and the proposed reorganisation of Education Boards, so that progress on education reform has slowed up considerably. The situation is now exacerbated by the global economic crisis, leading to a lack of funding for new schools, or even to transforming the status of existing schools to integrated. Some progress has, however, been made and currently there are sixty-two integrated schools attended by 22,000 pupils. Most new integrated schools come about by the activity and financial support of parents in particular areas. Their ongoing support is clear from a remark made by the Chair of Governors of NICIE in a recent Annual Report:[82] '... we educate 7% of children and some 79% of parents would like their children to be educated in an integrated setting.'

Noreen Campbell, CEO of NICIE, said in an article in the *Belfast Telegraph* that integrated education holds the key to a tolerant society.[83] She notes that the UN Convention on the Rights of the Child encapsulates the right. Chief Minister Peter Robinson 'reignited the debate in a speech last year, when he asked how we can justify a system that divides children on the basis of religion'.

The alternative of shared education is gaining in popularity, possibly because parents see it as a move in the right direction, even though this would generally mean shared sites and/or shared lessons but separate governance. Such arrangements fall far short of meeting the current demand for integrated education. Scarcity of funding for new buildings may be driving this initiative rather than ideological preference. Neither Sinn Féin, who hold the Education Ministry, nor the DUP appears to be disposed to pursue the spread of integrated education in our schools with any sense of urgency. 'A reasonable person would be forced to conclude that the Executive not only does not support Integrated Education but is also going out of its way to sideline it.'[84]

Integrated Education continues to be a major policy aim of the Alliance Party who had hoped for 10% integrated schools by 2010. Many members are involved as principals, teachers, governors and members of NICIE.


## WESTMINSTER AND EUROPEAN ELECTIONS 1979

In 1979 there were both Westminster elections and the first European elections. In the former, the twelve Alliance candidates obtained 11.7% of the popular vote, which was more than that obtained by the DUP. Yet because of the first past the post system in Westminster elections, the DUP won three seats but Alliance none. The best result was in East Belfast where Oliver Napier obtained nearly one-third of the votes: 15,066 (29.5%), just behind the UUP 15,930 votes (31.2%) for Bill Craig and DUP 15,994 (31.4%) for Peter Robinson. Two other candidates also stood, some of whose votes might have gone to Oliver Napier and enabled him to be elected, had they not stood.[85] George Chambers of the centrist NILP obtained 1,982 votes (3.9%) and Norman Agnew of UPNI (who supported the remains of Brian Faulkner's pro-power-sharing group) obtained 2,017 votes (4.0%). Peter Robinson continued to hold that seat and though Alliance candidates have often done well in East Belfast, they never come as close to winning again until Naomi Long's spectacular gain in 2010 with 12,839 votes (37.2%) against Robinson's 11,306 votes (32.8%).

Oliver Napier stood as the candidate in the first European elections also in 1979. The theme song played over loud speakers during the campaign was 'Oliver's Army', which was then a current pop song. His vote was a disappointing 6.8%. This, however, was the highest European vote obtained by an Alliance candidate in a European election until Anna Lo obtained 7% in 2014. Although STV proportional representation operated, the three Northern Ireland seats were split between DUP (Ian Paisley), SDLP (John Hume) and UUP (John Taylor and later Jim Nicholson). This pattern continued until 2004. Alliance candidates, David Cook, John Alderdice, Mary Clarke-Glass and Seán Neeson did successively poorly in European elections. Although Mary had much knowledge and experience of European affairs she was politically unknown. Seán Neeson was an excellent local politician as a councillor in Carrickfergus, but he lacked the charisma needed to project himself to the wider community in this type of election. He was a quiet, gentle person of great integrity, but lacked the hunger for power.

# THE HUNGER STRIKE AND THE RISE OF SINN FÉIN

The period from 1981 to 1993 (apart from the Prior Assembly from 1982 to 1986) was a time of decline in Alliance Party fortunes. The first problem was the hunger strike by Republican prisoners in the Maze, during which ten people died. They were demanding the return of some form of political status rather than being classed as ordinary criminals, which would include wearing their own clothes rather than prison uniform. They had been given 'Special Category Status', but in 1976 this had been withdrawn by the British Government. One of the hunger strikers was Bobby Sands who, while in jail and on hunger strike, stood as a candidate for the Westminster seat of Fermanagh-South Tyrone in a by-election following the death of Frank Maguire in April 1981. This was Sinn Féin's first venture into the electoral process in recent years. They had previously abstained, as they refused to recognise the legitimacy of the Westminster Parliament's jurisdiction over Northern Ireland.

Bobby Sands won the by-election but died on hunger strike so another by-election was needed in August 1981, this time won by Republican Owen Carron who had been election agent for Sands. Seamus Close stood for the Alliance Party, gaining 1,930 votes (3%), not enough to defeat Carron even if added to Ken Maginnis's 29,048 votes (45.6%) for the UUP. It marked the entry of Sinn Féin into the electoral process. As Sinn Féin's Danny Morrison famously said, they would proceed, 'With a ballot paper in one hand and an armalite in the other'.

Sinn Féin began to win seats in all elections from then on. They fielded candidates in a wider range of places, and so SDLP followed suit. Both parties were now contesting seats in the east of the province, formerly left to Unionist parties and the Alliance Party. Thus Alliance could no longer guarantee votes from Catholics who formerly had no other candidate to vote for. There was also a dearth of Young Alliance members in this period and many of the original members were getting older and tired, or disillusioned.

Initially it was the polarisation caused by the hunger strike that caused a decline in the Alliance vote. In the 1981 local government elections, the Alliance Party vote fell from 14.4% to 8.9%, yielding thirty-eight seats compared with the seventy seats gained in 1977. Unfortunately some of those new Belfast seats were lost in 1981 when only seven councillors were elected. However, Will Glendinning held his seat in Lower Falls in 1985 with 931 votes. His wife, Pip (a Catholic), also won a seat in Upper Falls in that election. In Newtownabbey the party bought a caravan for Gordon Mawhinney to use as a mobile advice centre, so Will and Pip used to borrow it on Saturday mornings to take to the Falls areas, as it was not safe to have a fixed advice centre there.

There were major gains in Ards where the number of councillors increased from three to five with Jim McBriar continuing to hold a seat from 1973 till 2011 when he lost his seat, but Deborah Girvan won a seat for Alliance instead. In fact in 1993 there were six Alliance seats when McDowell joined him and Kieran McCarthy and these three continued to holds their seats till 2005.

In Castlereagh there was an increase in seats from five to seven, the highest to be held in that council. Addie Morrow topped the poll in 1977 and continued to hold a seat there until after the 1985 election, when Peter Robinson of the DUP came on to the council, followed by his wife Iris Robinson in 1989. Peter Robinson dominated that council to the chagrin of the Alliance councillors. There was a decline to four in 1981, but that number remained steady until after 2005.

One extra seat was gained in each of Carrickfergus, Down and Larne. In Antrim two seats were held. In Lisburn three seats were held and one seat was held in both Ballymoney and Ballymena.

The performance of Alliance in North Down has been remarkable. The seven seats won in 1973 were all held in 1977. Only one was lost in 1981, to be recovered in 1985 against the trend. The decline to four in 1989 was followed by a recovery to five then six and still stood at six after 2005. One strange occurrence was that Brian Wilson originally held a seat for Alliance in Bangor West from 1981 till 1997 when he switched to Independent, then to the Green Party, continuing to hold a seat and topping the poll in four successive elections. A possible reason for this is that country people are more conservative. Also Alliance Party canvassers were not able to canvass widely in rural areas, compared with more compact city and town areas.

## ATKINS TALKS 1979 AND THE PRIOR INITIATIVE

In 1979 the Conservatives returned to power in government with Margaret Thatcher as prime minister and Humphrey Atkins as Secretary of State for Northern Ireland. The earlier Sunningdale Agreement and devolved Assembly of 1973/1974 had been brought down by the Ulster Workers' strike and the Constitutional Convention of 1975 had been unproductive. So Atkins initiated a new set of talks based on a government paper, 'The Government of Ireland: A working paper for discussion'. Initially these 'Atkins Talks' were attended by the Alliance Party, the SDLP and the DUP. The UUP refused to attend as they would not involve themselves in discussion of an Irish dimension. The DUP eventually also left. Discussions between the DUP, Alliance and SDLP proceeded from 7 January till 24 March 1980 without agreement.

In July 1980 the government published, 'The Government of Northern Ireland: Proposals for Further Discussion'. The paper proposed setting up a devolved Assembly with a compulsory power-sharing Executive, or a majority Executive with minority safeguards. Unionists opposed power sharing while Alliance and SDLP opposed a majority Executive. So on 27 November Atkins reported to Parliament that there was no prospect of a devolved Assembly. 1981 was dominated by the hungers strikes and prison issues.

In 1982 James Prior took over from Humphrey Atkins as Secretary of State and on 5 April published a new White Paper, 'Northern Ireland: A Framework for Devolution'. This proposed a new Assembly with seventy-eight members elected by STV proportional representation, as in 1973. It would have partial or 'rolling' devolution, but initially would have a scrutinising role of government departments, including study of draft legislation and making reports and recommendations to the Secretary of State, which he would lay before Parliament. An Executive of thirteen members could receive devolved powers if 70% of the Assembly members agreed. This devolution would be rescinded if that agreement fell below 70%. The Secretary of State would continue to control law and order functions and Westminster would decide on cross-border issues. Elections were held in 1982.

Nicholas Whyte commented:

Great interest centered on the performance of Sinn Féin [in these 1982 Assembly elections], fighting its first full election in many decades and on the inter-Unionist rivalry between the DUP and the UUP. The former had pulled ahead in the European election of 1979 and the Local Council Elections of 1981 but had suffered a setback in the 1982 by-election which followed the murder of Robert Bradford.

The results were seen as a positive step for the new electoral strategy of Sinn Féin which gained five seats and narrowly missed winning seats in Belfast North and Fermanagh and South Tyrone. The SDLP were disappointed with their fourteen seats and one of these was subsequently lost in a by-election to the UUP as Seamus Mallon was disqualified following a successful UUP election petition on the grounds that he was ineligible as he was a member of the Irish Senate at the time. On the Unionist side the UUP gained a clear lead over the DUP, while the UUUP failed to make an impact and, as a result, folded two years later [in 1984]. In the centre Alliance consolidated with ten seats including unexpected wins in North and West Belfast. The Workers Party failed to make a breakthrough despite respectable vote shares in places like North and West Belfast.[86]

The Alliance Party did particularly well in this election, obtaining ten out of the seventy-eight seats with a vote of 9.3% (a lower percentage than they obtained in 1973 and 1975). Seats were won in South Antrim (two seats), North Down (two seats), East Belfast (two seats), and one each in South Belfast, North Belfast, West Belfast and North Antrim. As Nicholas Whyte said:

> Alliance was very lucky to get ten seats; a shift of fewer than 900 votes would have put the party level with SF on seven seats each with one extra for the UUP. The Alliance gains were from UPNI and NILP compared with 1975, with one seat lost and another gained through the changes in constituency sizes.[87]

Alliance was rather fortunate in the way the transfer of votes went, as several seats were obtained with subsequent transfers after a low first-preference vote.

A particularly exciting battle was in South Antrim. James Knight described this election as, 'Near, if not above, the upper limit of practicality for a public single transferable vote election'.[88] The entire count took about forty-two hours, and the only STV election I know of which was of greater complexity was the Irish Free State's Senate election of 1925. There were twenty-six candidates fighting for ten seats. It was clear that Alliance would obtain at least one seat as they had done in 1973 and 1975. Nicholas Whyte's website comments:

> The results followed the first preferences, with Alliance's Gordon Mawhinney finishing on 5,100 votes to 4,651 for Frank Millar Jr of the UUP. (Millar was subsequently elected to the Assembly in a by-election for South Belfast. His father was also elected from North Belfast.). The 449 votes between Mawhinney and Millar were however not in fact the decisive margin. That had happened two counts earlier, when only 98 votes separated the SDLP's Clenaghan and Alliance's Close at the bottom of the pile. If the positions had been reversed, and Seamus Close been eliminated at that point, his votes would certainly have split more evenly than Clenaghan's votes, quite possibly enough to elect Millar of the UUP rather than the second SDLP candidate.[89]

Seamus Close was the lead Alliance Party candidate. Joan Tomlin was eliminated and the battle continued for the last seat, which was eventually won by Gordon Mawhinney for Alliance with Frank Miller of the UUP missing out. The count was one of the longest in the history of Irish elections and continued for three days.

Subsequently, after another UUP Assembly member, Queen's University lecturer in law, Edgar Graham, had been murdered by the IRA; Frank Miller was co-opted to the Assembly without an election. In East Belfast Oliver Napier and Addie Morrow both gained seats comfortably. In South Belfast David Cook took the second seat but Basil Glass just failed to gain another seat, coming sixth on the first count. In North Down John Cushnahan and Lord Henry Dunleath both gained seats comfortably. In North Antrim Seán Neeson took the eighth seat. There were very close results in North Belfast where Paul Maguire defeated Joe Austin of Sinn Féin by 184 votes and in West Belfast where Will Glendinning defeated William Dickson of the DUP by 244 votes and, as we have said, in South Antrim where Gordon Mawhinney defeated Frank Miller by 449 votes.

## ALLIANCE PARTY INVOLVEMENT IN THE PRIOR ASSEMBLY

The formation of this Assembly did not provide for any 'Irish dimension' (Council of Ireland or similar), so after the elections the SDLP and Sinn Féin Assemblymen refused to take their seats. The boycott by the Nationalist parties meant that the planned devolution never took place, while the UUP also intermittently boycotted proceedings. While the DUP were in favour of devolution the UUP had a strong faction who favoured continuation of Westminster rule.[90] In the Assembly, Alliance as the only non-Unionist group, acted as the opposition, which meant that Alliance had considerable influence. Although it had no legislative powers it had a scrutinising role and committees were set up to cover a range of policy areas. New party leader John Cushnahan for Alliance became chairman of the Education Committee, Seán Neeson was a Deputy Speaker and Will Glendinning was vice-chair of the Environment Committee.

A total of 118 committee reports were published over the next four years. Sydney Elliott commented, 'The best thing was committees and trying to work together and seeing what they could produce from that.'[91] Specialised committees were 'flavour of the month in terms of parliamentary reform' as they were also relatively new at Westminster.

Alliance members had several successful policy proposals approved by the Assembly and implemented by the Westminster Government.[92] Alliance Member David Cook put forward an Assembly Report on Planning, which was accepted by the British Government. Will Glendinning's proposals on homelessness were also approved by the Assembly and again accepted by the government. An Assembly Report on Landlord Agents Commission on leases and letting of land proposed by Gordon Mawhinney was similarly passed and accepted by the government. Gordon Mawhinney reported that six out of seven proposal made by the Assembly were accepted by the British Government for legislation. An account of the workings of this Assembly including the Alliance Party's participation is given in a book by Cornelius O'Leary, Sydney Elliott and R.A. Wilford.[93]

Education was a key area, as there was a major review of higher education in Northern Ireland during this period. A government committee was set up under Lord Chilver to carry out this review. The Assembly's Education Committee had a key role in meeting delegations from interested organisations. The main issue was that the University of Coleraine was not attracting students, whereas the Ulster Polytechnic at Jordanstown was very successful. Attempts to move successful courses from Jordanstown to Coleraine did not work. Just as it had been politically unacceptable to site the New University in the Catholic area of Derry/Londonderry, so it was deemed unacceptable to close down the Coleraine campus, which is what Lord Chilver recommended. So Minister Nicholas Scott decided in 1984 to merge the two institutions to form the University of Ulster, but with the Coleraine campus being the administrative centre, which is what happened. At the same time the two Colleges of Education at Stranmillis and St Mary's were formally incorporated as Colleges within Queen's University Belfast. They refused to merge, as St Mary's insisted on retaining the 'Catholic ethos' in training teachers for Catholic schools. It is difficult to know how much influence the Alliance-headed committee had on these decisions, as it only had consultative powers.

Some useful debates were held in the Assembly. At one point Gordon Mawhinney accused the DUP of being involved with Loyalist paramilitary groups. Following protestations from DUP members, the Speaker, Independent Unionist James Kilfedder, asked him to withdraw the remarks. When he refused he was excluded from the Assembly for a time along with party leader, John Cushnahan, who supported his comments.

Following the controversial signing of the Anglo-Irish Agreement (AIA) the Unionists (see chapter 4) tried to turn the Assembly into a debate about the AIA. Eventually in 1986, the Alliance Party refused to take any further part in an Assembly which refused to fulfil its proper function and withdrew. The Assembly was then formally closed down.

One unfortunate effect of the closing of the Assembly was that several Alliance Assembly Members who were formerly teachers were unable to get their teaching jobs back. Apparently the schools did not want teachers with a high political profile on their staff. They included party leader John Cushnahan, who did some lobbying work in the USA but then joined the Fine Gael Party in the Republic of Ireland. He was elected to a seat in the European Parliament in 1989, a seat he held until 2004, serving with distinction. Will Glendinning moved into the Community Relations Council and Seán Neeson set up a business enterprise in his home town of Carrickfergus.

## BY-ELECTION SUCCESSES

By elections in Northern Ireland for local government were by STV, but that effectively meant that it was by the Alternative Vote system, as proposed but rejected in a referendum in 2011 for all British general elections, as there would be only one seat and votes were transferred until someone reached over 50%. Between 1973 and 1979 there were eighteen by-elections at which Alliance Candidates won six council seats.

In Newtownabbey Claire Martin won a seat unopposed in 1975 and David Hilditch won in Carrickfergus. In 1976 George Jones topped the poll at a by-election in Newtownabbey, but lost at the third count. He did win a seat in 1977. Louise Devlin won a seat in North Down in 1976 and Arthur Barr won a seat in Derry in 1979, achieving 31% on the first count. In the following years Alliance won three more seats at by-elections. Anne Wilson won a seat in Bangor West for North Down in 1995 as did John Coates in Hollywood. Robin Cavan won a seat in Carrick. There were near misses in East Belfast and again in Bangor West. Usually there was a low turnout, so if Alliance worked hard to get their voters out, there was a good chance of success. Other by-election successes included John Blair winning a seat in Newtownabbey in 1982 and Barney Fitzpatrick winning a seat in Coleraine in 2006.

## BALANCE OF POWER

In many local councils Alliance held the balance of power between the Unionist block and the Nationalist block, which gave the party an opportunity to control who would win internal elections in that council. This was particularly important for the election of mayors or lord mayors. It was not intended that Alliance should seize all these positions but to ensure fair sharing.

The first opportunity came in Derry/Londonderry in 1975, where Alliance won four seats and held the balance of power between Unionists and

Nationalists (mainly SDLP). Thus Alliance was able to secure the post of the first non-Unionist Mayor of L'Derry, Councillor Ivor Canavan in 1975.[94] (He had been deputy mayor in 1974.) Subsequently the Nationalists obtained an overall majority in L'Derry, and at the 1977 elections Alliance only had two council seats, both of which they lost in 1981.[95] However, the tradition of sharing power, initiated by Alliance, has continued in Derry, the top two posts being rotated between all the parties including Sinn Féin and Paisley's DUP.[96]

Similarly in 1974 Alliance Councillor John Hadden was elected as chair of Omagh District Council, as the three Alliance councillors held the balance of power.[97] Michael McVerry was chair of Newry and Mourne District Council in 1974. In 1975 Roy Hawthorne became chair of Castlereagh[98] as Alliance was the largest party. Former Stormont MP Tom Gormley became vice-chair of Strabane[99] in the same year and in 1976 the former Stormont MP Bertie McConnell became Mayor of North Down Council,[100] Bill Matthews was Mayor of Coleraine in 1979. Jim McBriar was Mayor of Ards in 1983; Stewart Dickson and Seán Neeson were successively Mayors of Carrickfergus in 1982 and 1983 respectively. Seán Neeson was the first Catholic mayor in loyalist Carrickfergus in 1983. Seamus Close was the first Catholic Mayor of Lisburn in 1993. Brian Wilson was Mayor of North Down in 1993 followed by Susan O'Brien in 1995; Belfast City had its second Alliance Lord Mayor, David Alderdice (brother of John Alderdice), in 1998. In 1999 Janet Crampsey was Mayor of Carrickfergus and Marsden Fitzsimons became Mayor of North Down in 1999, followed by Anne Wilson (Brian Wilson's wife) in 2003. In 2002 Lisburn had become a city and the first Lord Mayor was Betty Campbell of Alliance. Then in 2004 Tom Ekin was elected as the third Alliance Party Lord Mayor of Belfast. In 2006 Lynne Frazer was made Mayor of Newtownabbey. Stephen Farry was Mayor of North Down in 2007, followed by Tony Hill in 2009, then Andrew Muir in 2013. Naomi Long was elected Lord Mayor of Belfast in 2009.

The quality of the Alliance Party candidates was generally much higher than that of other parties[101] – with some notable exceptions, especially in the SDLP. Thus the good councillors quickly established a personal reputation, ensuring their re-election, often coming top of the poll. In addition to those already mentioned, Dr Michael McVerry topped the poll in Newry and Mourne in 1973; Dr Aidan Lagan came top in Omagh in 1977, a year in which nine Alliance candidates topped the polls in their areas. Oliver Napier topped the poll in East Belfast twice (1981 and 1989). John Alderdice came top three times in the same area in 1989, 1993 and 1997. Seán Neeson came top four times in Carrickfergus (1985, 1989, 1993 and 1997).

Although the Alliance vote subsequently declined, the Nationalist vote increased over the years, so that in 1997 Alliance again held the balance of power on Belfast City Council.[102] The Unionists were totally against any form of power sharing with Nationalists, particularly Sinn Féin, but Alliance were able to use their balance of power to elect the first Nationalist Lord Mayor for Belfast, Alban McGuinness of SDLP,[103] then another Alliance Lord Mayor, David Alderdice, in 1998.[104] They also forced through a motion for the proportional distribution of committee and deputy chairs, against the opposition of the Unionists.[105]

In 2001 the number of Alliance councillors on Belfast City Council was reduced to three, but they still held the balance of power.[106] There was much pressure on them to elect the first Sinn Féin Lord Mayor, as Sinn Féin were now the largest party on the council.[107] They decided not to do this in 2001, but by 2002 the IRA had made two acts of decommissioning,[108] so Alliance decided to support Alex Maskey of Sinn Féin for Lord Mayor (along with the SDLP of course).[109] The Unionists tried not to recognise this appointment and refused to appoint a Unionist deputy mayor. In fact Alex Maskey was an excellent Lord Mayor for all the people of Belfast. Then in June 2003 Alliance's slim balance of power was used again to elect Martin Morgan of the SDLP as Lord Mayor against both UUP and DUP candidates. Margaret Crooks of the UUP was elected as Deputy Mayor with the votes of the APNI, the SDLP, Sinn Féin and UUP.[110]

Alliance continued to hold a slim balance of power so Tom Ekin became Alliance Lord Mayor in 2004 and in 2009 Naomi Long, now deputy leader of the Alliance Party, became perhaps the most successful and popular Lord Mayor of Belfast City. This gave her a great platform for the general election in 2010 when she took the East Belfast Westminster seat from sitting MP, Peter Robinson, who admittedly was having serious personal and domestic problems, involving his wife who was also a member of the Stormont Assembly. A report on this matter is still awaited in 2014.

There may have been several reasons for the decline in Alliance Party votes between the fall of the Prior Assembly in 1986 and 1993. Firstly Alliance had no MP and there was no Assembly to belong to, so their public persona was diminished, with just local councillors as their elected representatives. The media was never very kind to Alliance and in this situation hardly noticed Alliance. The next problem was a change in demographics. The Protestant population was declining compared with the Catholic population, as shown in Life and Times surveys.[111]

Two things were happening in the Catholic population. Firstly, with increased educational opportunities, more Catholics were joining the professions and many were moving into middle-class areas such the Malone Road in South Belfast. This resulted in enhanced votes for Nationalist candidates. The second was the growth of support for Sinn Féin. Many young people were joining Sinn Féin now it was committed to contesting all elections. This growth in support was not confined to West Belfast and the western counties, but also included North and South Belfast.

The Alliance Party desperately needed an elected Assembly to enhance its public profile. Sadly there was a missing generation of Alliance members. The original members were getting older and the next generation were not joining at that stage.

## HONOURS

It is difficult to find a complete list but among many Alliance Party members who have received honours have been: former Stormont MP Bertie McConnell, who received an OBE in 1977 having been Mayor of North Down in 1976 and a member of the 1973 Assembly and the 1975 Convention;[112] former party leader Oliver Napier, who was awarded a knighthood in August 1985[113]; Robert Cooper also was made a knight in 1998;[114] Seamus Close received an OBE in 1997;[115] and, in August 1996, Dr John Alderdice, then leader of the party, was made a life peer.[116] Other Alliance people to be honoured include Cecilia Linehan for her work with All Children Together and author Harry Barton who was made an OBE in 1985.[117] Former Assemblyman Hugh Wilson was made a Freeman of the Borough of Larne in the same year[118] and Councillor David Alderdice was awarded an OBE in 1999.[119]

## CONCLUSION

The Alliance Party reached a zenith in the 1977 local government elections with seventy councillors, and then winning ten Assembly seats in the 1982 elections to the 'Rolling Devolution Assembly'. Alliance Party members were now being trusted to take new positions such as heading the Fair Employment Agency. Other solid achievements were the setting up of the integrated school system, and the election of Lord Mayors of Derry in 1975 and Belfast in 1978, largely due to holding the balance of power. Oliver Napier came close to winning a Westminster seat in 1979, losing by 900 votes.

# 4

# 'There's trouble ahead':
# New political initiatives 1983–1993

## INTRODUCTION

The entry of Sinn Féin into electoral politics marked a time of difficulty for Alliance. It marked a decline in electoral performance and hence in numbers of party members. Pressure from the SDLP for greater co-operation with the Republic of Ireland was bitterly opposed by all Unionist parties and Alliance struggled to be heard. However, they took a stand in supporting the controversial AIA and succeeded in keeping local government going by legal action against Unionist factions who attempted to stultify district councils as part of their determined campaign against the AIA. There was considerable reconstruction leading to the important policy document 'Governing with Consent'. Eventually there was discussion about talks to try and find a way to a new devolved Assembly. Other attempts to seek some degree of reconciliation included the Opsahl Initiative and the Peace Train.

## GENERAL ELECTION 1983

In this election Margaret Thatcher consolidated her position as prime minister of the United Kingdom Parliament, following the victory over the Argentinians in the Falklands War.

The Alliance Party contested twelve of the seventeen seats in this election, five new seats having been created. Alliance obtained 8% of the overall votes, down from 11.9% in 1979, when all the then twelve seats were contested. The best result was for Oliver Napier who obtained 24.1%, again coming third, but well behind DUP's Peter Robinson, who was a clear winner with 45.3%. The best of the other results were David Cook with 25% in South Belfast up from 23.9% in 1979 again coming second to Revd Martin Smith (UUP) with 50.0%. John Cushnahan also came second in North Down with 22.1%. Seán Neeson was third in East Antrim with 19.9% as was Addie Morrow with 15.8% in the new Strangford constituency.

Seamus Close was also third with 11.3% in newly constituted Lagan Valley (originally part of the huge South Antrim constituency). Gordon Mawhinney obtained 11.9% in the newly constituted South Antrim, coming third. Paul Maguire won 9.1% in North Belfast. Modest results were obtained by others: Patrick Forde, 3.6% in South Down; Maria McGrath, 4.5% in the new East Londonderry; Dr Aidan Lagan, 3.2% in Mid Ulster; and Gerry O'Grady 2.1% in the new Foyle constituency. Alliance did not contest West Belfast, North Antrim, Fermanagh-South Tyrone, Newry and Armagh, Upper Bann. These results confirmed the decline in the Alliance vote, which commenced with the poor local government results in 1981 (38 seats from 8.9% of the popular vote). The frustration of the failure to secure a Westminster seat continued. It meant that Alliance was frequently ignored.

## NEW LEADER

In September 1984 Oliver Napier decided to step down after an immensely hard-working and courageous eleven years as party leader. He was replaced by John Cushnahan, who had previously been general secretary and quickly became active in establishing good relations with the press and other politicians.

## THE ANGLO-IRISH AGREEMENT 1985

In 1980/81 Margaret Thatcher had been taking a hard line on the IRA hunger strike but at the same time she began to seek co-operation with the Republic of Ireland government. Following the failure of the Atkins Talks in 1980, Thatcher led a high-powered delegation to Dublin and met the Taoiseach (Irish prime minister), Charles Haughey, in May 1980. The focus of the initiative was the relationship between the United Kingdom of Great Britain and Northern Ireland and the Republic of Ireland. A number of joint studies were commissioned concerning new institutional arrangements, security matters, economic co-operation and measures to encourage mutual understanding. The phrase 'totality of relationships between these islands' also entered the political vocabulary for the first time. After Garrett Fitzgerald took over as Taoiseach Margaret Thatcher met him in November 1981 and institutionalised co-operation between their governments with the formation of an Anglo-Irish Intergovernmental Council.

In March 1983, when the SDLP refused to participate in the Prior Assembly, they went off to Dublin and persuaded the Dublin Government to set up the New Ireland Forum.[120] The Alliance Party, UUP, and DUP refused invitations, but sent unofficial observers who reported the happenings. Sinn Féin was excluded. In May 1984 the Forum reported on its analysis of the political problems of Northern Ireland and three proposed solutions: 'A unitary state', A federal or confederal state' or 'Joint authority'.[121] However, following a two-day Anglo-Irish summit meeting at Chequers, a new statement emerged and Thatcher dramatically rejected the three main Forum proposals.[122] However, the joint studies between the governments continued and even after the dramatic attempt on her life by an IRA bomb at a Brighton hotel on 12 October 1984 Thatcher stepped up the co-operation, culminating in the signing of the AIA on 15 October 1985. It has been suggested that she was encouraged by US President Reagan to sign this agreement.[123]

The agreement affirmed the continuance of Northern Ireland in the United Kingdom as long as a majority wished. Thus it effectively ruled out a united Ireland, except with the consent of a majority in the north. It did not propose a change in the Irish Constitution to eliminate clauses 2 and 3 encapsulating an irredentist claim to all thirty-two counties of Ireland, which would include the six counties of Northern Ireland. This was intensely hated by the Unionists and disliked by Alliance. It encouraged cross-community devolution. It also proposed a north-south consultative body, jointly chaired by the Secretary of State for Northern Ireland, James Prior MP and the Irish Foreign Minister, Peter Barry, TD with a permanent Secretariat set up at Maryville in East Belfast.

Desmond Fennell points out that Britain and Ireland had quite different ideas of the application of this agreement.[124] British Prime Minister Margaret Thatcher was only interested in the defeat of the IRA, which the British Army considered to be impossible. The Irish aim was to 'concern itself with measures to recognise and accommodate the rights and identities of the two traditions in Northern Ireland', especially to recognise the Irish identity of northern Nationalists through political measures within the framework of the United Kingdom. All were supposed to bring about 'peace, stability and reconciliation' (to quote Mrs Thatcher's phrase).

The question for Alliance was should they support the AIA or not? A special party council meeting was held at Tullycarnet Bowling Club in

East Belfast. A very vigorous and at times heated debate took place. Several speakers, including former party leader Oliver Napier, abhorred the failure of the British Government to consult Unionists but others, led by party leader John Cushnahan, argued that the agreement provided the opportunity to 'trump the orange card' – in other words to show the Unionists that while they were accorded a veto in relation to the maintenance of Northern Ireland within the United Kingdom they did not have a veto over the arrangements for governing the province. A key point was the provision in the agreement that if 'responsibility in respect of certain matters within the powers of the Secretary of State for Northern Ireland should be devolved within Northern Ireland on a basis which would secure widespread acceptance throughout the community', this would in effect replace the agreement. After a long debate the Alliance Party Council overwhelmingly (137 to 2) agreed to support the AIA.[125]

The Unionist reaction to the AIA was vitriolic. The Unionist opposition resulted in boycotts of meetings with NIO ministers, boycotts of normal council business, rallies and riots for a period of several years.[126] There were no more talks during this period. Violence escalated on both sides. Loyalists attacked the RUC and even forced some officers out of their houses.[127] Unionists held a huge rally outside Belfast City Hall, jointly chaired by party leaders Ian Paisley and James Molyneux. Paisley shouted, 'Never, never, never, never!'

So the 'Ulster says No' campaign was launched, which, among other things, attempted to shut down council business in many of the local councils that they controlled.

In 1986 Unionists all resigned their fifteen Westminster seats to force by-elections in protest against the AIA. They did not contest West Belfast or Foyle, which were held by Sinn Féin and SDLP respectively. Where no other candidate was nominated the Unionist entered 'Peter Barry' (the Irish Foreign Minister as a 'paper opponent' in favour of the AIA!). 'He' saved his deposit in three of the seats. The Unionist results did not entirely go according to their intentions in that they actually lost a seat. Seamus Mallon won Newry and Armagh for SDLP.

Alliance put up candidates in several seats, including North Down where John Cushnahan won 25%, South Belfast where David Cook won 25%, East Antrim where Seán Neeson won 15%, East Belfast where Sir Oliver Napier won 17%, North Belfast where Paul Maguire won 17%. These figures were an improvement on the previous 1983 general election. Again Alliance did not win any Westminster seats.

The effect of this in the Assembly was that the Unionists tried to turn it into a Protest Forum, to which Alliance vehemently objected. On 5 December the Unionists set up a Grand Committee of the Assembly to examine the effects of the AIA, so on 6 December the Alliance withdrew from the Assembly, effectively ending it.

Unionist boycotts of council meetings continued, so in 1987 Alliance councillors David Cook, Seamus Close and Addie Morrow took High Court actions against Belfast, Lisburn and Castlereagh councils respectively demanding that they should resume normal business. In this they were all successful. Addie Morrow stated, 'After an Alliance member was kneecapped in West Belfast for opposing the hunger strikes, I was encouraged to take Castlereagh Council to court for refusing to operate. Peter Robinson told me that he would take my farm off me.'[128]

Unionist councillors in Belfast City Council agreed to pay the fine of £1,500 imposed on 23 February 1987 for their action. Gradually, however, the initial vehement opposition to the AIA declined through sheer exhaustion. The *Belfast Telegraph* published the results of an opinion poll of people in Northern Ireland.[129] One result showed that 68% of Protestants and 62% of Catholics felt that the AIA had made no difference to the political situation in Northern Ireland. The 'Ulster Says No' protest continued for a while including the display of 'Ulster Says No' banners in various places, particularly in Newtownards.

Margaret Thatcher was taken aback by the vehemence of the Unionist reaction to the AIA and subsequently regretted having signed it, saying Enoch Powell was right to oppose it. Some commentators also take that view.

However, in retrospect other commentators have endorsed the Alliance view that the AIA was a factor in bringing the Unionists eventually to the conclusion that power-sharing within Northern Ireland was worth conceding in order to ward off a slide towards increasing involvement of the Republic of Ireland in the affairs of the province. On 20 May 2011 the *Guardian* editorial said:

> ... a wind of change stirred that day [the signing of the AIA] which over the next quarter-century slowly carried all before it. Nationalists, Washington and the wider world now had something solid to point to as they persuaded republicans that progress could be made through the ballot box instead of the bullet. More profoundly, loyalists realised London would no longer wield a veto on their behalf. Once that penny dropped, the Downing Street declaration, the Belfast agreement and Dr No's learning to say yes were all a matter of time.[130]

## 1987 GENERAL ELECTION AND A NEW LEADER

There was a Westminster general election in 1987 at which Alliance again improved its performance, gaining 10.0% of the votes, with John Alderdice doing particularly well in East Belfast. He came second with 10,574 votes, which was 32.1%. Sixteen of the seventeen seats were contested, the exception being West Belfast. The best of the other results were: Neeson, 25.6% (2nd) in East Antrim; Cook, 21.3% (2nd) in South Belfast; Morrow, 20.3% (2nd) in Strangford; Cushnahan 19.4% (3rd) in North Down; Mawhinney 16% (2nd) in South Antrim; G. Williams, 12.5% (3rd) in North Antrim; Close 13.8% (2nd) in Lagan Valley

John Cushnahan resigned as party leader after the collapse of the Prior 'Rolling Devolution' Assembly, partly as he could not go back to his teaching post. At the election for a new leader the candidates were Seamus Close and John Alderdice. Despite never having held public elected office John Alderdice won and became the first Protestant party leader since Phelim O'Neill. His father was a Presbyterian minister. Generally the religion of the Alliance Party leader was not a matter of concern, but with such emphasis on perceived religion in the other parties perhaps, some members of council thought it was time to have a Protestant leader.

## LOCAL GOVERNMENT ELECTIONS 1985, 1989 AND 1993

Despite the 1986 and 1987 general election results, there were mixed fortunes in Alliance local government elections. Votes in 1985 local government elections fell to 7.1%, gaining thirty-four seats. This period was dominated by deep divisions caused by the AIA, as well as by the rise of Sinn Féin, which was now contesting and winning seats. Many pro-Union Protestants were alienated by the Alliance Party's support for the much-hated AIA.

Because of their principled stand over Unionist boycotts of some councils, Alliance Party fortunes revived somewhat in 1993 at the local government elections. The votes were up to 8.95%, yielding forty-four seats, compared with 6.9% in 1989 (thirty-eight seats). The best results were in Ards with six seats, up from four in 1989, and in Carrick with six seats, up from four in 1989. Frank McQuaid won a seat in Banbridge for the first time, which he held until 2010, when he was replaced by his wife Sheila. Anne Gormley, the daughter of Former Alliance Councillor Dr Aidan Lagan, won back a seat in Omagh and became deputy chair. In North Down Alliance gained one seat making five, which became six in 1997. An extra seat was won in Castlereagh bringing the total up to five seats. In Antrim there was an extra seat, bringing the total to two.

Newtownabbey held its four seats. In Craigavon, Coleraine, Larne and Lisburn the two seats in each were held, as was the seat in Ballymena. However, in Belfast only five seats were obtained compared with six in 1989, as Tom Campbell lost his North Belfast seat in Castle area. He did win it back in 1997, but then lost it again in 2001. Michael Healy lost his seat in Down by 2.4 votes. Afterwards he met a family of four who said they would have voted for him, but had not voted. The Strabane seat was also lost.

There was a strange effect in the Balmoral area of Belfast. Muriel Prichard and David Cook had both held their seats for Alliance from 1973 to 1981, but in 1985 Alliance candidate John Montgomery won a seat at David Cook's expense. (Muriel Prichard was not standing again.) In 1989 Mark Long took the seat for Alliance from Montgomery. Then in 1993 Phil McGarry took the Alliance seat and Mark Long lost. In 1997 the same thing happened when Tom Ekin won the seat and McGarry lost. Tom Ekin has held it for Alliance until 2014. Normally a sitting councillor would expect to retain his or her seat. This strange effect had consequences in 2010, when South Belfast decided to only field one candidate in the Assembly elections (see chapter 7).[131]

There was also a very sad event in the middle of the 1993 election, when Election Organiser Howard Johnston died suddenly.


## GOVERNING WITH CONSENT 1988

In 1988 Alliance produced a new key document, 'Governing with Consent',[132] which became their defining policy document until the Belfast Agreement in 1998. At a meeting of the Alliance Party Council in March 1988 party leader John Alderdice announced that he had set up a small study group to review the party's policy concerning the government of Northern Ireland. The group consisted of Gordon Mawhinney (deputy leader), John Alderdice (party leader), Dan McGuinness (party chair), Patrick Bell (policy convenor) and Paul Maguire (former Assembly member). The group reported to a residential strategy meeting in August and then to Council on 17 September, when the document was approved unanimously.

Since its formation in 1970 the Alliance Party had made detailed proposals regarding governmental structures required to produce a stable society in Northern Ireland. The initial proposals led to the 1973/1974 power-sharing

Executive. There were new proposals made for the 1975 Constitutional Convention and then further recommendations on the future government of Northern Ireland at the Atkins Conference in 1980. These were developed further during the life of the 1982–1986 Assembly.

After 1970, and the changes which had taken place, including the fall of the Assembly, the signing of the AIA and the beginning of political involvement by people from paramilitary groups, there was a need for some new thinking. In particular, Sinn Féin members were being elected to local councils and were likely to want to be involved in any future devolved Assembly. Despite every effort on the part of the Alliance Party representatives, the 1982 'Rolling Devolution' Assembly that never 'rolled' failed as a result of both Nationalist abstentionism and Unionist intransigence.

The 'Governing with Consent' document examined the various options for Northern Ireland including a United Ireland, independence, re-partition, integration, federation, joint sovereignty and devolution within the United Kingdom. The party again concluded that the option that would find the widest acceptance was going to be devolution.

Proposals were then set out for devolution. The legislature was to consist of one chamber (with the option of another representing community and vocational interests). The main Assembly would consist of eighty-five members (five for each of the now seventeen Northern Ireland Westminster constituencies), elected by the STV system of PR. It would sit for fixed terms of four years, similar to the Assemblies of 1973, 1982 and the Convention of 1975. Its powers would be covered within three categories. The first would be 'excepted matters' permanently dealt with at Westminster, such as national defence and security, electoral law and Supreme Court judges. The second would be 'reserved matters', in particular policing and justice that would remain with Westminster until the devolved system had progressed such that there was public confidence in the new institutions. Thirdly would be 'transferred matters' for which the Assembly would have powers transferred to it from Westminster. These would include agriculture, health and social services, economic development, the environment, education and finance. The scrutiny role would involve a series of back-benchers' committees with memberships and chairs in proportion and to represent the widest balance of the parties in the Assembly. The financial implications were also discussed.

'Composing the Executive within a devolved system had been the most intractable of all political problems'.[133] So it continued to prove. The proposal was for a small Executive drawn from and answerable to the Assembly.

'Our view is that the mechanism by which the Executive takes office should be by appointment by the Secretary of State ... acting according to a set of criteria'.[134]

These criteria were unspecified except in the most general terms. It was suggested that the Executive to be formed must:

A   Be widely representative of the community as a whole
B   Reflect, so far as is practical and subject to c below, the balance of the parties in the Assembly
C   Include no person who supports the use of violence for political ends
D   Where the Executive failed to command acceptability in the Assembly, provision would be made for the Executive to act merely on a caretaker basis to enable discussions to go on without direct rule being re-invoked or for direct rule to be re-invoked in the case of irretrievable breakdown
E   Allocation of portfolios would be a matter for the Executive itself

In view of the difficulties experienced in getting other parties (especially Unionists) to agree to devolution proposals, there must be clear criteria of accept-ability. It was suggested that if at least 15% of the Assembly members required it, there could be a vote on that once in a parliamentary year. For an acceptability motion to be carried it should be supported by at least 70% of the members of the Assembly. The document emphasised the importance of this weighted majority which would have been similar to that required in the 1982 Northern Ireland Act.

Among options was the suggestion that a constitutional scheme for devo-lution as a single package could be presented for approval to the electorate in the province in a referendum. If the referendum carried, the effect would be to entrench the scheme concerned and any future changes would also require a referendum.

There was then a section about Constitutional Protections for individuals who should be protected by incorporation of the European Convention on Human Rights that would in effect be a Bill of Rights. In addition if there was an aggrieved minority in the Assembly, of, perhaps, 30% of Assembly members, they should have the right to lodge an appeal against a political decision of the majority, which would then be referred to Westminster.

The next section was on the Anglo-Irish context, which had been a sticking point in all previous negotiations and Assemblies. There was a need to establish good working relationships between Belfast, London and Dublin as well as between London and Dublin. The document stated:

In relation to transferred matters the devolved Assembly and Executive should be free to enter into whatever they consider to be the most convenient and advantageous relationship with the institution in the Republic of Ireland. Practical co-operation across the border between the respective authorities, North and South, makes sense. Examples might be in relation to economic development of border regions, tourism, energy and agriculture.

Regarding reserved and excepted matters the United Kingdom Government should give the right of consultation to both administrations in Dublin and Belfast. Hence the Anglo-Irish Inter-governmental Conference could be superseded by a new tripartite institution connecting all three executive authorities.[135]

## FURTHER PROGRESS AND SOME REVIVAL IN THE 1980s AND 1990s

There was little inclination for new initiatives for a number of years, due to on-going violence and the negative attitudes to the AIA. IRA violence continued, as did Loyalist violence and murder. In 1987 there was the terrible bombing of a Remembrance Day parade in Enniskillen. Eleven people were killed and sixty-three injured. One interesting outcome was the courageous act of Methodist Gordon Wilson who offered forgiveness to the perpetrator, after his daughter Marie died holding his hand following the explosion. He became a peace campaigner and a member of the Irish Senate. Sadly Gordon died a few years later. It was not until 2001, fourteen years after the Enniskillen bomb, that Sinn Féin support returned to its 1985 level.

Meanwhile, following the demise of the Prior Assembly, members of the Alliance Party joined with some from SDLP, UUP and DUP for talks in Duisburg, West Germany, on 14 October 1988. Little progress was reported from the meetings. Later, in 1988, came the Forum for Peace and Reconciliation, which Alliance attended. No Unionists were ready to participate fully in talks, though a representative from UUP with unofficial observer status was present.

In order to try to find a way round this impasse Tom King, then Northern Ireland Secretary, and his successor Peter Brooke were to engage in a round of 'talks about talks' with the local parties. This process was to last from 1988 to 1991 and eventually, in early 1991, Brooke was able to declare some measure of success. As a result he announced that an agreement had been reached for formal talks to begin at the end of April 1991.

Peter Brooke took over as Secretary of State in July 1989 from Tom King and on 3 November 1989 he made a speech in which he admitted that the IRA could not be defeated militarily.[136] He also said that he could not rule out talks with Sinn Féin if there was an end to violence. In a further speech on 9 November 1990 he said that 'Britain had no strategic or economic interest in Northern Ireland and would accept unification of Ireland if that was the wish of the people of Northern Ireland'.[137]

On 14 March 1991 Peter Brooke announced to the House of Commons that talks involving the four main parties in Northern Ireland would take place during a gap in the operation of the Anglo-Irish Conference meetings.[138] These talks were the first of a series lasting from March 1991 to November 1992 that became known as the Brooke/Mayhew Talks. They were to involve a three-strand process. This process was to include relationships within Northern Ireland (Strand 1), between Northern Ireland and the Republic of Ireland (Strand 2), and between the British and Irish governments (Strand 3).

It was expected that all strands would commence within a short period of time and that in the end 'nothing would be agreed until everything was agreed'. The Alliance Party was actively involved in these talks. Their position papers were based on the 'Governing with Consent' document of 1988.[139]

The talks progressed in a desultory manner, interrupted by protests and walkouts by Unionists, especially by Ian Paisley. They folded on 3 July 1991. Peter Brooke had talks to try and restart them throughout the autumn till December 1991. Almost inevitably, however, once the negotiations got underway, difficulties soon emerged. These centred on the fact that procedures and arrangements for the talks had not been settled. Thus there were to be wrangles over procedures, the venue for talks and over the choice of an independent chair for the north-south strand.

## 1992 ELECTIONS AND NEW PRIME MINISTERS

On 9 April 1992 a general election was held in the United Kingdom and John Major was re-elected prime minister, having taken on the position in 1990 following Margaret Thatcher's resignation. In the Republic of Ireland Albert Reynolds became Taoiseach. The Alliance Party won 8.7% of the votes overall, with John Alderdice coming second in East Belfast with 29.8%. Gerry Adams, then president of Sinn Féin, lost his seat in West Belfast to Dr Joe Hendron of the SDLP. On 11 April 1992, Sir Patrick Mayhew replaced Peter Brooke as Secretary of State and on 27 April it was announced at the Anglo-Irish

Intergovernmental Conference that there would be a three-month break in its meetings to allow the Brooke/Mayhew Talks to recommence, which they did at Stormont on 29 April.

On 12 June work began on Strand 2 and Strand 3 of the process, even though discussions on Strand 1 were at a standstill. The agenda was discussed for Strand 2. On 19 June, talks continued between Stormont and London. On 1 July it was agreed to involve politicians from the Republic of Ireland in the Strand 2 talks. These continued till the end of July and resumed in September, though on 8 September Ian Paisley walked out.

Following further talks in the autumn around Strands 1 and 2, some of which were boycotted by the DUP, the UUP had 'a change of heart'.[140] Their proposals now included power sharing and an Irish dimension, while the SDLP line softened its aim from complete unity to joint authority. Jim Molyneux, then leader of the UUP, led a delegation from the UUP to talks in Dublin with the Irish Government from 21 to 23 September 1992. The talks were based on Strand 2. The DUP did not attend. On 26 September 1992 the DUP returned to the resumed Brooke/Mayhew Talks at Stormont.

As before, the real negotiations began almost immediately but within a short period of time problems soon arose as the negotiations began to address the major issues. To begin with, in Strand 1 there were to be sharp differences between the SDLP and the UUP, DUP and Alliance over the arrangements for the governance of Northern Ireland. At the same time in Strand 2 the UUP and DUP were adamant that the question of cross-border relations could only be addressed when and if the Irish Government agreed to amend articles 2 and 3 in its constitution, which laid territorial claim to Northern Ireland. In reply the Irish delegation made clear that they would only countenance such a move in the event of an overall settlement.

With the exchanges having failed to achieve their objective of reaching a comprehensive settlement not surprisingly there were to be recriminations amongst some of the participants, each eager to blame someone else for the collapse of the talks. The British and Irish governments were anxious to take something positive out of the process, with both stressing that they believed a basis had been laid for future discussions. To a certain extent this was to be borne out when all-party talks resumed later in the 1990s and the agenda was once again to consist of the three strands of the 1991-1992 period along with the proviso that 'nothing would be agreed until everything was agreed'. In addition, the negotiations of 1991-1992 marked the first serious attempt to address some of the key questions since the collapse of the Sunningdale Agreement and the power-sharing Executive in May 1974. This was a very significant point.

During these talks a consensus was reached between Alliance and SDLP on the concept of internal governing arrangements. Mark Durkan, Seán Farren and Dennis Haughey had reached a point of agreement.[141] David Ford and Addie Morrow believed that Seamus Mallon, Eddie McGrady, Joe Hendron and others could have agreed to the proposals presented by Durkan, but it was blocked by John Hume. Gordon Mawhinney said, 'The public held this view that John Hume was striving for peace. But as far as we saw it, he was the sole individual in the Talks who was frustrating the movement to reach agreement.'[142]

It was suggested that Hume was seeking to incorporate Sinn Féin into the outcome. David Ford said, 'I think that it is a legitimate basis of argument that Hume personally ensured that we didn't reach another 1974-style deal'.[143]

Whilst no agreement was reached, the very fact that the talks had taken place was in itself significant. For instance Irish ministers had been able to travel north to Stormont to engage with Unionist representatives in an attempt to end the political stalemate without being met by demonstrations and protests. Similarly a delegation from the UUP had gone to the Republic of Ireland for talks with the Irish Government and these marked their first formal discussions in Dublin since 1922. Although the DUP had refused to follow the UUP on its visit to Dublin, on occasions the DUP too had also engaged with the Irish delegation.

Even though it had proved impossible at this juncture to provide answers to problems such as the form of devolved government for Northern Ireland or the exact nature of how relations between the north and south should be managed, significant developments were to occur. For example, although the SDLP and the Irish Government had been reluctant to abandon the AIA, they were also seemingly prepared to explore the possibility of its replacement with a wider settlement, something which, as we have seen, was provided for in the AIA itself. In addition certain elements within Unionism had decided to consider the need for new thinking if a political settlement was ever to be found. This meant having to address the need to prove to Nationalist opinion that any new form of devolved government for Northern Ireland would have to ensure they had a meaningful say in its administration. Also the 'Irish dimension' could not be simply ignored and a political structure was needed to manage the relationship between Belfast and Dublin. The differences remained sufficiently great, however, that in the period 1991-1992 the conditions to allow a settlement to emerge did not yet exist.

In particular two main obstacles remained to be overcome. Firstly, the level of trust needed to reach a compromise between the different parties at the negotiations had not yet been reached, given the level of mutual suspicion.

Secondly, even if it had proved possible to reach an agreement, its long-term prospects of being successful would have to be judged against the background of the on-going campaigns by Loyalist and Republican paramilitaries. In essence, therefore, the Brooke/Mayhew Talks seemed to hold out the possibility of a political settlement being reached at some point in the future, but that time had not yet come.

On 6 November 1992 the Irish Coalition Government collapsed and a general election was called for 25 November 1992, which resulted in change of power to the Fianna Fáil Party led by Albert Reynolds. The British and Irish governments then launched the Downing Street Declaration in 1993.

After the collapse of the Prior Assembly the Unionists were absorbed in combating the consequences of the AIA and were not interested in talks with anyone. Their principal objection was that it allowed the Irish Republic to have a say in the affairs of Northern Ireland, through the Maryville Centre and the north-south consultative meetings. Even when talks did resume they would only participate during gaps in time when the North-South Meetings were not taking place. The Nationalists (mainly SDLP) were more interested in developing relations with the Republic of Ireland such as the New Ireland Forum. Alliance had no MPs, no longer any Assembly members, so their only political influence was through local councils and in some of these the Unionists refused to work them because of their antipathy to the AIA. Although they submitted papers and entered discussions during talk's processes, Alliance people were rather ignored in this period.

Alliance did surprisingly well in the local government election of 1993, obtaining forty-four seats with 7.6% of the votes. Over the next two years they also picked up three more seats at by-elections.

## THE OPSAHL INITIATIVE[144]

During this period an independent initiative was set up. The idea came in 1991 from Robin Wilson, editor of *Fortnight* magazine, and Professor Simon Lee of Queen's University Belfast. It was called 'Initiative '92 – A Citizens' Inquiry' and was chaired by Professor Torkel Opsahl from Norway. A team of eminent observers was set up which included Lady Faulkner of Downpatrick (widow of former Stormont Prime Minister Brian Faulkner), Professor Ruth Lister, solicitor Mr Eamonn Gallagher, author and Massachusetts Professor Padraig O'Malley, Professor Marianne Elliott and Methodist minister Revd Eric

Gallagher. Accountant Andy Pollak helped to facilitate the proceedings and edited the report, which was published in 1993. The commission sought verbal and written evidence from a wide range of citizens of Northern Ireland, indeed anyone who wished could contribute.

The Alliance Party made one of the first formal oral submissions on 20 January, led by party leader John Alderdice, accompanied by Addie Morrow and David Ford. The Alliance submission was based on the papers submitted for various talks. They had concerns that the SDLP was taking a more extreme position than it had twenty years ago regarding power-sharing. Written submissions were made from party members, David Cook, Brice Dickson, Will Glendinning, Brian Eggins, Patricia Mallon and Glyn Roberts individually.

David Cook was concerned about direct rule continuing indefinitely. He opposed joint authority but suggested a confederation scheme.

Professor Brice Dickson of the University of Ulster made several submissions and was quoted several times by others. In one article he said that 'an obvious way of countering extreme nationalism and extreme loyalism was to emphasise the benefits of having both nationalities'. In another he complimented the Fair Employment Acts, but said that discriminatory attitudes still prevail among the 'establishment' and among ordinary people. Professor Dickson considered the necessity to hold talks involving members of paramilitary groups including the IRA and the UDA.

In his contribution, Brian Eggins discussed the effect of deleting Articles 2 and 3 of the Irish Constitution – abolition would allay fears of Unionists, but would not materially affect people's attitudes.

Will Glendinning made two submissions, one concerning the problems and possibilities of joint sovereignty and the other about the best way to 'sell' a deal to each community.

Patricia Mallon was concerned that while everyone knows that there are still 'no-go' areas this was denied by the RUC and by political leaders such as John Hume and Margaret Thatcher.

Glyn Roberts made detailed suggestions for a devolved government with some degree of partnership with the Irish Republic. His proposal included an elected Executive confirmed by a weighted majority vote of 80% in the Assembly. Like many others he was in favour of a Bill of Rights and a Civil Rights Commission to monitor its operation

Dr B. Cullen of Queen's University, Belfast, considered that within the Catholic Nationalist community there was a wide spectrum of opinion including people who consciously support the 'consciously' pro-union Alliance Party.

Submissions came from the widest possible range of people including all political parties and their members, Church leaders, civic leaders and members of peace and cross-community groups such as Corrymeela, the Peace People and the Cornerstone Community Sisters of the Cross and Passion. Gordon Wilson, Glenn Barr, Anglican Sister Anna, Fr Patrick McCafferty, Fr Denis Faul, Fr Brian Lennon, Revd Sydney Callaghan, Archbishop Robin Eames, Bishop Samuel Poyntz, Sir Kenneth Bloomfield, David Bleakley, Edna and Michael Longley, Polly Devlin, were among many other prominent citizens who contributed.

A 440-page report was published in 1993, edited by Andy Pollak.[145]

The commission covered: politics and the constitution; culture, religion, identity and education; the economy and society; Sinn Féin and the para-militaries; the constitutional parties; law, justice and security; and the two communities – a widening gulf? A key chapter was 'A Modest Constitutional Proposal'. This included the following conclusions:

- The Unionist community accepted that power would have to be shared with Nationalists
- While the Unionists acknowledged that an Irish dimension existed, they refused to accept that the Republic of Ireland could have any executive role in Northern Ireland. All-Ireland proposals from some Nationalists were put forward as if a Unionist community did not exist
- There was widespread disagreement on the form north-south relations should take; from 'good neighbourliness' to 'co-operation on matters of mutual interest' to an executive role for the Republic
- It was agreed that the economies of the two parts Ireland would be inextricably linked to a single-market Europe
- Northern Ireland should be as self-governing as possible
- A Bill of Rights was universally endorsed as necessary
- Proportionate or equal power sharing should give literal expression to the equality of the two traditions
- Special majorities would be required to pass legislation
- There would need to be veto rights to protect the interests of the minority

## THE PEACE TRAIN

Much of the violence in Northern Ireland was not cross-community violence but involved IRA violence against Catholics, often accused of being 'touts' giving information to the security forces, and Loyalist paramilitary violence against

Protestants. It was difficult to operate the rule of law in some areas, and the IRA and the Loyalist paramilitaries operated their own crude techniques.

During the late 1980s there were considerable attacks on the railway between Dublin and Belfast by the Provisional IRA, mostly as bombs (or hoax bombs) left on the line causing great disruption of services and inconvenience to all.

So in 1989 writer and broadcaster Sam McAughtry set up the 'Peace Train'. He was supported by Chris Hudson, MBE in the Republic. A train was hired out for the day, which brought hundreds of people across the border from all over Ireland as a symbolic gesture to protest the bombing of the railway line. This was followed by a rally at Belfast City Hall. Another rally was held at Oriel Football Park in Dundalk.

Many other prominent figures supported the Peace Train including Alliance Party's John Alderdice and Eileen Bell, Unionist MP Ken Maginnis, the Secretary of State for Northern Ireland, the British Foreign Secretary, the Taoiseach Charles Haughey, Proinsias De Rossa, MEP, politician Tom French and southern secretary Seán Ó Cionnaith.

For two years, the Peace Train ran between Dublin and Belfast. In 1991, it travelled from Belfast to Dublin and then, on the 'immigrant route' through Holyhead to London Euston. British MP for Derbyshire North East, Harry Barnes, recalled:

> The peace train left Belfast at 11 a.m. yesterday and, following a ferry crossing, finally arrived at Euston at 7.14 a.m. today. The people on the Peace Train then boarded two double-decker buses with open tops and came to Westminster. The buses were driven by an Irish Catholic and a Northern Ireland Protestant, to demonstrate unity. We had a fantastic rally in the Grand Committee Room and an effective press conference in the Jubilee Room. Moreover, at Euston, we heard a telling expression of views by a broad range of people.

The Peace Train's activities had been extended to Britain because the IRA has been involved in attacking railway targets here. There were deaths at Lichfield and Victoria, and bombings at Paddington. A section of line was taken out at St Albans and there was regular disruption of morning rail services. Harry Barnes considered that 'it seemed entirely appropriate that activities that had been effective in Ireland and Northern Ireland should be extended to this country to show that we are not prepared to knuckle under in the face of paramilitary activity here'.

The people who supported the peace train did so irrespective of their views on the border, and irrespective of their political differences on other matters. They were united in saying that such matters should be dealt with through the normal political processes of democracy, participation and involvement. The movement has quickly gained momentum, and both its support and the scope of its activities have grown.

## OTHER PEACE INITIATIVES

With the failure of the Brooke talks it was hoped that this and other peace initiatives such Families Against Intimidation and Terror (FAIT) started by Nancy Gracey and again actively supported by Alliance Party members such as Eileen and Derek Bell would change the climate of opinion and increase the likelihood of successful political talks. Other peace groups included 'Enough is Enough', 'Hands off my Mate', 'Consensus' and 'Women Together'. These groups all wanted to see an end to the violence, development of proper politics and justice given to victims.

## CONCLUSION

The years from 1980 to 1993 were largely a time of struggle for the Alliance Party. Due to the AIA, so vehemently opposed by the Unionists with their 'Ulster Says No' campaign, there was little political progress in this period. Alliance had made good use of the time to develop policies, gain respect and influence. Their representatives also took legal action to keep local government going despite Unionist efforts to disrupt it. Eventually, as the impact of the AIA, faded some talks resumed, culminating in 1993 in the joint British and Irish governments' 'Downing Street Declaration', giving hopes for some movement in the near future. Also in 1993, Alliance's electoral fortunes revived when they won forty-four local government seats with 7.6% of the vote. Alliance also participated actively in a number of other peace initiatives, such as the Opsahl Initiative and the Peace Train.

# 5

# 'Hope springs eternal': Towards the Good Friday Agreement 1993–1998

## INTRODUCTION

After so much struggle and dissension this period began as a time of optimism. The joint governments' Downing Street Declaration led to ceasefires by the paramilitaries and the setting up of a negotiating Forum, much along the lines suggested in the Alliance Party's 'Governing with Consent' policy document. This resulted in the Good Friday Agreement, endorsed by a referendum in both the north and south of Ireland in 1998. However, in the subsequent Assembly election, Alliance was disappointed to win only six seats. Party leader John Alderdice was made Speaker and given a peerage. He was replaced as leader by Seán Neeson. Getting the Assembly working was problematic owing to the IRA's reluctance to disarm. So, following Alliance's suggestion, a decommissioning body was set up and Lord Alderdice became a member. With Eileen Bell as a member of the Committee of the Centre the Alliance Party was referred to as 'The conscience of Northern Ireland'.

## THE DOWNING STREET DECLARATION

As there had been no progress in any of the talks' processes, the two new Premiers issued a joint statement known as the Downing Street Declaration on 15 December 1993. The declaration confirmed the right of the Irish people to self-determination. Only if a majority of the population in Northern Ireland voted for it, would the province be transferred to the

Republic of Ireland. For the first time it declared the sole right of the people of Ireland, north and south, to solve the issues between them by consent. This statement encouraged Republicans to rethink their attitudes towards a negotiated agreement. A commitment was made by both governments to seek a constitutional settlement, which could include paramilitary-linked parties such as Sinn Féin in any discussions. But firstly they had to renounce violence. The declaration was at first rejected by Unionists, but was in fact the first step towards meaningful discussions.

## AMERICAN INFLUENCE IN THE NORTHERN IRISH PEACE PROCESS

Americans have always had an interest in Ireland as there is a large American-Irish diaspora. Since John F. Kennedy was US President from 1960 to 1963, he and nearly all successive presidents have discovered their Irish roots and have visited Ireland. St Patrick's Day is very much celebrated in New York and many Irish politicians visit the USA for the occasion. Following the demise of the Prior Assembly in 1986, former Alliance Party leader John Cushnahan worked as a lobbyist in Washington DC for a time.

Following the end of the Cold War in 1989, there was an end to ideological paradigm favourable to the armed struggle of IRA. An essay by Laure Laroche,[146] supervised by Professor Jennifer Todd of University College Dublin, discussed 'how the end of the Cold War changed the terms of international relations' so that there was less emphasis on the 'special relationship' between Great Britain and the USA as well as developing European integration. There was a growth in the American-Irish lobby, especially 'with inputs from the US elite – Tip O'Neill, Edward Kennedy, Daniel Moynihan, Hugh Carey'.

Laroche referred to older links involving funds for the War of Independence, support for 1950s IRA border campaign, and the $3 million raised by NORAID for the Republican cause in 1986. NORAID was set up in the 1920s by Michael Flannery 'to raise fund to help Irish Republicanism'. It was revised in 1968 and was accused of funding the Provisional IRA, especially through Martin Galvin who had never accepted the peace process.[147]

Even so, Laroche admitted that the major movement towards a peace process was that a local movement had already begun with Sinn Féin's political and electoral struggle after the hunger strikes of 1981, the achievement of the AIA in 1985, which she calls 'the single most important defeat for unionism since the abolition of Stormont'. Then the end of Sinn Féin's policy of abstentionism followed in 1986 (except that they still do not take their elected seats in the Westminster Parliament). The US began dialogue with the Irish Government in 1987. The changing international situation may have influenced Republican and Loyalists in their decision to declare ceasefires. Laroche considered that the post-Cold War situation was a catalyst of the peace process and needed to be taken into account.

Congressional Speaker Tip O'Neill along with New York Governor Hugh Carey and senators Edward Kennedy and Daniel Patrick Moynihan worked together from 1977 to develop a 'peace accord' opposing violence. After the signing of the AIA in 1985 they produced an Irish peace package and encouraged presidents Carter and Reagan to bring pressure on the British Government. In 1981 O'Neill, along with Senators Kennedy and Moynihan, created the Friends of Ireland organisation.[148]

Just days before the United States President Bill Clinton was scheduled to make his historic visit to Northern Ireland, the British and Irish governments were making last-minute efforts to issue a document on decommissioning which would receive the president's support. Amazingly, on 28 November 1995, after a week of intense diplomacy, Prime Minister John Major and Taoiseach John Bruton agreed on the Joint Communiqué over the phone on the eve of Clinton's arrival in London. The document discussed the twin-track policy 'to make parallel progress on decommissioning and all-party negotiations'.[149] Both governments committed themselves to launching all-party talks by February 1996. In parallel, they 'agreed to establish an international body to provide an independent assessment of the decommissioning issue'.[150] The governments asked Senator George Mitchell of the United States to chair the independent body. Former Finnish Prime Minister Harri Holkeri and Canadian Chief of Defence Staff General John de Chastelain were also asked to serve on the independent body. Perhaps most important of all, President Clinton arrived in London on 29 November 1995 and endorsed the Joint Communiqué. The next day he became the first serving United States President to visit Northern Ireland.[151]

In January of 1998, Senator Kennedy visited Northern Ireland to meet with its opposing political parties and to address its people about the need for peace. He spoke at the University of Ulster and supported the inclusive peace talks chaired by Senator George Mitchell that led to the Good Friday Peace Agreement and the most promising opportunity for lasting peace in the three-decade-old conflict in Northern Ireland.[152]

## SINN FÉIN AND THE HUME–ADAMS TALKS

Sinn Féin began to be involved in politics in Northern Ireland in 1981, during the hunger strikes when Bobby Sands stood for Fermanagh-South Tyrone in the Westminster elections and won, despite being on hunger strike from which he subsequently died. They also contested the 1981 local government elections and then the 1982 Assembly elections.

Following the Enniskillen bomb in 1987 Sinn Féin president Gerry Adams began to think about where Republicans were going. Sinn Féin was becoming an organised political party under his leadership in both Northern Ireland and the Republic of Ireland, so in 1988 he started secret talks with John Hume, leader of the SDLP. These talks began in January and continued throughout 1988 till August. 'I think people in Sinn Féin were realising that they were not going to achieve a United Ireland by paramilitary activity and needed to think of an alternative strategy.'[153] This led to secret contacts with both the British Government, under Peter Brooke as Secretary of State, and the Irish Government under Charles Haughey, though both denied that they would negotiate with terrorists.

Jason Ingraham describes the Hume–Adams Talks in 'The Irish Peace Process' recorded in the CAIN WEB Service:

The current peace process began in April 1993 when John Hume, leader of the Social Democratic and Labour Party (SDLP), and Gerry Adams, leader of Sinn Féin (SF), met to discuss the future of Northern Ireland. Their meetings focused on the idea of self-determination for the people of Ireland, and they hoped their discussions would lead to a historical agreement between the British and Irish governments. No official documents were produced, but commentators generally agree on what was discussed by Hume and Adams. A key element of this discussion was that Britain should be willing to allow the people of Ireland to decide their own political future. This meant that they had to be willing to accept the possibility of a united Ireland. Furthermore, they were to call on Britain to declare it had no 'selfish, political, strategic, or economic interest in Northern Ireland'.[154] This statement was in response to Peter Brooke's, then Northern Ireland Secretary of State, statement on 9 November 1991 which claimed that Britain had no 'selfish, strategic, or economic interest in Northern Ireland'.

In previous years, SF had shown hints that they wished to peacefully and democratically reach a political settlement in Northern Ireland.

Through their coming together, Hume and Adams signalled a change in the Nationalists' approach to the Northern Irish situation which would, eventually, entail Republicans being willing to abandon violence. In this approach, Nationalist leaders hoped to appeal to a much larger percentage of the Nationalist community and to the Irish people of the Republic. It was clear that violence had reduced support for the Nationalist cause in the Republic of Ireland. The task of SF would be to convince the Irish Republican Army (IRA) that they could achieve their political aims without the use of paramilitary force.[155]

These negotiations provided the groundwork for what was later to be the Belfast Agreement, the Downing Street Declaration and the Joint Framework Document and led to the IRA ceasefire in August 1994. Irish Taoiseach Albert Reynolds, who had played a key role in the Hume–Adams dialogue through his Special Advisor Martin Mansergh, regarded the ceasefire as permanent. However, the slow pace of developments, in part attributed to the political difficulties of John Major's government and the consequent reliance on UUP votes in the House of Commons, led the IRA to end its ceasefire and resume the campaign of violence.

Sinn Féin was unhappy with the progress so they withdrew the IRA ceasefire on Friday 9 February 1996. The IRA statement said that the ceasefire was ended because, 'the British government acted in bad faith with Mr Major and the Unionist leaders squandering this unprecedented opportunity to resolve the conflict by refusing to talk with Sinn Féin'.

One hour later the Provisional IRA detonated a large lorry bomb near South Quay DLR (Docklands Light Railway) station in the London Docklands, killing two people, injuring forty, and causing £150 million worth of damage.

After a summit in London on 28 February, the British and Irish prime ministers set a date, 10 June 1996, for the start of all-party talks, and stated that participants would have to agree to abide by the six Mitchell Principles and that there would be preparatory 'proximity talks'. These started at Stormont on 4 March. The DUP and the UUP refused to join and Sinn Féin were excluded. So elections were announced to a Forum of 110 delegates for all-party talks.

On Monday 20 May 1996 Gerry Adams, President of Sinn Féin, said that his party was prepared to accept the six Mitchell Principles, if the other parties agreed to them. Following the elections the Forum met on 10 June with nine parties, Sinn Féin still excluded. On 15 June 1996 the Provisional IRA attacked Manchester city centre, detonating a massive explosion which injured 212 people and caused widespread damage to businesses in the surrounding area.

Following a British general election in May 1997, Tony Blair became the Labour prime minister. He endorsed the Framework Documents, the Mitchell Report on decommissioning, and the criteria for inclusion in all-party talks. He stated that he valued Northern Ireland's place in the United Kingdom, and suggested that the Republic of Ireland should amend Articles 2 and 3 of its constitution, and indicated that officials would meet Sinn Féin to clarify certain issues. In June there was a general election in the Republic of Ireland. The ruling coalition government of Fine Gael, Labour and Democratic Left was defeated by a coalition of Fianna Fáil, Progressive Democrats, and independent members. Bertie Ahern became Taoiseach. Sinn Féin won its first seat in the Dáil Éireann since it had ended its policy of abstentionism in 1986.

Eventually, on Friday 18 July 1997, John Hume and Gerry Adams issued a joint statement. Gerry Adams and Martin McGuiness called on the IRA to renew its ceasefire. So on Saturday 19 July the IRA announced the renewal of its 1994 ceasefire as of 12 p.m. on 20 July. On Friday 29 August the new Labour Secretary of State for Northern Ireland, Marjorie Mowlam, accepted the IRA ceasefire as genuine and invited Sinn Féin into the multi-party talks at Stormont, following which representatives of Sinn Féin entered Stormont to sign a pledge that the party would abide by the Mitchell Principles. Thus the multi-party talks resumed on 11 September 1997.

## THE FORUM ELECTIONS 1996

In accordance with the Alliance Party suggestion in 'Governing with Consent', it was decided to have a Negotiating Forum to which delegates would be elected. The method of election was not to Alliance's liking. It involved a list system of proportional representation with provision for parties obtaining a certain percentage of votes to receive two top-up seats. This was to allow minor parties the chance for active participation. Alliance put up multiple candidates (fifty-eight in all), spread over all constituencies. They won five seats: East Antrim (Seán Neeson), East Belfast (John Alderdice), South Belfast (Steve McBride), North Down (Sir Oliver Napier) and Strangford (Kieran McCarthy), but none in Lagan Valley. However, two top-up seats were allocated to Seamus Close and Eileen Bell, thus giving Alliance seven seats.

Of the other parties, the UUP had thirty seats, the DUP, twenty-four; the SDLP, twenty-one; Sinn Féin, seventeen; and the UK Independence Party, three seats. The top-up system also gave two seats to the Ulster Democratic Party (UDP) representing the UDA (Gary McMichael and John White), two to the Progressive Unionist Party (PUP) representing the UVF (David Ervine and Hugh Smyth), also to a new moderate party the Northern Ireland Women's Coalition (NIWC) with Monica McWilliams and Pearl Sagar. The UK Unionist Party (UKUP) had Cedric Wilson and, surprisingly, Conor Cruise O'Brien, former Minister for Posts and Telegraphs in Liam Cosgrave's Republic of Ireland Government of 1973. Labour was represented by Malachi Curran and Hugh Casey. The idea was that all relevant parties should be represented in the Forum, including those representing loyalist paramilitary groups.

## FORUM TALKS AND THE MITCHELL PRINCIPLES

Before the talks could start some ground rules had to be agreed, especially to allow the participation of Sinn Féin. US Senator George Mitchell was appointed to chair the proceedings and established what became known as the 'Mitchell Principles'. These were six ground rules agreed by the Irish and British governments and the political parties in Northern Ireland regarding participation in talks on the future of the region. All involved in negotiations had to affirm their commitment to:[156]

- Democratic and exclusively peaceful means of resolving political issues
- The total disarmament of all paramilitary organisations
- Agree that such disarmament must be verifiable to the satisfaction of an independent commission
- Renounce for themselves, and to oppose any effort by others, to use force, or threaten to use force, to influence the course or the outcome of all-party negotiations
- Agree to abide by the terms of any agreement reached in all-party negotiations and to resort to democratic and exclusively peaceful methods in trying to alter any aspect of that outcome with which they may disagree
- Urge that 'punishment' killings and beatings stop and to take effective steps to prevent such actions

These principles were accepted by Sinn Féin on 21 May 1996, so the talks could start on 10 June.

The basic model of a power-sharing Assembly being considered was fairly similar to the Alliance Party document, 'Governing with Consent'.[157] Although Alliance played a major part in these negotiations to reach the Agreement, which all participants eventually signed,[158] they were left without major influence in the new Assembly. Allan Leonard has presented the role of Alliance in these discussions.[159] A summary of his conclusions follows.

The role taken upon itself by Alliance was essentially to smooth the process so as to encourage its success. Position papers were regularly presented by Alliance, but with its small representation, most of the work was between the larger parties, UUP and SDLP with major attempts to include Sinn Féin. Alliance had a 'policing role' to ensure the rigorous upholding of the Mitchell Principles, against a use or threat of the use of force.

'Alliance tabled indictments against the UUP and DUP for their actions at Drumcree in July 1996; against the UDP for a breach of cease-fire in January 1998 and against Sinn Féin for a breach of the IRA cease-fire in February 1998'.[160]

Leonard notes that, 'while Alliance was thanked privately, it was not thanked publicly, either by the other parties or the governments'.[161] Clearly Alliance 'was willing to sacrifice popularity, for the sake of ... long term interests of society'. The second role was that of a 'weathervane', that is to signal whether a proposal by one party was likely to be acceptable across the board.[162] This role required Alliance representatives to reject the 'Mitchell draft', because, though Alliance could have accepted it, they felt that it 'could not be sold to Unionists' because of the wording about north-south relations. This resulted in Monica McWilliams, leader of the Women's Coalition, accusing Alliance of 'being a Unionist party, by providing political cover to the UUP'.[163] Apparently Nationalists did not need such cover and were well able to defend themselves.

The third role was 'making political space for "Others"'.[164] Regrettably Alliance did not or could not oppose the idea of Unionist and Nationalist designations for voting purposes in the Assembly, but would not accept either designation for itself. Alliance attributes the achievement of the allocation of the designation 'Other' to its direct appeal by John Alderdice to the British prime minister.[165] One of the main proposals in the Agreement was the principle of 'sufficient consensus'. Although Alliance conceded this principle they were opposed to a total consensus, which would give every party a veto, regardless of size. Alliance saw itself as part of the centre ground, appealing both to moderate Unionists and moderate Nationalists.

Stephen Farry said, 'It would be nice to have the extremes on board, but if you don't ... then you could still move forward, put something in place, implement it, show that it works, and then convince them that you'd been right, in the long term.'[166]

The DUP and UKUP removed themselves from the talks, so 'sufficient consensus' was easily achieved.

In the final 1998 Agreement it was stipulated that:

> Members of the Assembly will register a designation of identity – Nationalist, Unionist or other [and] Arrangements to ensure key decisions are taken on a cross-community basis, (i) either parallel consent, i.e. a majority of those members present and voting, including a majority of the Unionist and Nationalist designations present and voting, (ii) or a weighted majority (60%) of members present and voting, including at least 40% of each of the Nationalist and Unionist designations present and voting.[167]

In retrospect we wonder why, having got the designations 'Others', did Alliance not insist that the 'sufficient consensus' should include a majority of Unionist, Nationalist *and other* or at least 40% of majority of the Unionist, Nationalist *and other* designations?[168] Having once voted against the Mitchell Draft, perhaps they should have voted against the final Agreement unless that option was included. Maybe that would not have been acceptable to the major Unionist and Nationalist groups, as it would give Alliance a veto, but it would have made for a more logical arrangement. The alternative, avoiding designations, would be for weighted majority voting of (say) 65%, which would avoid a specific veto.[169] Accepting the Agreement with this mode of designations was very damaging for Alliance, effectively disenfranchising them.

John Alderdice's main aim was to obtain an Agreement, even at the expense of political space for the Alliance Party. A cartoon published in *The Irish Times*, shown in Alan Leonard's thesis,[170] shows Alderdice with arms stretched out, as if going between the Unionist group and the Nationalist group. An account of the negotiating process involving Alderdice and Oliver Napier was published in *The Observer* on 12 April 1998:

> Inside Hillsborough Castle around 10pm on Tuesday, just hours after he had flown from Downing Street to Belfast with the Northern Ireland talks teetering on the verge of collapse, Tony Blair received a poignant history lesson.
>
> Lord Alderdice, the bearded leader of the centrist Alliance Party, brought his colleague Sir Oliver Napier to see the prime minister in his makeshift offices on the third floor of the Stormont building.

The room was already cluttered with draft treaties, notes and coffee cups. The team of six who accompanied Blair were busy installing themselves, arranging meetings and taking briefings.

Alderdice introduced Blair to Napier who had served in the ill-fated 1974 power-sharing executive, brought down by loyalist political opposition backed up with paramilitary muscle and the Ulster Workers' Strike.

Napier told Blair about his experiences as a Minister in the executive and particularly of the deal which brought it into being. He recalled the experience of Brian Faulkner, the Ulster Unionist leader who headed it, and how he had been pressurised by Ted Heath into signing something he not could sell to his fellow Unionists. 'Faulkner went too far too quickly and was destroyed by Paisley,' Napier told Blair.

The parallels with the dilemma facing David Trimble that Tuesday evening were too obvious to spell out. He needed a package he could sell to his increasingly restive party. Blair should not repeat Heath's mistakes.

Napier's memory was all the more pressing because by that stage it seemed that the UUP were poised to reject the first draft of Senator George Mitchell's document. Trimble had studied it overnight and the negotiations had reached a nadir with his colleagues rejecting it out of hand. His deputy John Taylor colourfully declared that he would not touch the document 'with a 40-foot bargepole'. Trimble himself described it as a 'Sinn Féin wish list'. They even claimed large parts of the document had been kept from them by the Irish government, operating a pan-Nationalist front with Sinn Féin.[171]

Of course at the time, negotiations reached a very delicate stage and Prime Minister Tony Blair came over to try to urge the participants towards agreement. There were phone calls to US President Bill Clinton. Mo Mowlam, who was Secretary of State, describes the last night of frustration and tension with Sinn Féin threatening to walk out, then the UUP objecting to the issue of prisoner releases and decommissioning of IRA weapons. They were mollified by a side letter from Tony Blair. After that even Ken Maginnis and John Taylor were satisfied, but Geoffrey Donaldson refused to countenance power sharing with Sinn Féin before IRA arms were decommissioned and walked out.[172]

The fourth contribution from Alliance was to obtain agreement for the electoral system to be used in Assembly elections. The Alliance suggestion of eighteen six-member constituencies prevailed. Members were to be elected by STV with no 'top up' as suggested by the NIWC. In retrospect Alliance might have fared better, electorally with a top-up system.[173]

In general the compromises Alliance was making were approved by 87% of Alliance supporters, according to 'an opinion poll taken towards the conclusion of the Multi-Party Talks'.[174]

## THE GOOD FRIDAY AGREEMENT

The Agreement's main provisions included:[175]

- The principle that any change to the constitutional status of Northern Ireland could only follow a majority vote of its citizens
- Commitment by all parties to use 'exclusively peaceful and democratic means'
- The establishment of a Northern Ireland Assembly with devolved legislative powers
- The cross-community principle for any major decision taken by the Assembly
- Establishment of a 'power-sharing' Northern Ireland Executive using the d'Hondt method to allocate ministries proportionally to the main parties;
- Abolition of the Republic's territorial claim to Northern Ireland via the modification of Articles 2 and 3 of its constitution. As a result, the territorial claim which had subsisted since 29 December 1937 was dropped on 2 December 1999
- Establishment of a North-South Ministerial Council and North-South Implementation Bodies to bring about cross-border co-operation in policy and programmes on a number of issues
- Establishment of a British-Irish Inter-governmental Conference (replacing the former Anglo-Irish Inter-governmental Conference, established by the AIA), which gave a consultative role to Ireland concerning matters not devolved.
- Establishment of a British-Irish Council, comprising representatives from the governments of the United Kingdom, Ireland, Scotland, Wales, Northern Ireland, Guernsey, Jersey, and the Isle of Man
- Conditional early release within two years of paramilitary prisoners belonging to organisations observing a ceasefire
- Establishment of the Northern Ireland Human Rights Commission
- Establishment of a two-year time frame for decommissioning of paramilitary weapons
- Repeal of the Government of Ireland Act 1920 by the British Parliament

- Introduction of legislation to place a duty to promote equality of opportunity on public authorities in Northern Ireland
- Normalisation of security measures, e.g. closure of redundant army bases
- Reform of the police led by the Independent Commission on Policing for Northern Ireland
- Recognition of the birthright of all the people of Northern Ireland to identify themselves and be accepted as Irish or British, or both, as they may so choose
- Confirmation that the right to hold both British and Irish citizenship is accepted by both governments and would not be affected by any future change in the status of Northern Ireland

The Agreement was not ideal, especially for Alliance, who would have preferred a model involving integrative – inter-group co-operation, establishing majoritarian but ethnically neutral decision making rather than the consociational model which institutionalises sectarianism. An article by Neeson and Farry discusses the problems in detail and is presented in the next chapter.[176] Many of the problems they anticipate have happened in practice.

There was a review process included in the Agreement, mainly concerning its operation.[177] It was invoked at a later time (see chapter 6), but the Nationalists appeared to consider the basic principles of the Agreement to be 'set in stone' and refused to contemplate any substantial changes.


## REFERENDUM ON THE GOOD FRIDAY AGREEMENT

The 'Belfast Agreement' was finally signed early on 11 April (but dated for Good Friday 10 April) 1998, hence it is commonly known as the Good Friday Agreement. Formally it is just called 'The Agreement'. The DUP campaigned vigorously against it. The Orange Order was against it as were six of the Unionist MPs. An all-Ireland referendum was held on 22 May. In Northern Ireland the turnout was 81%, of whom 71% voted 'Yes' to the Agreement and 29% voted 'No'. There were then some arguments as to whether a majority of Protestants (Unionists) voted 'Yes' or not. It was generally considered that at least 51% voted 'Yes'. However, this included the Loyalist PUP and UDP members, who were keen to see their prisoners released. In the Republic of Ireland the turnout was 56%, of whom 94% voted 'Yes' and 6% voted 'No'.

## ASSEMBLY ELECTIONS

Following the Good Friday Agreement referendum, elections to the new Assembly took place in 1998. Alliance obtained 6.5% of the vote but only six seats.[178] Elliott and Flackes commented that 'The Assembly elections in June ought to have been good for Alliance since so much of the new institutions reflected party views'.[179]

The Alliance members of the Legislative Assembly (MLAs) were: John Alderdice, Eileen Bell, Seán Neeson, Seamus Close, David Ford and Kieran McCarthy. They were unlucky in several areas. In South Belfast Steve McBride was third in the order of first preference votes with 4,086 votes ahead of Monica McWilliams for the NIWC with 3,912 and Carmel Hanna of SDLP with 3,882, but as the transfers mounted he was overtaken by Monica McWilliams, then by Carmel Hanna of the SDLP, as well as by Esmond Birnie (UUP, with 2,875 and Mark Robinson with 2,872, so he lost out by 151 votes. On the final count he had 4,832 votes to Hanna's 4,983.

As Nicholas Whyte pointed out, 'There were 143 undistributed UUP votes from McGimpsey's and Birnie's surpluses, which would have gone a long way to making up the difference, so the effective margin of defeat was more on the order of 15 votes than 151.'[180]

In East Antrim Seán Neeson obtained 20% of the vote, the highest of all the Alliance candidates. He was second to Roy Beggs and elected on the first count. It was hoped that Stewart Dickson could also be elected. He had 1,921 first-preference votes, just behind Danny O'Connor of SDLP with 2,106. When Neeson's surplus of 159 was distributed at Stage 4, only 105 went to Dickson (giving him 2,174) and 20 to O'Connor who then had 2,210. At Stage 7 Dickson had 2,744 votes to O'Connor's 2,977, so Dickson was then eliminated. The aim in the campaign was 'vote management', that is to get people to vote more evenly between Neeson and Dickson giving Dickson a higher first preference and hence a better chance of winning a seat. The strategy did not work.

In all previous Assembly elections Alliance had won two seats in North Down. This time there was again competition from the NIWC. Eileen Bell came fourth with 3,669 and the other Alliance candidate, Gavin Walker, with 1,699, was just behind Jane Morrice of the NIWC who had 1,808. Marietta Farrell of SDLP was just ahead of both of them, with 2,048. Walker was eliminated at Stage 7 with 2,095 votes to put Eileen Bell in over the quota. Morrice had 2,478 and Farrell had 2,238 at this stage. Farrell was eliminated at Stage 10, leaving Morrice elected without reaching the quota.

In East Belfast John Alderdice came second and was elected on the first count with 6,144 votes (18%). The second Alliance candidate, Richard Good, was in seventh place (for six seats) with 1,000 votes. At the third stage only 65% (281 votes) of Alderdice's surplus of 487 votes transferred to Good, the rest being split between David Ervine of PUP, Reg Empey and Ian Adamson of UUP with some going to David Bleakley (Labour) and Pearl Sagar (NIWC). Good picked up further votes, notably 976 from Jones of SDLP when he was eliminated at Stage 13, giving him 2,974, but not enough for a seat. As we have seen previously, transfers from Alliance candidates did not go entirely to other Alliance candidates.

## THE ALLIANCE PARTY POSITION AFTER THE ELECTIONS

The election results left Alliance without enough seats to qualify for a place in the Executive and an Assembly divided along sectarian lines, contrary to Alliance policies. Lord Alderdice then resigned as party leader and became the Speaker of the Assembly.[181] Even this was controversial[182] as Seamus Close had been given to understand that he would be made Speaker.[183] Martina Purdy says Lord Alderdice was 'initially appointed, amid some controversy ... and kept in post when no other candidate came forward'.[184]

Clearly there were last-minute discussions that resulted in John Alderdice's appointment. Whatever happened, behind closed doors, John Alderdice was made the new Speaker and Close made it public that he felt betrayed.

Seán Neeson was elected to take over as party leader.

The results of the election after the Good Friday Agreement were disappointing for the Alliance Party, with only six MLAs and hence no chance of qualifying for a ministerial post.

## POOR ELECTION RESULTS

One can only speculate but here may be several reasons for this poor electoral outcome. Many people have emotional loyalties to the party they usually support and it is hard to persuade them to vote otherwise, regardless of policies, leaders, past performance in previous events, or campaign promises. This is true in most elections in Britain and elsewhere but perhaps more so in Northern Ireland, where tribal support is so dominant. Perhaps also on this occasion people wanted to ensure that their tribal party obtain the maximum possible number of seats in the new Assembly

Alliance Forum members may have played a crucial part in securing the Agreement, but people are not necessarily grateful. At the end of the war in 1945 the UK electorate soundly rejected successful war leader Winston Churchill and voted in Clement Atlee and the Labour Party. Former SDLP deputy leader Seamus Mallon who was Deputy First Minister with David Trimble gave an interview on RTÉ reported in the *Irish News* and commented about voters switching to Sinn Féin: 'SDLP having mortgaged their credibility' to bring Sinn Féin in from the cold in the Hume Adams talks, but some 'took for granted that an electorate would forever remain grateful'.[185]

Probably many of the general populace were unaware of the part Alliance had played in obtaining the Agreement, as press coverage of Alliance Party activities was still very poor. Even if they were aware would they have been grateful? It's unlikely.

Probably a major factor was the poor electoral campaign run by the Alliance Party on this occasion. Considerable money was wasted on an ineffective TV presentation involving puppets, meaning perhaps that there was not sufficient and enthusiastic contact with voters on the doorsteps.


## SETTING UP THE ASSEMBLY AND EXECUTIVE

There was a great deal of wrangling to get the Assembly up and working and an Executive selected. David Trimble, leader of the UUP, was approved as First Minister and Seamus Mallon, deputy leader of SDLP, was approved at the same time as Deputy First Minister. But the UUP still had problems with having Sinn Féin in government before the decommissioning of IRA weapons had taken place. Their slogan was 'No guns, no Government'. So it was not until December 1999, after an abortive attempt on 14 July, that the Assembly and Executive began work. Even that was short-lived as Trimble resigned in early February 2000, after only seventy-two days of operation, owing to lack of movement on IRA arms decommissioning. It resumed again in November 2001. But it collapsed again in 2002 after an alleged IRA break in to Sinn Féin's Stormont offices.

## EILEEN BELL ON THE COMMITTEE OF THE CENTRE

During these periods of operation Alliance Party deputy leader Eileen Bell, MLA[186] was a member of the Committee of the Centre which oversaw the work of the Office of the First Minister and Deputy First Minister. She told them that they:

> … must deal with sectarianism on the streets … they have not really done that [and] promote community relations and equality for all … We have made a difference in committees … I was one the first persons to put forward the idea of a children's commissioner … we set up the children's committee. We now have a very good man in this post. We have also done a lot of work on the periphery of the health service such as MENCAP, children with behavioural problems such as autism.

Eileen Bell and others constantly pressured the Assembly on the issues of community relations. The Alliance group voted against the Programme of Government because it lacked concern for sectarianism 'in our schools, in our offices and on our streets'. Eileen Bell twice submitted press releases, complaining about deficiencies in the Assembly's Executive programme. She emphasised three areas: inequality, community relations and the 'inability to recognise that our society is made up of more than two communities'.[187] She said, 'One of the main weaknesses of the programme is the continued assumption that we live in a two-community society and that diversity should still be regarded as the difference between the Unionist and Nationalist; between Catholic and Protestant.'

She repeated these complaints in another press release in September 2002, saying that the Executive had ignored community relations.[188]

## DECOMMISSIONING AND THE INTERNATIONAL MONITORING BODY

Alliance MLAs were the original proposers of the International Monitoring Body (IMB) to supervise decommissioning of paramilitary arms (particularly from the IRA), which was a matter of great controversy within the UUP. When John Alderdice stood down from the Assembly he became a member of the IMC. Eileen said that some people referred to the Alliance

Party as 'The conscience of Northern Ireland'.[189] The Alliance MLAs were effectively acting as an opposition. In particular, Alliance MLA Seamus Close (an accountant) scrutinised the finances of the Assembly and Seán Neeson criticised their attitude towards education, retaining the 11 Plus examinations and not sufficiently encouraging integrated schooling.

The problems of implementation of the Agreement and the progress of the Alliance Party during his period are described in the next chapter.

## CONCLUSION

Despite making major contributions to the negotiation of the Good Friday Agreement, Alliance had a disappointing election, winning only six seats. They sacrificed some of their own potential political success in order to achieve agreement. However, John Alderdice (now Lord Alderdice) was made Speaker. There were continuing problems in implementing the Agreement.

# 6

# 'Problems and setbacks': Implementing the Good Friday Agreement 1998-2005

## INTRODUCTION

Despite the success of setting up the Good Friday Agreement, there were many problems in implementing it, mainly concerned with decommissioning of IRA weapons. It led to disagreements within the UUP and the beginnings of its subsequent decline, as some members disagreed with David Trimble's policies and left to join the DUP. At the same time the Alliance Party was also having very mixed electoral fortunes. A major survey of Alliance members and subsequent analysis by Evans and Tonge[190] predicted a decline and suggested a merger with the Unionists. Despite, or because of these factors, there was a major review of Alliance Party mission, aims and objectives carried out in 1998. At the end of this process there were some signs of renewal of fortunes.

## PROBLEMS OF 'DECOMMISSIONING' AND DESIGNATIONS

The Alliance Party representatives at the Forum were cock-a-hoop when the referendum went in favour of the Agreement that they had helped to negotiate on Good Friday 1998. Indeed a photograph appeared in *The New York Times* showing the Alliance Party celebrating the results of the referendum with party leader John Alderdice spraying champagne! They had jollied and pushed and persuaded the other parties to come to an agreement that included Sinn Féin (linked to the IRA) across to the PUP (linked to the UVF), but excluding

Paisley's DUP. At the end Geoffrey Donaldson of the UUP ominously did not go along with his party's acceptance and later joined the DUP.

There was still unfinished business, principally the decommissioning of IRA arms, but no mention at that stage of Loyalist arms. Despite that, the prisoners on both sides were to be released on licence in order to keep those with paramilitary wings on board.

But much had been sacrificed by the Alliance Party against its own interests. Although many features of the (by then) rather dated 'Governing with Consent' were included, the Agreement was a carve-up, that entrenched the sectarian divisions, so that voting in the subsequent Assembly required 50% of Nationalists and 50% of Unionists to pass appropriate legislation, known as 'parallel consent'. The appointment of ministers was not to be done by cross-community voting in the Assembly, but by the strange d'Hondt method, introduced by Mark Durkan of the SDLP (according to himself). That arrangement effectively left Alliance disenfranchised, as they rightly refused to consider themselves belonging to either camp, but were given the designation 'Other', after appealing to the prime minister, though they would have preferred to be called 'Centre'. Their votes were not to count, except in the overall total.

During the negotiations Trimble had argued for a weighted majority in decision-making. Even in May 1999 Seamus Mallon thought that the Ulster Unionist leaders were unhappy with the notion of 'parallel consent' and were trying to reverse it. He told the governments that the issue was a 'deal breaker' and he would walk away if it was not included.[191]

The referendum was followed by elections to the new Assembly. Against the expectations of both the Alliance Party and many independent observers, Alliance did much worse than expected with 6.5% of the vote, winning only six seats, which was not enough to qualify for an Executive place. Alliance received a dispiriting, heavy blow in the disappointing level of support given to its candidates by the electorate, after the party had offered sustained sacrificial effort on the altar of political progress.

## STEPHEN FARRY AND SEÁN NEESON'S ANALYSIS OF THE AGREEMENT

Following the Good Friday Agreement, the then Alliance Party leader Seán Neeson and General Secretary Dr Stephen Farry wrote a detailed analysis of the Agreement, its background, its operation and its drawbacks.[192] They said that there was a need to move from conflict management to conflict resolution, and to downgrade territorial aspirations.

Firstly they gave an analysis of the Northern Ireland problem:

> It is primarily ethno-Nationalistic focussed on a clash of identities; Unionist and Nationalist. It is not fundamentally about religion, though the terms Catholic and Protestant often serve as convenient labels for Nationalists and Unionists.

This may well underplay the religious dimension. Anti-Catholicism is rife among some Protestant/Loyalists, though generally this is not reciprocated by Catholics/Nationalists against Protestants.

Farry and Neeson continued, quoting Colin Irwin, 'In Search of a Settlement: Summary Tables of Principal Statistical Results':

> At core it is a conflict in which Unionists and Nationalists seek to maximise the power and benefits for those associated with them. There are contests for control of territory and 'groups rights'. They aim to maximise the level of resources perceived to be going to each section of society. Substantial segregation is the norm. Despite public demands for integrated education 97% are in Protestant (state) or Catholic schools with few shared symbols.
>
> Orange marchers – claim the absolute right to march anywhere, the absolute right to determine which groups parade the neighbourhoods. The law is ambiguous. 1996 at Drumcree nearly brought civil war.
>
> It is not a pluralist society. There is strong correlation between religion and political party. There are few cross-cutting cleavages such as class, ideology, gender, or simple differences of opinion. Most elections are tribal head-counts. There is concern for the distribution of support for the more moderate and more extreme factions within Unionism and Nationalism. Furthermore politics have become more polarised over the course of the 'troubles'. This is over-simplistic. Many do not associate with Protestantism or Catholicism. In 1998 election 9% did not vote Unionist or Nationalist. In an opinion poll 33% expressed strong or moderate association with the centre ground, 40% Unionist and 29% Nationalist.[193]

One should be wary of opinion polls. The late John Whyte repeatedly warned researchers in Northern Ireland of the dangers of using survey data, as he argued that respondents tend to give a more moderate response or pro-officialdom answer rather than offering their real views.[194]

A possible solution might have included re-partition which is an option recognised for the divided society but it is an affront to liberal democracy. The other possibility is joint authority between British and Irish governments, with little scope for local decision-making.

Timothy Sisk describes two sorts of power-sharing: integrative (inter-group co-operation, establishing majoritarian but ethnically neutral decision-making) and devising (ethnically blind public spaces).[195] Alliance is philosophically more in tune with this model.

The option taken for the Agreement was consociational democracy.

The article then goes on to discuss the Alliance Talks Agenda and consociationalism and an assessment of the terms of Agreement. Many of the proposals put forward by the Alliance Party are reflected in the Agreement. The Alliance Party accepted the Agreement in full, though it will not by itself bring about a liberal, pluralist, non-sectarian society.

It was a classic compromise. Alliance introduced the concept of 'sufficient consensus', borrowed from the South African experience. A temporary voting arrangement was needed to reach agreement. It was a political deal. Each party had to sacrifice some of their aspirations to benefit from the peace and stability provided by an agreed form of government.

Neeson and Farry also said that the Agreement had many weaknesses. They thought the idea of power-sharing was a step forward, but it did not make provisions for powers to vary tax rates.

The major concerns were the designations Nationalist or Unionist or Other. These are very problematic. Unionist and Nationalists are given greater political rights than Others. Thus the institutionalisation of sectarianism disincentives people from voting for Others as they will have less influence in the Assembly. This could create barriers to the growth of the important centre ground. This could have been minimised by the use of non-qualified weighted majority voting for contentious issues. However, the use of parallel consent or weighted majorities can cause problems giving a hostage to fortune if one group has difficulty delivering votes, risking blocking by anti-agreement forces.

Rather than allowing the Executive to be created voluntarily by parties who together (or singularly) can obtain the support of weighted majority of Assembly members, the Executive is to be formed, or imposed institutionally, according to a set formula. This does facilitate all-inclusive government subject to parties having sufficient democratic support, but it can create unwilling partners in government and pose major problems for co-ordinating action between departments and the creation of a budget and a coherent programme of action and a Northern Ireland Government could quickly become fragmented.

Farry and Neeson then analyse further deficiencies in the Agreement:

> Further deficiencies in the Agreement limit its ability to perform as a regional government. There is an asymmetrical balance between Northern Ireland as a Regional Government co-operating or competing with the Republic of Ireland as a sovereign state (although limited inter-alia as a member of the European Union). The absence of tax varying powers exacerbates this imbalance.

They discussed Strands 2 and 3 under the headings: Human rights, safeguards, and equality of opportunity, decommissioning, security, policing and justice, prisoners, validation, implementation and review and conflict management.

There is then a detailed discussion of consociational government in practice – and the long-term threats to the Agreement. The Agreement was sold to Unionists as strengthening the Union and to Nationalists as a route to a united Ireland. This dichotomy was hardly enough to command loyalty to the Agreement. To work it requires that the more moderate leaders such as SDLP and UUP be stronger than more extreme parties, DUP and Sinn Féin. If the latter become bigger there is enormous pressure on continued existence of the consociational arrangements. Anti-system parties on either side can exploit dissatisfaction if they think they are not getting a good deal out of the Agreement.

It requires that the Alliance Party act as effective and constructive opposition to SDLP and UUP, to build support for themselves from disaffected UUP and SDLP members (is that a contradiction?). There is a danger of extreme parties overwhelming the moderate ones, especially with the existing voting system. With a weighted majority there is less danger.

It is better if divisions are cross-cutting rather than reinforcing. That is if religious, class, ideological differences intersect rather than collide with each other. Four or five segments are judged to be optimal for consociationalism. In Northern Ireland there are just two communities, so it is fundamentally destabilising to the Agreement. There is need for greater pluralism.

Consociationalism carries democratic limits. There is too much interest on the rights of the groups and not enough on the rights of individuals. It reinforces divisions. It is not pleasant for those not associated with one or the other group. It is not flexible enough to cope with demographic changes. Placing minority groups on the same footing as larger groups infringes the larger groups' perceptions of democracy and further strains the system.

There is a lack of opposition and identifiable alternative government. Consequently elections carry less significance and the same parties and individuals tend to be present in successive governments. Problems with accountability, corruption, conservatism and lack of vision or imagination can be anticipated. It distorts the economy and is wasteful in duplicating services.

Finally liberal, cross-community non- or multi-ethnic parties do not prosper in consociationalist systems, as opposed to more general power-sharing. Ultimately it is hoped that a re-alignment away from ethno-Nationalist politics towards issue-based politics can occur in Northern Ireland.

We will see that many of these problems have indeed arisen and are threatening the stability and maybe the existence of the power-sharing Assembly.

In the short term, they say, minor disputes could erupt into major crises. Formation of the Executive took excessive time. There was no progress on decommissioning. David Trimble unwisely drew a line in the sand over decommissioning. If he moved forward he risked splitting his party. He needed to carry three-quarters of his MLAs to pass the minimum threshold.

The first Executive was not properly representative – a 50/50 split should be 5/4/1 Unionist/Nationalist/Others and a fractured centre ground lost an Alliance Party seat to the SDLP. It was a recipe for weak government. Neeson and Farry presumed that the DUP and Sinn Féin would take their ministerial positions.

There were tensions from the marriage of democratically based parties and those with paramilitary links. It is not sustainable to be in government with those who have private armies. The politics of the Assembly was already dominated by difficulties within the UUP. Every crucial vote was threatening the durability of the Assembly.

In conclusion they called it a 'band-aid' approach to conflict resolution. It was not going to produce long-term peace and stability. Yet they regarded it as a solid foundation and said the Alliance Party was committed to making it work, to express concerns of the centre ground and be a constructive opposition.

## POLICING IN NORTHERN IRELAND

One criticism which might justifiably be levied against the Alliance Party's response to the Belfast Agreement was its apparent failure to grasp fully the need for root and branch reform of policing.

The Royal Irish Constabulary (RIC), established by Sir Robert Peel in 1822, was replaced by the Royal Ulster Constabulary (RUC) when Northern Ireland became a political entity. The identification of the RUC with Protestant Unionism was much stronger than that of the RIC with the Anglo-Irish ascendancy. RIC members were, for example, forbidden to vote or to join political or religious organisations except the Freemasons, in order to maintain their reputation for impartiality.[196] In contrast, an Orange Lodge for police officers was established in Belfast within three months of the RUC's birth.

From the beginning, the expression of Nationalist identity was discouraged throughout the province and suppressed by legislation under the Public Order Act 1951 and Flags and Emblems Act 1954. The greatest burden for the RUC was, arguably, the Special Powers Act 1922 which was renewed and applied consistently until 1973.

For reasons summarised above, there was an antagonistic relationship between the police and the minority Catholic population and so Catholic membership of the RUC never reached a one-third quota recommended by Sir Dawson Bates' Committee in 1922. The figure peaked at fewer than 22% in 1923 and declined to below 8% by the year 2000 when the Catholic population had reached approximately 46%. It should be noted, however, that: 'Under-representation by Catholics could not be attributed directly to the RUC, in that recruitment was open to all who met the requirements, but resulted mainly from the partisan use made of the force by the Stormont governments.'[197]

Their lack of operational autonomy meant that under the Stormont regime the Minister of Home Affairs could and did direct the Inspector General (later named the Chief Constable) as to where Orange processions would be allowed to parade. Inevitably, ministerial control of policing brought the officers on the ground into conflict with the Nationalist population.

With the unrest surrounding the activities of and opposition to the Civil Rights Association and the People's Democracy and the emergence of the IRA – the Stormont Government faced an overtly political and violent challenge which had to be policed. Fifty years of one party-rule in Northern Ireland had been conveniently ignored by Westminster, the result being no evolutionary change in a region of the UK, a supposedly liberal democracy.

A seriously deteriorating security situation in 1969 prompted Westminster to appoint Sir John Hunt, conqueror of Mount Everest, to chair a small committee to recommend measures which would attempt to change the RUC from being largely a colonial style police force into a liberal force on the British model. The political context was such that few of the recommendations were implemented.

One of the Alliance Party's first principles was to support the rule of law.[198] At the same time, Alliance was often critical of hard-line security policies.[199] The power-sharing Executive of 1973–74, in which Alliance shared power with SDLP, selected Alliance Party leader Oliver Napier as Minister of Law Reform. Executive members intended to set up an all-party committee 'to investigate the way forward in achieving effective and acceptable policing so that the RUC would receive universal approval'.[200] Unfortunately, the Assembly collapsed so the committee was never set up.

Despite this apparent acknowledgment of a pressing need for reform, Alliance Party leaders were slow to recognise Nationalists' problems with the RUC, continuing to support the status quo until Seán Neeson became leader. Following the collapse of that Executive, and despite having been sharing power with the SDLP, Oliver Napier declared that he ruled it out in future unless that party fully supported the RUC.[201] This principle was reiterated in the Alliance Party's submission to the Atkins Talks in 1980[202] and in its party leader's speech in 1982.[203] When John Cushnahan became party leader he continued to express the same sentiment in the Prior Assembly,[204] as well as in his conference speeches of 1986 and 1987.[205, 206]

In 1987 Cushnahan, in a letter to Prime Minister Margaret Thatcher, threatened to review support for the AIA unless SDLP called on Catholics to join the RUC.[207] In a conference speech, he deplored SDLP's refusal to wholeheartedly support the police – which formed a major block to political progress.

The Alliance Party argued that no military solution could be found, unless there was political agreement first in order to isolate the IRA from the community that supported it. With progress towards talks in the 1990s, SDLP insisted that there must be reform of the police before it would win their party support. Unionists said there was no need for reform. Even Alliance was half-hearted about the need for reform.[208]

The main reason behind this seeming short-sightedness by Alliance policy-makers was probably their fear of a collapse of morale in the RUC during the long period when they were under constant attack from malevolent forces. With all their flaws, the RUC were the 'thin black line' between the province and utter mayhem. However, by the 1990s it should have been clear that real change was needed. In a policy statement in 1995 the party rejected the idea of major structural changes in the RUC, instead focusing on changes at government level and in dealing with individual complaints. The Alliance Party Election Manifesto of 1997 talked only of RUC reform in minimalist language[209] and the party submission to the Patten Commission made no serious criticism of the RUC, restricting its suggestions to symbolic changes in name and uniform.[210]

Determination on the part of Prime Minister Tony Blair, cross-party talks encouraged by paramilitary ceasefires and international support brought the Belfast Agreement and what the British Government hoped for: 'the opportunity for a new beginning to policing in Northern Ireland with a police service capable of attracting and sustaining support from the community as a whole.'[211]

There being no meeting of minds among the local parties, Tony Blair took a decisive step in appointing Chris (later Lord) Patten to chair an Independent Commission on Policing for Northern Ireland. The Patten Report, published in 1999, produced a reflective analysis of the best from world policing of divided societies, in order to guide ambitious plans for police reform.

In contrast to relatively weak central party policy, when former Alliance Party Lord Mayor of Belfast, David Cook, was chair of the Police Authority (1994-1996), he, along with colleague and journalist Chris Ryder, suggested major changes to the RUC. The highly publicised division in the Police Authority in 1996 stemmed from internal disagreements over issues relating to policing changes and the pace of proposed reforms.

Author Roger McGinty reported on the situation and the outcome as follows:

> In May 1995 the Police Authority embarked on its own consultation to contribute to a Government White Paper on Policing. 600,000 households were contacted. There were less than 8,000 replies. This inflamed tensions between those within the police authority. The majority favoured a minimalist approach to reform of the RUC. The Chair (David Cook) and one other [presumably Chris Ryder] were in a favour of far-reaching reform, especially regarding the accountability of the Chief Constable to the Police Authority and to the public. After public rows there was a vote of no-confidence in the Chair, David Cook who refused to resign.[212]

The two 'rebels' were, however, subsequently sacked from their positions by the Secretary of State, Sir Patrick Mayhew. An out-of-court settlement of a libel case was eventually arrived at some years later and an agreed statement by the duo was read out in court. It noted with approval the Patten recommendations and brought the libel action to a close with undisclosed damages awarded.

Cook and Ryder explained:

> This libel action was reluctantly commenced solely to authoritatively establish that at all times we acted with complete propriety and integrity in our work as members of the Police Authority from July 1994 until we were dismissed and we are glad that it has now been publicly endorsed to our satisfaction.

When Seán Neeson became leader of the Alliance Party there was significant progress made in grasping the importance of structural change of the police service, if it was to win the support of the whole community. He asked Steve McBride to write a critique of the Patten Report, which was largely favourable.[213] Neeson gave his verdict on Patten:

> We want to see the blueprint for single integrated and professional police service that is representative of, and responsive to, and which carries the confidence of the entire community. As we are satisfied that the Patten report largely meets these objectives we are prepared to endorse the bulk of its recommendations. Some clarifications, some safeguards needed and one particular proposal [for *50:50 Catholic: non-Catholic recruitment*] that we simply reject. Quotas will detract from the principle of merit, are illegal under NI and European law, and are not actually necessary.[214]

Patten was endorsed at a special meeting of the Alliance Council and a press release followed on 5 December.

In the Assembly the DUP tabled a motion trying to unite Unionist opposition to Patten. The Alliance Assembly Group tabled an amendment:

> This Assembly believes that while the Patten Report causes pain to many, it can provide a new beginning for policing in Northern Ireland, responsive to and representative of the entire community to give full support to the proposed police service and to encourage people to join.[215]

Seán Neeson introduced the amendment, which was then supported by David Ford, with a winding up speech by Seamus Close. SDLP and the NIWC joined Alliance in supporting the Amendment. All the rest (including Sinn Féin who just wanted to see the RUC disbanded) voted against.

When the Patten Report was made a Bill, Alliance General Secretary Stephen Farry announced Alliance Action on the Police Bill. While generally supportive, he again warned against the 50:50 recruiting proposal. The Bill was debated in Westminster and the Labour government included the 50:50 quotas in the final Bill.[216]

By 2007 all political parties had signed up to support the PSNI, which in spite of opposition from many interests achieved a Catholic membership of more than 30% by 2010 as a result of 50:50 recruitment. Since the Patten reforms were implemented the Chief Constable is operationally independent of political interference; transparency and accountability are demanded by the Policing Board and the Ombudsman's Office; the uniform has changed and the regalia been depoliticised. Undoubtedly, the PSNI still faces enormous challenges from dissident Republicans and Loyalists who refuse – often violently – to accept the Belfast Agreement and its implementation for different reasons.

While Alliance came rather late in the day to realise the crucial importance of a police force being transformed into a police service, the party has not been found wanting in giving full support to the PSNI, a hugely important part of the justice system, most visibly since the current party leader David Ford accepted the mantle of Minister of Policing and Justice, when responsibility was devolved from Westminster in 2010.


## GETTING THE ASSEMBLY TO WORK

Meanwhile, the elected MLAs were having great difficulty in setting up the Executive and getting started. It was agreed that David Trimble, leader of the UUP, should be the First Minister and that Seamus Mallon, deputy leader of the SDLP, should be the Deputy First Minister, but the UUP were not prepared to support Sinn Féin MLAs as ministers (which would happen under the d'Hondt procedure) until there was evidence of the decommissioning of IRA weapons. This issue had been addressed in the Agreement, but with no specific timetable. There was considerable pressure on David Trimble within his own party from people such as Geoffrey Donaldson and others who were not happy with the Agreement.

During a visit to the USA the strain between Trimble and Mallon became obvious. On 15 August the Omagh bombing atrocity had taken place, in which twenty-nine people and unborn twins died. While the atrocity was 'claimed' by the 'Real IRA', an organisation opposed by Sinn Féin, this killing of innocent civilians aggravated already tense political relationships. US President Bill Clinton came to visit Northern Ireland in September and a deadline of 31 October was set for implementing the Agreement.

Meanwhile, David Trimble and John Hume were awarded the Nobel Peace Prize for their role in getting the Agreement accepted and Secretary of State Mo Mowlam was made 'European Person of the Year'.

By 18 December there was agreement that there should be ten ministerial departments rather than six. There was some decommissioning of Loyalist Volunteer Force (LVF) weapons but the UUP was still holding back. On 8 March 1999 there was agreement between the British and Irish governments about north-south and British-Irish bodies. A new deadline of 10 March was set for implementation and George Mitchell reluctantly returned as negotiator to Northern Ireland. The deadline was then put back to 2 April – near the anniversary of the signing of the Agreement. On 31 March 1999 there were talks at Hillsborough followed by the 'Hillsborough Declaration' which promised that an Executive would be in place within a month supported by an 'act of reconciliation'. No progress was made, and talks were moved to Downing Street in London and an 'Absolute Deadline' was set for 30 June.

On 1 July a new proposal, 'The Way Forward', was issued. General John de Chastelain, chair of the Independent International Monitoring Commission (IIMC), said that there was progress on decommissioning, as he had met the IRA leadership. The UUP was still divided. Pressured by the prime minister, Mo Mowlam called a meeting of the Assembly on 14 July to set up the Executive, but only the DUP, SDLP, Sinn Féin and Alliance were in attendance.

As Martina Purdy put it:

> The speaker had to call on Trimble to nominate and gave him five minutes to make up his mind, and in effect the speaker was addressing a row of empty Ulster Unionist benches. The Alliance Leader, Seán Neeson, condemned the nomination process as outrageous and lambasted the UUP absence as unforgiveable. None the less, one by one the ministers, all Nationalists, were nominated, first by John Hume and then by Gerry Adams. As the rules stated that there must be no less than three Unionists and three Nationalists, the Executive was immediately dissolved. Then in dramatic style Seamus Mallon rose to deliver his personal statement, resigning as Deputy First Minister.[217]

It had been agreed at a special Alliance Party Executive, held at Stormont the night before, that if asked, in the absence of the UUP, Alliance Party leader Seán Neeson would nominate someone for a ministerial seat, but Mo Mowlam aborted the procedure because the UUP failed to turn up. Seamus Mallon resigned as Deputy First Minister to be replaced by Mark Durkan. It was now necessary to have a formal review of the whole Agreement, to be carried out by US Senator George Mitchell.

While Alliance continued to attend all these consultations and contribute their input, they had little influence with only six MLAs in the Assembly.

## COLLAPSE OF ASSEMBLY AND A FORMAL REVIEW

In London there was a cabinet reshuffle and Peter Mandelson replaced Mo Mowlam as Secretary of State for Northern Ireland. On 15 November there was a report from the Independent International Commission on Decommissioning (IICD), headed by Canadian General John de Chastelain. By the next day each party had made a statement about the current position.

On 20 November there was a new Mitchell 'Review of the Peace Process' report, which Mo Mowlam thought was less favourable to the Unionists than the earlier report, 'The Way Forward', in July. [218] However, this time the UUP went along with it and a government was set up in December 1999. David Trimble, however, signed a post-dated letter of resignation which would operate if there was no actual decommissioning by the end of January 2000. There was none and so in early February 2000, Trimble resigned and the Assembly was again suspended. A new Way Forward was proposed on 29 February. By May 2000 there was some progress on decommissioning, so a deadline of June 2001 was set for its completion. The executive was up and running and David Trimble was back in place as First Minister. There was good progress, the ministers were doing good jobs and the economy was improving.

January 2001 brought the resignation of Peter Mandelson as Secretary of State and his replacement by John Reid. David Trimble was in trouble in his own party because there was a drift of UUP members to the DUP, including Geoffrey Donaldson, Peter Weir and Pauline Armitage, because they were not satisfied with David Trimble's approach and were generally not happy about aspects of the Agreement.

## WESTMINSTER AND LOCAL GOVERNMENT ELECTIONS 2001

Westminster elections followed. Probably unwisely, Alliance decided to prop up the UUP by refraining from putting up a candidate in the key seat of Upper Bann, which was Trimble's seat. It saved Trimble for the moment. Alliance also did not stand in North Down, so the UUP's Sylvia Hermon won the seat from UKUP MP Bob McCartney. Both these decisions were unpopular among some Alliance Party members. It was a short-term tactic aimed to keep the Assembly operating with David Trimble as First Minister. In the longer term the tactic was unsuccessful and resulted in the Alliance Party being labelled as Unionist with a small 'u', which was hardly surprising and definitely counter-productive.

Once again Alliance put dedication to progress the peace agenda ahead of its own interests as a party. In 1999 there was a European election. Seán Neeson was the Alliance Party candidate but only got 2.1% of the vote, so for the 2001 election he was deselected as the Westminster candidate.

Seán Neeson was de-selected as Westminster candidate in East Antrim to be replaced by John Matthews. It was a very poor election for Alliance, as they won only 3.6% of the total votes from ten seats contested. At the same time there were local government elections in which Alliance had its worst performance ever, winning only twenty-eight council seats with 5.1% of the vote, so Seán Neeson resigned as Party Leader. There was an election for this post on 6 October between Eileen Bell and David Ford. David Ford won by eighty-six votes to forty-five. David Ford, who had been general secretary of the party and was a councillor for Antrim Town and an MLA for South Antrim, was identified with the more Liberal, internationalist wing of Alliance, while Bell was a more traditionalist, bridge-building candidate. Notably, David Ford was also the only Alliance MLA to be a member of the Liberal Democrats at the same time.[219]

There was still no decommissioning by the summer of 2001, so Trimble resigned again and the Assembly was suspended. There were further talks at Weston Park. Finally, on 23 October, John de Chastelain announced that the IRA had put 'all' its weapons 'beyond use'. This action had been observed by Methodist minister Revd Harold Good and Redemptorist Priest Fr Alex Reid. So the Assembly was reconvened yet again on 6 November. The requirement to re-elect David Trimble and Mark Durkan as First and Deputy First Ministers was for an overall majority and a 50 per cent majority in both the 'Nationalists' bloc and the 'Unionists' bloc. Defections by UUP members to the DUP created a deficit of 'unionist' votes. The Unionist vote was deficient due to the resignation of Peter Weir and Pauline Armitage from the UUP group. Under pressure from the Prime Minister three Alliance MLAs reluctantly obliged by re-designating three of themselves temporarily as 'unionists' to get Trimble and Durkan elected. They were Sean Neeson, Eileen Bell and David Ford.[120] This was a very controversial decision and was made a major feature of a questionnaire by Jocelyn Evans and Jonathan Tonge.[221] In addition one of the Northern Ireland Women's Coalition Party, Jane Morrice, re-designated as 'unionist' and the other, Monica McWilliams, as 'nationalist'. But Seamus Close was disgusted, saying:

If Tony Blair was on his knees in this room at this moment there would not be a snowball's chance in hell of me changing my designation … It was the best opportunity in the history of the Alliance Party to stand and say no![222]

## EVANS AND TONGE SURVEY OF ALLIANCE PARTY MEMBERS 2001

Evans and Tonge's article, 'The Future of the Radical Centre in Northern Ireland after the Good Friday Agreement', 'Explores the implications of the consociational basis of the Good Friday Agreement and the effect of tactical re-designation upon the political centre in Northern Ireland'.

Tonge and Evans said:

The 1998 Good Friday Agreement (GFA) offered the prospect of a new political dispensation in Northern Ireland. As long-standing advocates of devolved power sharing, the Alliance Party of Northern Ireland (APNI) endorsed the Agreement. Yet the Agreement posed theoretical and practical problems for Northern Ireland's main bi-confessional centre party. The consociational underpinnings of the GFA appeared to institutionalise a Unionist-Nationalist dichotomy within Northern Ireland politics, at odds with the APNI's view that the construction of 'one community' was required (Alliance Party of Northern Ireland, 2000). Since the party's establishment in 1970, it has clung to a belief that a third tradition, post-Nationalist or post-Unionist, could be established. In practical terms, the GFA threatened to further reduce the narrow centre ground formed by Alliance.

The commencement of decommissioning of weapons by the Provisional IRA in October 2001 briefly improved prospects for Northern Ireland's political institutions. Yet the considerable size of the anti-Agreement wing of unionism has ensured that the Good Friday Agreement, which essentially requires dual community support, has so often appeared fragile. The lack of a pro-Agreement Unionist majority has caused Alliance to compromise its stated principles of being neither Nationalist nor Unionist.

Trimble failed to obtain majority Unionist support and his subsequent re-election was thus dependent upon re-designation by sufficient Alliance MLAs. Although only temporary, the re-designations of three MLAs occurred against the wishes of the majority (60%) of Alliance party members. Indeed, two other Alliance MLAs declined to redesignate (the sixth Alliance MLA, Eileen Bell acts as Speaker). Furthermore, re-designation compromises long-held Alliance principles and may have profound implications for the continued existence of centrist politics.[223]

Evans and Tonge then concentrated on the perception that Alliance is really a 'Unionist' party, as perceived by the SDLP and the UUP and some 28% of the Alliance Members in their survey, which indicated that 64% Alliance members were Protestant, 21% Catholic and 15% of no religion.

Asking whether Alliance should permanently redesignate as 'Unionist' on the basis of the actions of three MLAs, they suggest there might be three possible scenarios for the future of the party. The first is 'The collapse of centre politics per se in Northern Ireland', which they think unlikely. The second possibility, equally unlikely, they suggested, is 'That of a revival in Alliance fortunes'. 'The third scenario is the swallowing of the existing centre by the SDLP and the pro-Agreement UUP'.

## DISCUSSION OF EVANS AND TONGE

Consociationalism is a political method of attempting to get diverse political parties to work together sharing power. Arendt Lijphart described this procedure in 1975.[224] It was basically what had been used in the ill-fated Sunningdale power-sharing Assembly of 1973–1974. Lijphart considered it the most appropriate method but was pessimistic about its future prospects. But he makes no distinction between linguistic, ethno-nationalistic or religious causes.

However, as John McGarry and Brendan O'Leary have pointed out, the basic version leaves many problems to be addressed.[225]

They found six weaknesses in original consociatiovial theory:

1  Neglect of external actors
2  Trans-state self-determination dispute
3  Principle of consent
4  Merits of STV vs List system elections
5  Allocation of ministerial portfolios
6  Conceptual refinements

Such a settlement requires more than just consociational institutions. Minimally, these would include all-island and all-Ireland cross-border institutions and institutions linking the two sovereign governments of the United Kingdom and Ireland.

McGarry and O'Leary consider that:

Anti-consociationialism is the 'staple political diet' in NI including
Unionists, Nationalists, Alliance and others. 'There is uncritical acceptance of permanent ethnicity, not resolving conflict but setting it in
marble. It is incompatible with stable democracy. It is 'impermanent',
dysfunctional, and unworkable. It is a parody of real democracy. It is
segregational – condoning ethnic cleansing.[226]

To an extent its application in the Good Friday Agreement has worked.
An essential approach was to involve assistance from 'external actors'. It was
probably President Reagan of the USA who prompted Prime Minister Margaret
Thatcher to sign the AIA in 1985. Subsequently other Americans, including
Speaker Tip O'Neill, Senator Edward Kennedy and eventually President Bill
Clinton, became involved. Prime Minister John Major, aided by Taoiseach
Albert Reynolds, made some progress with the Downing Street Declaration of
1993, but little real progress was possible until, following the Hume-Adams talks
and encouraged by President Bill Clinton, there was an IRA ceasefire in 1994.

In the years after the signing of the Good Friday Agreement and the
referendum, Unionist support for it was indeed 'fragile'. With the difficulties
around the decommissioning of IRA weapons, there was a drift of support
away from First Minister David Trimble and his UUP towards Paisley's DUP
which was at that time vehemently against sharing power with republicans,
i.e. Sinn Féin. The DUP was probably still suspicious of the more moderate
but Nationalist SDLP under John Hume and Seamus Mallon.

The centrist Alliance Party had always tried to divorce itself from the
sectarian Unionist–Nationalist arc, but in trying to act as a bridge-building and
facilitating party found that it needed to help pro-Agreement UUP. But at the
time Tonge and Evans fell into the old trap of labelling Alliance as a 'Unionist
party with a small 'u'. As they discovered in their survey, some 28% of Alliance
Party members agreed with that designation, as did the other parties.

It has always been the intention of the Alliance Party to avoid being labelled
as Unionist or Nationalist. They wished to be non-sectarian or even anti-
sectarian. The official line is that people in Northern Ireland should be free
to vote for a Unionist or Nationalist position and that Alliance will accept
the will of the majority. That has in effect meant that Alliance accepts that
for the present Northern Ireland will remain part of the United Kingdom,
as expressed in a referendum of 1973 and from the clear expression of views
in voting patterns and opinion polls.

But because of their obsession of the larger political parties with the 'border
question' they are always trying to pigeonhole Alliance as a Unionist party.

Alliance constantly finds it difficult to avoid this labelling. The way in which many members avoid the sectarian implications of the word 'Unionist' is to call themselves 'pro-union'.

It is not surprising that Evans and Tonge, in their analysis of the opinion poll they ran among Alliance Party members, push the party in the Unionist direction. Because of the history of Northern Ireland and community fears the strongly sectarian basis of most parties persists. Alliance has always recognised the need to encourage full participation in government of people drawn from both sides of the traditional divide and realistically this can only currently be done by encouraging power sharing between Unionist and Nationalist/Republicans parties. However, Alliance feels it must avoid itself being seen as on one or other side of this divide.

The effect of consociationalism on the Good Friday Agreement has been to consolidate the sectarian divide, giving power to the extreme 'elites', now Sinn Féin and the DUP.

Ian Paisley did not consider Alliance to be a Unionist party in any sense when he said in 1981, 'Basically the Alliance Party has the same spirit as the Roman Inquisition, and would silence and put to death all who would raise their voices in protest against the errors, pernicious doctrines and idolatrous practices of the Roman Catholic Church'.[227] Perhaps he had in mind the fact that Alliance Party leader Oliver Napier was a Catholic?

Evans and Tonge's analysis of the possible future for the Alliance Party was based in the premise of it being a Unionist party manqué. At the time of their survey and analysis the fortunes of the Alliance Party were at low ebb, having poor elections results in 1998 and 2001.

Evans and Tonge attempted to speculate about the possible future for the Alliance Party, suggesting that it should permanently re-designate as 'Unionist', thus making their votes in the Assembly more effective. Of their three suggested options for the centre, they rightly agree that the centre is unlikely to disappear, but it might be absorbed into the SDLP or the UUP as a new centre group. The Alliance Party clearly had no intention of disappearing or being absorbed into the SDLP/UUP. Evans and Tonge considered that a 'revival of Alliance Party fortunes' was unlikely. Contrary to that suggestion a revival is what happened. Following the extensive President's Review (see below) and its implementation, fortunes began to change. Alliance was lucky to retain all six Assembly seats in the 2003 elections with only 3.7% of the vote. Two major policy initiatives came out of the review process. The first was the emphasis on the cost of division, that the sectarian divisions in society cost £1 billion per year. Deloitte's analysis confirmed this and put the cost at £1.5 billion. The second initiative was the development of the 'Shared Future' strategy. Both are described later. The general populace became aware of these points and probably mainly supported them, but because of the sectarian nature of the Executive, neither has even now been properly addressed. This shows up the major fault in the consociational nature of the power sharing Assembly, as we have just discussed. The other major events were the election of Chinese Anna Lo to the Assembly and the rise of the charismatic Naomi Long to be Lord Mayor of Belfast, MLA for East Belfast and then MP for East Belfast.

As we shall see, in the event there was a revival of Alliance electoral fortunes and a decline in the fortunes of the SDLP and the UUP, as the DUP's and Sinn Féin's demands and pre-conditions moderated.

At this point the Alliance Party produced a new document, 'A Review of the Assembly Designations and Voting Systems' (November 2002).[228]

In October 2002 there was a further hiatus, when the police raided Sinn Féin offices at Stormont because of an alleged Provisional Irish Republican Army spy-ring and intelligence gathering operation. It involved the arrest of Sinn Féin's Northern Ireland Assembly group administrator Denis Donaldson (who subsequently identified himself as a double agent and was found murdered in Glenties, County Donegal in 2005), his son-in-law Ciarán Kearney, and former porter William Mackessy for intelligence-gathering. The event was dubbed 'Stormontgate'. As a result Trimble resigned again and so direct rule was re-established. Meanwhile in the newly designated 'City' of Lisburn, Betty Campbell of the Alliance Party was elected as the city's first Lord Mayor.

## REVAMPING THE ALLIANCE PARTY –
## THE PRESIDENT'S REVIEW

In 1998 John Alderdice was made Speaker of the new Assembly, so he resigned as party leader, to be replaced by Seán Neeson. Seán decided that the party needed a revamp. A new radical review known as 'The President's Review' was clearly needed.

Following the July 1998 Alliance Party Council and the succeeding Executive, the party president, Dr Phillip McGarry, was given the task of carrying out a review of the overall policy and strategy direction of the party. In addition an Alliance Members Questionnaire was issued in October of the same year. This firstly aimed to discover the range of religious affiliations of party members. It asked them to suggest the top three future goals for the party over the next five to ten years. It asked members where they perceived themselves on the Nationalist/Unionist spectrum, on the political left/right spectrum and what keywords they would favour to describe the Alliance Party. Finally it asked them which of a range of activities they had participated in.

Philip McGarry was greatly assisted by Naomi Long and Peter Whitecroft. He visited the meetings of twenty-one associations. He spoke to many other individuals and groups and received many written submissions. Thirty people are named as sending in written submissions. A Strategic Operational Planning Group was set up to 'refine strategies and operations in specific areas'.

The report began by critically reviewing the 1998 Assembly election results. It then considered general strategy and policy. It continued with a discussion of the principle of equity, people before territory, the challenge of the SDLP and of the NIWC and female representation. The report went on to consider the Alliance image and public relations. McGarry then proceeded to consider Organisation and Administration of the party. This section considered central organisation, local organisation and fund-raising, relations with other organisations, young Alliance and local councillors. After a brief summary the report listed the twenty three recommendations and sixty optional ideas. The report of 'The President's Review' [229] was presented to Party Council in December 1998.


## THE ALLIANCE PARTY'S STRATEGIC PLAN 2000–2002

The Strategic Operational Planning Group was set up in January 1999 and consisted of Jayne Dunlop, Richard Good, Michael Long, Gerry Lynch, Peter Osborne, John Wallace and Seán Neeson.

The Party Council had agreed that:

> The party should operate on the basis of a continuous strategic and operational planning process on a three year cycle. This process will be the responsibility of the party executive. Initially a Strategic Operational Planning Group (SOPG) will be set up to process the recommendations of the Review and address the various optional ideas which have come forward from members. The group will report back to Council in March 1999 on the work it has carried out and set in place the mechanism for a continuing strategic and planning programme. [230]

The SOPG published its report, *The Alliance Party's Strategic Plan 2000 – 2002* [231] in June 1999 when it was presented to Party Council by Seán Neeson and unanimously approved.

It firstly set up a vision statement which said:

The Alliance Party of Northern Ireland's vision is of a permanently peaceful, stable, and truly democratic society, which cherishes diversity and is committed to human rights, equality of citizenship and social justice.

It then stated 'Our Mission':

The Alliance Party puts people first. We aim to replace sectional politics and to create an inclusive, fair, prosperous and peaceful society through innovative and distinctive policies.

We aim to expand the centre ground by maximising the number of elected representatives at every level and creating and sustaining a vibrant and effective party organisation.

It listed six aims, which each covered two pages, giving more detailed objectives and timetables for their implementation and naming which group would be responsible for each objective. At the end were two appendices, the first giving a Planning Timetable and the second a Policy Development Programme.

The six aims were:

- To increase the number of elected representatives at all levels of government, and increase the party's political influence
- To develop distinctive, radical and innovative policies
- To improve the party's communication with the media and the electorate
- To develop effective and efficient internal structures and communication
- To develop an effectively funded and managed organisation
- To increase the number of members and their involvement in the party

This was an ambitious but necessary programme and it is interesting to see how far it was implemented and how effective it was. The effectiveness will be seen in the progress of the Alliance Party over the first decade or so of the twenty-first century. A further major policy paper on Community Relations was produced in 2002 called 'Building a United Community'.[232] It was presented to Council on 7 December 2002 and launched on 8 January 2003.

## NEW ASSEMBLY ELECTIONS 2003

In 2003 there were more Assembly elections. The results showed a dramatic shift in major party fortunes. There had been defections from the UUP to the DUP, resulting in 30 seats for the DUP and for the UUP only 27, so the DUP was well positioned to block progress of the Good Friday Agreement. Similarly Sinn Féin won 24 seats and the SDLP only 18. Alliance was fortunate to hold their six seats with only 3.7% of the vote, compared to 6.5% in 1998. Some of the seats were won with very narrow margins. The Women's Coalition was wiped out by losing both its seats; the UKUP lost 5 seats, leaving it with only one. The PUP lost one of its two seats. A remarkable win was that of Dr Kieran Deeney who won a seat as an independent, standing to support the Omagh Hospital threatened with closure. He would not accept the Alliance designation or any other, but would tend to vote with Alliance. Thus the Assembly and Executive could not resume as before and there was a reversion to direct rule from Westminster.

Despite this poor Assembly election result there were two more successes in local government with Anne Wilson being elected Mayor of North Down and Jim McBriar being elected Mayor of Ards Council. In 2004 Tom Ekin was elected Lord Mayor of Belfast.

In 2004 the Independent Monitoring Commission was set up to monitor any continuing paramilitary activity by Republican or Loyalist groups. Lord Alderdice was one of the four commissioners. Prior to its removal in January 2011 the IMC made 22 reports to both British and Irish governments which included a recommendation for the devolution of policing and justice.

## 2004 AND 2009 EUROPEAN ELECTIONS

In 2004 Alliance supported an independent candidate John Gilliland, outgoing President of the Farmers Union, who was also supported by the Workers' Party, the Conservatives, Labour and a number of independent councillors. He obtained 6.6% of the vote, was 4th in the count and survived the first round of eliminations. Then in 2009 a new young and enthusiastic candidate, Ian Parsley, then deputy Mayor in North Down, won 5.5% of the vote, which was the best since Oliver Napier's 6.8% in 1979.

## 2005 WESTMINSTER ELECTIONS AND
## LOCAL GOVERNMENT ELECTIONS

In the 2005 Westminster elections Alliance contested twelve of the eighteen seats. The overall vote was again very poor at 3.9%. Seán Neeson was back as the candidate for East Antrim and he obtained the best result of 15.3%.

Naomi Long came third standing for the first time in East Belfast. She won 12.2%, down from David Alderdice's 15.8% in 2001. David Alderdice stood in North Down and received 7.6% of the vote, coming third also. Seamus Close obtained 10% in Lagan Valley, also third, as was Kieran McCarthy in Strangford with 9%. Perhaps the electorate punished Alliance for standing down in favour of two Unionists in the previous election?

The Strategic Plan had had not yet made a positive impact on the electorate, except in EU elections and the winning of some Mayoral positions.

At the local government elections in the same year Alliance made a marginal improvement with 5.0% of the overall vote, gaining five seats, but losing three to give a total of 30. In Belfast Máire Hendron won a seat back from Sinn Féin in Pottinger, coming fifth. This was partly due to a dispute with the local Sinn Féin organisation about the murder of Robert McCartney outside Magennis's bar on May Street, Belfast on 30 January 2005, carried out by two IRA volunteers. Naomi Long and Tom Ekin held their seats, both coming second in Victoria and Balmoral respectively. Mervyn Jones held his seat also in Victoria, coming sixth. David Ford won a seat in Antrim coming third in Antrim Town. Alan Lowther won back the seat in Antrim South East formerly held by David Ford but lost in 2001. He came fifth. Tom Campbell won a seat in Newtownabbey, to join Lynne Frazer who was again fourth in the University area. Later two other councillors switched to Alliance: John Blair, who had held a seat for Alliance in 1989 and 1993, won a seat as a Ratepayers Candidate in 2005. Independent Councillor Billy Webb also switched to Alliance. Ian Parsley won an extra seat in the Holywood area of North Down, but two seats were lost in Carrickfergus and one lost in Ards.

Although a gain of two seats was not substantial, the wins by David Ford, Naomi Long and Ian Parsley were very significant for future developments in the party.


## CONCLUSION

Following the Good Friday Agreement there was much argument about the decommissioning of IRA arms, so much so that the Assembly staggered from crisis to crisis and by 2002 the UUP had lost so many seats to the DUP that direct rule had to be resumed. Alliance Party fortunes were also very poor with 6.5% and 6 seats in the 1998 Assembly election, 2.1% in the 1999 EU election, 3.6% in the 2001 general election and 5.1% in the local government election of the same year, giving 28 seats – the lowest number ever.

In 2003 in a new Assembly election brought a fall in Alliance vote to 3.7%, yet surprisingly all six seats were held. While the controversial decision of 3 Alliance MLAs to redesignate temporarily as "Unionist" to avoid collapse of the Assembly can be criticised the question has to be asked – was the alternative a return to unrest and even violence?

Following a major review of Alliance Party Mission Aims and Objectives, another change of leadership and the publication of a substantive paper on *Building a United Community*, there were some signs of improved fortunes, with the gain of several mayoralties and some important if modest gains in the 2005 local government elections.

# 'Back in government': Revival, two ministries and an MP 2006–2011

## INTRODUCTION

Contrary to the predictions of Evans and Tonge in the analysis of their 2001 survey,[233] there was a distinct revival of the fortunes of the Alliance Party over the next few years, so that after the 2011 Assembly election the party had eight MLAs from which they gained two ministers. In the local government elections they had forty-four councillors elected, the best result since 1993. Best of all, for the first time Alliance had a member elected to the Westminster Parliament.

How had this come about?

## RECOVERY

A major factor in the Alliance Party recovery was that Naomi Long, a young charismatic civil engineer, became a highly successful and popular Lord Mayor of Belfast City in 2009. She had been elected to Belfast City Council in 2001, and then succeeded John Alderdice as MLA for East Belfast in 2003. Naomi was elected as deputy leader of the Alliance Party in 2006. This formed the platform from which she beat sitting MP Peter Robinson and captured the East Belfast Westminster seat in 2010.

Leading up to this election was the appointment of David Ford as Minister for Policing and Justice by a cross-community vote in the Assembly.

There was also a resurgence of young people joining the party and becoming active, perhaps encouraged by Naomi's example. Young Alliance with Ian Parsley as chair for four years had engaged with other young people and showed that Alliance is a party of the future.

Meanwhile QUB Alliance Chair Michael Bower and his team used a highly successful Freshers Fayre as the springboard for progress in the Student Council elections, which saw Alliance's representation jump from two to eleven. Alliance then scored a major upset in electing our first ever member (Stephen Martin) to Queen's University Senate.[234]

Another triumph was the election of Chinese-born Anna Lo to the Assembly for South Belfast in 2007. She was the first Chinese person ever elected to a European parliament, an event that was acclaimed worldwide. A further arguably significant event was the candidature of charismatic North Down Councillor and Deputy Mayor Ian Parsley in the EU election of 2009, when he won the highest Alliance vote since Sir Oliver Napier in 1979.

In addition Alliance had a number of successes in local councils, with Lynne Frazer becoming the first Alliance Mayor of Newtownabbey in 2006. Similar achievements were when Betty Campbell became the first Lord Mayor of Lisburn when it was made a city in 2002. Anne Wilson became Mayor of North Down in 2003, followed by Stephen Farry in 2007 and Tony Hill in 2009. In 2004 Tom Ekin became Lord Mayor of Belfast City. There were also several deputy mayoral Alliance appointments.

## ST ANDREWS TALKS AND 'AGREEMENT'

With the Assembly in abeyance and back to direct rule, negotiations for devolution had been in the doldrums. Alliance delegates attended and made contributions to a new series of talks at St Andrews in 2006 but were, however, largely ignored. The talks nevertheless resulted in the St Andrews Agreement,[235] the terms of which the DUP appeared to find acceptable. From time to time later, when it suited their purposes, the DUP claimed that they did not fully support the St Andrews Agreement, which they said was foisted on them by the British and Irish governments. David Ford commented: 'Despite all that remains to be done, there is now at least a sense of hope for a shared future'.[236]

Predictably, as on various previous occasions, it took some time to implement the St Andrews Agreement. Deadlines were set for 13 October, 17 October, and 10 November, with no results until the following year. Another set of elections were held in 2007, at which there were further erosions of the UUP and the SDLP positions.

## 2007 ASSEMBLY ELECTIONS

At last there were encouraging signs for Alliance's fortunes. In the 2007 Assembly elections not only were all the six MLAs returned easily with increased votes, but a new MLA was elected for South Belfast. Naomi Long was elected for East Belfast on the first count with 5,583 votes; significantly only fifty-three fewer than Peter Robinson, new leader of the DUP and eventually to become the First Minister.

David Ford was third elected in South Antrim on the fifth count, Seán Neeson was also third elected in East Antrim, but again Stewart Dickson was eliminated. Both Stephen Farry (North Down) and Kieran McCarthy (Strangford) were third elected in their constituencies. Trevor Lunn was fourth elected in Lagan Valley. Anna Lo (South Belfast) was also fourth to be elected.

Brian Wilson was again elected in North Down for the Green Party and Kieran Deeney in West Tyrone, as an independent supporting the retention of the Omagh hospital, joined the Others group in the Assembly. That gave a centre group of nine Others.

## NEW ASSEMBLY AND EXECUTIVE

The Assembly was now dominated by the DUP and Sinn Féin who had opposite policies! Overall the DUP now had thirty-six seats, a gain of six. Sinn Féin had twenty-eight seats, a gain of four, but the UUP were reduced to eighteen seats, a loss of nine (which could have been worse). The SDLP won sixteen seats, a loss of two. Dawn Purvis of the PUP held her seat, but Robert McCartney of the UKUP lost his seat.

Amazingly having spent many years saying 'Smash Sinn Féin', Ian Paisley now agreed to share power with his former enemies and hence become the First Minister himself, with Martin McGuinness as Deputy First Minister. He had supposedly received instructions from God about dealing with Sinn Féin.[237] On 26 March Ian Paisley and Martin McGuiness made a historic and bewildering announcement that they would restore the Assembly on 8 May. They seemed to enjoy a surprisingly good personal relationship, so much so that they became known as the 'chuckle brothers'. The d'Hondt system was run to select the ten ministers. Alliance still did not have enough MLAs to qualify for an Executive ministerial post. There was no election and no requirement for cross-community support within the Assembly.

The ministers were each nominated by their party leaders. Hence they tended to run their departments according to their own party policies, regardless of the needs of the whole community. This led to many log jams in policymaking and failure in decision-making. There was disagreement about how to charge for water supplies, while Sinn Féin were in favour of eliminating academic selection at 11 Plus by examination, the Unionists disagreed and private selection examinations continued to operate in the grammar schools. More recently Sinn Féin has refused to accept British Government proposals to modify the allocation of benefits, despite some successful negotiation by Minister Nelson McCausland of the DUP.

The DUP took four ministries: Finance and Personnel, Environment, Business and Culture Arts and Leisure, Enterprise Trade and Investment. Sinn Féin took three ministries: Education, Regional Development and Agriculture and Rural Development. The UUP took Health, Social Services and Public Safety, and Employment and Learning (which included higher education), whilst the SDLP took on Social Development.

So Alliance MLAs formed an unofficial 'opposition' and were effective in challenging and questioning the workings (and often non-workings) of the Executive. A particular concern that registered with many people was the party's emphasis on the cost of segregation, as discussed on p. 133.

Seamus Close was particularly effective in scrutinising the financial aspects while Eileen Bell became regarded as the 'conscience' of the Assembly.

During this Assembly there were some clashes with First Minister Ian Paisley. His most venomous barbs were not aimed at Sinn Féin, the enemy turned partner in government, but at the middle-of-the-road Alliance Party. In December 2007 Alliance Party leader David Ford remarked in the house about 'laying one-self open to abuse' merely by asking questions. Paisley replied, 'I am sorry that when he does not get it the way he likes it, he considers it abuse. I have never abused the Honourable Member; if I had he would not be sitting in this place today'. Quite how the First Minister would have had the power to eject Ford from 'his place' was not explained. Paisley's quip was met by laughter.[238]

In 2008 there was a local council by-election in Dromore. The DUP were expecting to win the seat having already three of the five seats in that area. David Griffin stood for Alliance and obtained 10% of the vote. Despite some quarrels within the UUP David's transfers went mainly to them and the DUP candidate was defeated.[239] Jim Allister's Traditional Unionist Voice (TUV) candidate had also eaten into the DUP vote.

Ian Paisley Jr MLA, who had been made a junior minister, found himself
in trouble over his excessive expenses from three sources; as his father's
parliamentary assistant for caseload work in South Antrim, as an MLA
and as a junior minister. On top of that there were questions about the
expensive constituency office in Ballymena, rented from property developer
Seymour Sweeney and costing three times more than any other MLA's
office. So Paisley Jr was forced to resign from his junior ministerial position
on 18 February 2008. Alliance leader David Ford commented, 'Ian Paisley's
behaviour has severely damaged the credibility of the Executive. However,
the questions being asked relate to his behaviour as an MLA. This would
suggest that he must resign as an MLA too.'[240]

Finally, on 30 May 2008, Ian Paisley Sr resigned as First Minister and
Alliance leader David Ford said history would judge, 'whether Ian Paisley is
remembered for 40 years of saying no or one year of saying maybe'.[241]

Many people considered that Paisley's vehement anti-Catholic rhetoric
through his own Free Presbyterian Church and as an elected politician were
very largely personally responsible for the Northern Ireland 'Troubles'.[242]
He often called on others to repent in sackcloth and ashes, but showed no
sign of repentance himself.


## A SHARED FUTURE

Alliance had always supported the idea of sharing, but it had received
little support in practice. Alliance's own policy paper, 'Building a United
Community',[243] approved by Council in December 2002 and published in
January 2003, was followed by a British Government initiative which led
to the publication of a document called 'A Shared Future'.[244] It was hoped
that it would be developed by the Assembly. During the time of the first
dysfunctional Assembly led by Trimble and Mallon and then by Trimble and
Durkan no progress was made towards sharing in the interests of the whole
community.

Alliance continued to press for a shared future and continued to emphasise
the cost of divisions within society. The OFM-DFM developed a draft
document on the Shared Future but it was not publicised or processed for
some time. Indeed on one BBC *Hearts and Minds* programme, Sinn Féin's
John O'Dowd ominously laughed at Stephen Farry for promoting the idea
of a shared future. This issue continued to cause problems and at the time of
writing has still not been properly resolved and implemented.

Political parties based on support from one section of the divided community (Unionist or Nationalist) naturally aim to maximise their votes at each election. They try to control the areas where their community predominates. Thus they have little incentive to promote mixed housing or integrated schooling. They have established a segregated system in many areas. Perhaps they see Alliance as a threat to these arrangements. If people mixed together they might get to know people of the other persuasion and might get to like them and even listen to them. Cross-fertilisation or cross-contamination might result. Their children might make friends with 'others' at school. Their politicians might lose votes to the 'others', and perhaps lose their seats and hence their salaries. Flags and painted kerb-stones help to remind 'their' people who they belong to and to discourage 'others' from living in their area. They don't want successful Alliance Party ministers showing the rest how to run departments in a shared, cross-community manner. That might break down their apartheid and lose them votes. Their personal career success and financial comfort would appear to be dominant priorities, regardless of the financial cost to society of £1.5 billion per year due to duplication of facilities – far removed from concerns for post-conflict transformation in their sadly divided society.

## EUROPEAN ELECTION 2009

The next European election was to be in 2009. It was not possible to find a cross-community candidate such as John Gilliland who had obtained 6.6% vote in 2004. Some doubted the wisdom of running an Alliance Party candidate at all. Ian Parsley, a North Down councillor who had been very active in working as Policy Officer for the party, was considered. He had been elected as Deputy Mayor of North Down Council. At a key Party Council meeting he spoke displaying such charisma and persuasion that doubters were quite won over and he was selected to be the candidate. He ran a vigorous and effective campaign, and received considerable media publicity. In the election he obtained 5.5% of the vote, which was the best the party had achieved since Oliver Napier's 6.8% in 1979. During this election campaign it was noted from doorstep canvassing that there was high support for Alliance in East Belfast in particular.

Jim Allister, formerly MEP for the DUP, had resigned because he disagreed with the DUP decision to share power with Sinn Féin. He set up his own Traditional Unionist Voice party (TUV). In the European election he obtained more first-preference votes than the successful DUP candidate, Diane Dodds, but failed to be elected because of how the STV voting system worked.

Alliance was devastated when immediately after the election Ian Parsley defected to the Ulster Conservatives and Unionists New Force (UCUNF), a new link up between the British Conservative Party and the UUP. The idea was that elected MPs for this party group from Northern Ireland would be in the next Conservative government at Westminster. This obviously appealed to Parsley as a more likely opportunity for his political ambitions to be progressed, rather than in the Alliance Party who had no MPs. He had been active in the Conservative Party when he was in England. How wrong his judgment was! Although Conservative candidates had occasionally stood as such in Northern Ireland they had received only derisory numbers of votes, which did not augur well for the new link-up. They had occasionally won council seats in North Down. Significantly Lady Sylvia Hermon was the UUPs only MP (for North Down), originally elected with the help of Alliance votes when they deliberately did not stand in the 2001 Westminster elections. She did not approve of the link with the Tories and in fact voted mostly with the Labour government!

East Belfast Councillor and MLA, Naomi Long was elected in June 2009 as Lord Mayor of Belfast, the fourth Alliance Lord Mayor and only the second woman to hold that office. She was highly successful in the role and received extensive publicity.

## DEVOLUTION OF POLICING AND JUSTICE

When the British Government saw that the Assembly and power-sharing Executive were working tolerably well, they suggested that it was time to devolve the last and most sensitive area, Policing and Justice.[245] In 2006 they published a 'Road Map'[246] to restore that devolution by 26 March 2007. With a new executive up and running all parties had to agree to support the Police Service of Northern Ireland, with a view to Stormont taking control of policing by May 2008. Crucially, the DUP said it was an aspirational date to which they were not committed. Since the Patten Report[247] there was a policy of requiring 50% of new applicants to the PSNI to be Catholic and 50% non-Catholic. This was necessary to bring the percentage of Catholics in the police up to 30% by 2010.

So in January 2007 Sinn Féin agreed for the first time ever to support the police. The DUP dragged its feet about devolution of Policing and Justice, claiming they were waiting for 'adequate public confidence'. The DUP and

Sinn Féin also agreed that neither of their parties should take on the related ministerial role. The SDLP clamoured that the post should go to them by the d'Hondt system, but the DUP and Sinn Féin disagreed. The media, particularly Liam Clarke in the *Sunday Times*,[248] started proposing that Alliance and particularly David Ford should have this ministry, even though they did not qualify according to the d'Hondt system. The issue was extensively debated at Alliance Party Executive and Council, where there was great difference of opinion expressed. Some thought it would be a 'poisoned chalice' and that Alliance would get blamed for everything that went wrong on the security front; others thought it was too good a chance to decline and that members would never forgive the party if they did not accept. There were many other concerns, such as that if Alliance had a minister, they would be in the Executive and could no longer act as an 'opposition'.

In the summer of 2008 David Ford announced publicly that he would not accept the post, even if it was offered.[249,250]

Meanwhile Stephen Farry and his wife, Wendy, researched the requirements for the new ministry and produced a long policy document covering the various areas of policing, justice and the prison service.[251] Areas of concern were:

> Delays in bringing young offenders to court; identifying reasons for anti-social behaviour and for offending; paying greater attention to rehabilitation and the mental health and personality problems of offenders;. [Alliance] favoured greater police visibility and rationalisation of District Policing Partnerships (DDPs) and Community Safety Partnerships; large scale reform of the prison service to cover governance and accountability and review of the Prison Ombudsman's brief; revision of sports law and spectator control, a code of practice for victims and witnesses; sentencing guidelines – which would be welcomed by a public seeking fairer and more consistent sentences.
>
> Historical enquires, 'peace walls', public display of flags and hate crime will all receive attention if the Minister's ambitious plans for reform are shared and he receives approval across the Executive.[252]

A shortened version of this Farry document was debated at the Alliance Party Council on 12 September 2009. The DUP and Sinn Féin continued to press that Alliance should take the ministry, as it could not be trusted to either a Unionist or a Nationalist MLA. As has happened on a number of occasions noted earlier, when a sensitive cross-community post is needed, people look to Alliance to take it on.

Before this decision could be implemented there needed to be a small change in Westminster legislation after which devolution had to be approved by a vote in the Assembly. Prior to this happening, a conference was held at Hillsborough Castle in March 2010 at which this issue was debated along with proposals to change the role of the Parades Commission.

Eventually it was suggested that Alliance might consider accepting the post with conditions attached. If the party's own policy proposals on policing and justice were agreed to and the Assembly's Executive published the long-awaited paper on the 'Shared Future' – known as Cohesion, Sharing and Integration (CSI). This proposal was put to a special meeting of the Alliance Party Council and a packed meeting approved it, with only one person dissenting.

The proposal stated that the Assembly should vote on the issue and the result should be approved by cross-party consent, ignoring the d'Hondt system. Still the SDLP and the UUP did not approve. The UUP voted against the devolution at all and then proposed Danny Kennedy for the post! The SDLP put up Alban McGuinness, but neither of these candidates received sufficient cross-community votes, so David Ford was elected without the support of either the UUP or the SDLP.

The CSI document was published and put out for consultation. The content was, however, a great disappointment. Alliance criticised it for being long on rhetoric but lacking in specific action plans.[253] Indeed it was publicly criticised by Duncan Morrow of the Community Relations Council, who produced an extensive report,[254] by Revd Dr Norman Hamilton, Moderator of the Presbyterian Church,[255] and by many other groups and organisations. It was not about sharing, but about equality of provision of resources for each separate community. It was 'a sectarian sharing out', not real sharing. It was really a recipe for benign apartheid.

News was made in 2010 by the appointment of John Larkin QC, a former Alliance Party member, as the first Attorney General for Northern Ireland since direct rule in 1972. He was the first holder not to be a politician sitting in the Parliament of Northern Ireland or Westminster.[256]

## WESTMINSTER ELECTION 2010

With the next Westminster election imminent, there was a dream that maybe Alliance would have a chance of winning the East Belfast seat. Naomi Long was considered to be the obvious candidate, but she was at first rather reluctant. She liked her work on the city council, but was perhaps less attracted to the rather dysfunctional Assembly.

Alliance ran a very vigorous and effective campaign, focussed on East Belfast. Even though fighting their own elections, many people from other constituencies were drafted in to help. Electors were surprised to see David Ford (by now Minster of Policing and Justice) knocking on their doors.

James McClure described the campaign in *Alliance News*:[257]

### Yes, She Did!

Stuffing, sticking, canvassing and delivering. This sums up exactly the Alliance Party's effort to elect our first ever MP, Naomi Long. While canvassing could not officially begin until the election was formally called, there was still plenty of preparation work to be done behind the scenes – leaflets had to be written, labels needed, printing and delivery routes had to be organised.

Our canvassing in East Belfast began in earnest on 7 April, little under a month before the general election, scheduled for 6 May. This meant all hands to the pump in the constituency – and the hands most certainly came! Canvassers and deliverers came to 56 Upper Newtownards Road from Lisburn, Derry, Antrim, and everywhere in between. We held canvassing sessions daily from Monday to Friday and also on Saturday morning. The Justice Minister even managed to fit in a number of canvassing sessions into his busy schedule.

We also had stickers and stuffers based in the office at all hours of the day and night!

The May Bank Holiday certainly wasn't a holiday for the Alliance Party! In the last week of the election, we had around 7,000 target letters (with the addresses handwritten by willing volunteers) to deliver and thanks to members of the party, we got them to voters in good time to remind them why it is important to vote Alliance. Constituents commented on how impressed they were with the personal touch of the target letter and recognised the effort we had put in.

This year we were also able to introduce new forms of campaigning to East Belfast and across the World Wide Web, A viral cartoon was produced of 'Super Naomi' which was posted on YouTube, Facebook, the Alliance Party Website and other social networking websites. This widened the target base and many people, especially young people, were able to see that the Alliance Party can branch out into new forms of media to show that we are a party of the present and of the future. We were also able to produce a cartoon election Address which was delivered to around 15,000 homes.

6 May came quickly and before we knew it, we were in the office at
5.00 ready to deliver 'Elephants' to likely Alliance voters to remind how
important it was for them to vote this time. Then it was time to give the
people lifts to polling stations and finish some last minute on-line and
polling station canvassing before arriving at the count centre to hear
the result. Election Day was 24 hours long for some of us as we didn't
manage to get to bed until 6.00 am the following morning once we
had quite justifiably, spent a few hours celebrating!

The morning after the night before in the Constituency Office
was certainly an experience! Horns tooted as people drove past the
office, constituents sent hundreds of E-mails from the early hours of
the morning, voters hand delivered congratulations cards, telephone
calls we received showed how truly happy people were to see Naomi
elected and David Ford popped in to celebrate with some cake!

Cynics of the Alliance Party and some media spectators suggested
that our election victory was an attack against our only viable
opponent, rather than success for the Alliance Party. This, as many
volunteers saw on the doors, including myself, was definitely not
the case. The people of East Belfast and across Northern Ireland are
beginning to see more clearly that the Alliance Party is the only party
to support that will cut out sectarianism from our society. This had
become clear in the most recent elections and I am convinced that
our success on 6 May was not a one-off success. I am convinced
that the Alliance Party will continue to grow and will be even more
successful in the future.

So the huge effort was not in vain; Naomi Long won East Belfast with 12,839
votes (37.2%) against sitting MP Peter Robinson with 11,306 votes (32.8%),
a majority of 1,533 votes. Overall Alliance candidates obtained 6.3% against
3.7% in 2005, contesting all eighteen seats, an improvement of 46%. Anna
Lo got 5,114 (15.0%) votes in South Belfast, coming fourth behind Alasdair
McDonald who held the seat for the SDLP, ahead of Jimmy Spratt (DUP)
and Paula Bradshaw (UNCUNF) who subsequently left the UUP and
joined the Alliance Party (she was Ian Parsley's girlfriend, and Ian eventually
saw the error of his ways and returned to the Alliance Party). Trevor Lunn
came third in Lagan Valley with 4,174 votes (11.4%). Gerry Lynch came
third in East Antrim with 3,377 votes (11.1%), Deborah Girvan was fifth in
Strangford with 2,828 (8.7%). Alan Lowther was fifth in South Antrim with
2,605 (7.7%), where Sir Reg Empey, the UUP party leader, failed to win a seat

and subsequently resigned as party leader. Stephen Farry was third in North Down with 1,876 votes (5.6%), against Ian Parsley standing for (UCUNF), with 6,817 votes (20.4%). This seat was held by Lady Sylvia Hermon as an Independent with 21,181 votes (63.3%).

Ominously the two constituencies in which the vote went down slightly were North Down and East Antrim, where Alliance might hope to win extra Assembly seats.

## ASSEMBLY ELECTIONS 2011

After the successes of 2010, there was great expectation for continuing gains in the Assembly elections of 2011. A fairly ambitious and (for Alliance) expensive programme was in place. Leading up to the elections in May there was the Party Conference at the Dunadry Hotel in February. The guest speaker was Enda Kenny, soon to become Taoiseach in the Republic of Ireland. Sir Oliver Napier and his wife Briege were able to come, though the founding leader of the party was not in good health. Ian Parsley, having repented of his excursion into UCUNF, was also there. There was a discussion panel about the Shared Future issue. Party leader David Ford thought that maybe the party would win eleven Assembly seats.

In the event Alliance won a disappointing 7.7% of votes and one extra MLA in East Belfast. Naomi Long MP had stood down from the Assembly to give her time to the Westminster job and Chris Lyttle had taken over as MLA. He held his seat and Judith Cochrane, a Castlereagh councillor who had masterminded the very successful Alliance Party's fortieth anniversary dinner in 2010 and contributed hugely to Naomi Long's campaign for Westminster, also won a seat. Anna Lo topped the poll in South Belfast with 6,390 votes. Perhaps there should have been a second candidate in that constituency? Gordon Kennedy suggested that in South Belfast there have been some strange results when the sitting councillor was not re-elected but replaced by someone else (see chapter 4).[258] Also in the Assembly election of 1998, Steve McBride appeared well place to take a seat, coming third with 4,086 votes but lost out in transfers to SDLP and NIWC candidates (see chapter 5). As they wished to ensure Anna Lo was re-elected they were cautious. Anna had 3,829 votes when first elected in 2007.

Unfortunately Anne Wilson just missed out on winning a second seat in North Down, where Stephen Farry was re-elected. It was hoped that she would take the seat vacated by her Green Party husband Brian Wilson,

as the Green Party was doing badly everywhere else. However, Stephen
Agnew just held the Green Party seat. Anne Wilson started with more
first-preference votes than Leslie Cree, who was elected for the UUP,
and was just ninety-nine votes behind Stephen Agnew on the final count,
with sixty-two of Stephen Farry's votes being undistributed. The Alliance
vote in North Down went up to 18.6% (an increase of 8.6%), though the
Westminster vote in 2010 was slightly down compared with 2005, probably
due to Ian Parsley's vote as UCUNF candidate. The situation in East
Antrim was similar. Former party leader Seán Neeson did not stand again
and his Assembly seat was taken by Stewart Dickson. Geraldine Mulvenna
missed out on a second seat as her transfers were needed to elect Stewart.
The Alliance vote was only 1.8% up compared with 2007. Often Alliance
had polled well in Carrickfergus and East Antrim. Perhaps the strategy
was wrong, or their expectations were too high, or perhaps the nature of
an Assembly election was so different from local government elections,
in which Seán Neeson had four times topped the poll and Stewart Dickson
had come top twice in his electoral area.

The other possible extra seat might have been in North Belfast, where
Alliance had won Assembly seats in 1973, 1975 and 1982. Newtownabbey
Councillor Billy Webb was a strong candidate, but was 536 votes short at the
sixth count, when he was eliminated.

A number of new members had been joining Alliance from other parties,
mainly from the UUP and the SDLP, as they saw something attractive
about Alliance or were dissatisfied with their own party. At party Executive
it was agreed that such new members should not be considered as Alliance
candidates immediately. In the event this rule was bent in some cases.
In Upper Bann, popular Freddy Mercury impersonator Harry Hamilton,
who had been the UCUNF candidate for Westminster, was allowed to
stand together with Sheila McQuaid, now Banbridge Councillor, who had
taken her husband Frank's Banbridge Council seat due to his ill health.
Sheila got about the same vote as in 2007 (786 votes). Harry Hamilton got
1,979 votes as an Alliance candidate, but much less than the 10,639 he got
for the UCUNF in 2007.

Then Alliance had a slice of luck. David McClarty had been a UUP
MLA for East Londonderry but was de-selected by the UUP. He stood as
an independent and came top of the poll, leaving the official UUP candidates floundering. This disappointment for the UUP left the party short
when it came to selecting ministers by the d'Hondt rules. Despite much
pleading by the UUP, David McClarty declined to rejoin them. So, with

eight MLAs, Alliance now qualified for a ministry. Dr Stephen Farry thus became Minister for Employment and Learning. David Ford was again selected by cross-community vote to continue as Minister for Policing and Justice. Seemingly he had become the most respected minister by the Civil Service.

Stephen Farry inherited the tricky job of determining whether students should pay higher fees, as was happening in England, and was urged by both vice-chancellors of Queen's University Belfast and the University of Ulster to do so. As he told Party Council, he was inclined to stay with party policy of not raising fees by more than allowance for inflation, a policy supported by all the other parties.

## LOCAL GOVERNMENT ELECTIONS 2011

Local government and Assembly elections took place on the same day. The increased Alliance Party vote was reflected in these elections with the number of council seats going up from thirty to forty-four. There were two extra seats in Belfast, leading to six councillors and two in Castlereagh also giving six councillors there – the same number as the DUP. There were recovered seats in Craigavon and Ballymena and two in Coleraine, which included Barney Fitzpatrick's seat won in a by-election. In Ards and Larne there were gains of one extra councillor each.

Newtownabbey saw three gains to five councillors, though two of these, Billy Webb and John Blair, had held seats as 'Ratepayer' councillors and had switched to Alliance. In Down, Patrick Clarke, formerly a member of the SDLP, won a seat for Alliance for the first time in over twenty years, an event that received considerable publicity. Sheila McQuaid retained her husband's former seat in Bainbridge since he had to withdraw from politics because of ill health.

David Griffin failed to win a new seat in the Dromore area of Banbridge, where he had done so well at a by-election in 2008 and had hoped to make a gain. In North Down and Carrickfergus, where Alliance had hoped for gains in Assembly seats, the number of councillors remained at six and three respectively. In Antrim the total remained at two. Former SDLP councillor Oran Keenan in Antrim had switched to Alliance but this time he lost his seat.

## CONCLUSION

Sir Oliver Napier was very proud to see the party he had started doing so well by gaining an MP for the first time. In addition, Alliance had the best Assembly and local government election results for many years, though not as good as in the Assembly election of 1982 or the local government elections of 1973 and 1977. Despite the negative aspect of Alliance's electoral record, to have two ministers in an Assembly that was actually working and not in immediate danger of being pulled down was an even greater achievement. This was a great personal reward for Sir Oliver following the Fortieth Anniversary Dinner in 2010, to which he was able to go and give an address. Sadly he passed away on 2 July 2011, after an exemplary life well lived spiritually, professionally, politically.

# 8

# Flags, Haass and elections
# 2012-2014

## INTRODUCTION

The period 2012 to 2014 was dominated by four events: the flags dispute at Belfast City Hall, the Haass Talks, and elections to the eleven new councils and the European elections. The Haass Talks were intended to resolve the three issues – flags, parades and the past – at a series of five-party talks chaired by Americans Richard Haass and Meghan O'Sullivan. In May 2014 there were elections to the eleven new councils and to the European Parliament.

## THE FLAG PROTESTS

A major crisis developed in November 2012. The Union flag had been flown daily over Belfast City Hall, but Republicans had started to object. Sinn Féin had become the largest party on the city council since the 2011 elections. They wanted to see either no flag or joint flying of the Irish tricolour with the Union flag. Of course the Unionist group objected very strongly. It was, and is, a very emotional issue. In November 2012 Sinn Féin, supported by the SDLP, put forward a motion to council to stop flying the Union flag at all.

Alliance Party Councillor Máire Hendron proposed a compromise amendment that the Union flag should just be flown on seventeen designated days, as was already the case in Unionist-dominated Lisburn City Council, Craigavon Council and also at Stormont over the parliament buildings. It had also been recommended earlier by the Equality Commission for Northern

Ireland, an independent body formed after the Good Friday Agreement for the purpose of examining issues of this nature. Its current Chief Officer Michael Wardlow said in November 2014:

> Regarding the official displays of flags, particularly the Union Flag, we proposed that the principles contained in the Flags (NI) Order, which applies to Government buildings and lists designated days for flying the Union Flag, should form the basis of a regulatory framework for official displays of flags by local councils.

The amendment was supported by SDLP and Sinn Féin councillors (thus recognising that their first preference to stop flying the flag would fail to get majority support), but opposed by all Unionist (UUP, DUP, PUP) councillors. As Alliance held the balance of power on the Belfast City Council with six council seats, the amendment passed. So the flag is now flown only on the seventeen designated days. It was a good and proper democratic decision.[259]

In the weeks before the vote on the flag issue, the DUP had printed and distributed over 40,000 leaflets, mainly in East Belfast, made out in Alliance Party colours, calling on people to protest about the Alliance proposal. The UUP assisted the DUP in distributing the leaflets.

Alliance Councillor Máire Hendron said she was 'disgusted' by the leaflet. She said, 'I cannot be clearer when I say the Alliance Party has not formed a pact with Sinn Féin or the SDLP over the future of the flag at Belfast City Hall'.

She accused the DUP in particular of 'underhand tactics' ahead of a council vote on the issue. However, in response to complaints from Alliance, the DUP said it had 'nothing to apologise for'. The UUP has confirmed its councillors were involved in distributing the leaflets and said flag policy was an emotive issue for Unionists. The leaflets were printed in the Alliance Party's distinctive yellow colours and included the telephone numbers for its headquarters and East Belfast office. Over the previous two weeks, they had been posted through doors across Belfast, ahead of the upcoming debate on flag policy that was due to take place at the council on 3 December.

On the day of the vote five police officers were hurt during disorder in Belfast that erupted minutes after the council had voted to change its policy on the Union flag. A number of loyalist protesters had tried to force their way into Belfast City Hall where the vote took place.

The result of the vote was bitterly resented by many of the Unionist and Loyalist people, as well as councillors, especially in East Belfast.

They refused to accept the democratic decision made by the council. Street protests began which involved major confrontations with the police. Flag protest marches from East Belfast to the City Hall were held every Saturday morning. These marches were not authorised, but the police seemed at a loss as to how to deal with the situation, which was regularly riotous and involved many police and other people getting injured. They did take video shots of the marchers, especially those causing rioting, and were able to prosecute a number of them. The protests caused major disruption of city centre trading, and many shoppers just stayed away, damaging the business of many traders.

First Minister Peter Robinson MLA and his DUP colleagues, while stating that they condemned the violence, openly supported the flag protests. The protests appeared to be organised via social media on mobile phones from dark, quasi–anonymous groups of so-called 'loyalists'.

The protestors then turned their attention to the Alliance Party deputy leader, Naomi Long MP, now Westminster MP for East Belfast. Although as an MP she was no longer a Belfast city councillor, she was made the scapegoat for the flags decision. Her advice office on the Lower Newtownards Road in East Belfast came under frequent attack with bricks, petrol bombs and other missiles. She herself received death threats. Threats were also made to other Alliance Party councillors in East Belfast, Bangor and Carrickfergus. Alliance Party councillor Laura McNamee was threatened in her East Belfast home and moved out on 4 December. 1,500 protestors gathered in Carrickfergus on 5 December and burned down MLA Stewart Dickson's advice centre, which was an Alliance Party office. In Bangor, Alliance councillors Michael and Christine Bower had their home attacked.

Fortunately the East Belfast office was well protected and the damage to it was fairly minimal. Naomi Long insisted that she was going about her business as a democratically elected MP, working for and supporting her constituents in East Belfast:[260]

My colleagues and I have been asked, in light of all that happened, whether we think Alliance did the right thing in supporting the change. That is a question which I can answer simply and honestly – yes. Though I am no longer a city councillor, I believe my colleagues took a decision that was principled, respectful and which took full account of the equality and legal advice when they tabled a brave compromise that brought Belfast City Council in line with the majority of the councils in Britain by voting to fly the union flag on designated days only.

But it was not only Alliance that was affected by those protests and the violence which surrounded them – they damaged our economy greatly, causing widespread disruption to the daily lives of people across Northern Ireland, all the while placing the police under extraordinary pressure and drawing precious resources away from tacking other crime and the threat from dissident republicans.

Unionist parties in particular on the flags issue have made a series of promises to people that they simply cannot keep, such as promising that the Union flag will fly 365 days a year at Belfast City Hall. Making false promises pre-election may win votes and even placate people in the short term, but how much angrier and frustrated will they be when those promises fail to be kept?

As suggested by Neeson and Farry in their analysis of the Good Friday Agreement,[261] there were some Loyalists who felt that they had got nothing out of the Agreement and were resentful. They had long relied on jobs at the shipyards, aircraft factory Shorts and other places in East Belfast handed on from their fathers, and now many of these traditional jobs had gone. Many were living on benefits, and were open to the malign influence of paramilitary hoodlums. Whereas in South and West Belfast, the impression was that many Catholics had got themselves educated and were taking professional jobs. The flag issue was used as an excuse to hold violent street protests and to attack the Alliance Party, particularly Naomi Long.

Flags have always been a contentious issue in Northern Ireland, with Unionists insisting that the union flag is the flag of their country and can and should be flown anywhere at any time. It is flown from lampposts and other street furniture all over the place. Often flags are left up till they become tattered and disintegrate, ignoring the view of others that this is an insult to the Queen. Resulting from the flag protest in Belfast, there was an increase in the flying of flags in many other places, including outside the Catholic church on a roundabout in the Ballynafeigh area of South Belfast which had long been a very peaceful mixed area. Attempts were made to fly the flags inside Catholic Church property in Garvagh, County Londonderry. Of course some Republicans insist on flying the Irish tricolour from time to time though usually just in places where there is a Nationalist majority. This adds to the antagonism of Loyalist protestors who recall the days prior to 1987 when it was illegal to fly the Irish flag in Northern Ireland.

Although violent protests have subsided the issue continues to prevail and poison community relations, with no end in sight despite efforts in the Haass Talks to achieve agreement.

## THE HAASS TALKS

In the autumn of 2013 former US Special Envoy to Northern Ireland and current president of the Council on Foreign Relations Dr Richard Haass and former US National Security Council staff member and current Harvard Professor Meghan O'Sullivan were invited from the USA to lead a series of talks on three remaining contentious issues. These were dealing with the past, the flying of flags and marches.

This talks process had its genesis within a proposal from the Alliance Party. In May 2012, Alliance withdrew from the cross-party working group established to devise a Strategy for Cohesion, Sharing and Integration, on the basis that it was a closed process lacking in ambition, and ultimately doomed to fail. In early 2013, in the aftermath of the flags protests and civil unrest, David Ford wrote to the other party leaders suggesting a new process to address shared future issues, chaired by an independent figure of international standing and involving civil society.

Within the 'Together: Building a United Community' strategy released by the First Minister and Deputy First Minister in May 2013, there was a commitment to a fresh cross-party process to address three long-running, corrosive issues for Northern Ireland: Flags, parades and dealing with the Past.

The five parties in the Executive all participated. Two people were nominated from each party to take part. For the Alliance Party they were Naomi Long MP and Chris Lyttle MLA. Their appointment was endorsed by Party Council in September, and they were given the authority to negotiate and to take decisions on behalf of the party in the talks, in line with existing party policy on the issues in question. This was most recently articulated in the 'For Everyone' document (February 2014).[262]

For the DUP one of their nominees was Revd Mervyn Gibson, chaplain to the Orange Order but not an elected representative. The timing of these talks was very unfortunate as protests about the Union flag continued weekly and there was an on-going protest at Twaddell Avenue, near the Crumlin Road in West Belfast, about the Parades Commissions refusal to allow an Orange parade to 'complete' its march from 12 July 2012 past the Ardoyne shops area, populated mainly by Catholics, who very much objected.

The talks continued up to Christmas and just afterwards. Many useful suggestions were made. The Haass proposals were drafted and re-drafted several times, but no agreement was forthcoming. The SDLP and Sinn Féin would have agreed and Alliance agreed with most of the material, but the DUP and UUP would not agree. At one point UUP leader Mike Nesbitt

MLA said he was inclined to accept the proposals, but then changed his mind and rejected them outright.

The best account of the Haass Talks, their origins, contents and the attitudes of the other parties is probably given in the Alliance Party's own account, which follows.[263]

## Alliance Delegation

Party leader David Ford appointed deputy leader Naomi Long and OFMDFM Spokesperson Chris Lyttle as the Alliance delegates to the talks. Their appointment was endorsed by Party Council in September, and they were given the authority to negotiate and to take decisions on behalf of the party in the talks, in line with existing party policy on the issues in question. This was most recently articulated in the 'For Everyone' document (February 2014).

The delegation was in turn supported in the negotiations by David Ford, Stephen Farry, Richard Good, and Christine Robinson, plus some external advisers, with staff assistance from David Young, Nuala McAllister, Kate Nicholl, and Ben Lloyd.

## Public Submissions

Consistent with the Alliance aspiration, submissions were sought from individuals and organisations to better inform the process. Over 600 submissions were received; many of which reinforced the Alliance perspective.

## Alliance Positions

Alliance was guided by three cross-objectives: to entrench the rule of law, to develop recognition that all space is shared space, and to promote respect for diversity.

All along, Alliance's preference was for a comprehensive agreement, involving all parties, across all three issues. In the event that this was not forthcoming, progress on the past would constitute a major breakthrough. In the absence of agreement in any or all areas, Alliance wanted Richard Haass to set out his commentary on the necessary proposals to deliver change in each of the areas in line with the key underlying values of a shared future and the rule of law.

## Parades

On parades, the party had relatively few issues with the Parades Commission that could not be addressed through some minor changes to how it conducted its business. Instead, Alliance regarded the real issues as a common understanding of shared space, and a clear commitment to the rule of law through respecting and abiding by decisions made by regulators. The party was prepared to consider changes to or a replacement of the Parades Commission but this had to be balanced by clear commitment to the necessary values, and stronger accountability measures over illegal or offensive behaviour.

## Flags

On flags, the party wanted to see a consistent, Northern Ireland-wide approach to the flying of the Union flag on government and council buildings. The only logical position in this regard was the use of designated days. The party also proposed a system for the regulation of the unofficial flying of flags on lampposts and other street furniture. This is often conducted by paramilitaries, and is less about celebrating culture than marking out territory. Polls show that around 80% of the population object to flags on street furniture. Therefore, Alliance proposals for regulation in themselves constituted a compromise.

## The Past

The party has long believed that Northern Ireland could not simply draw a line under the past, and that moreover addressing the past in a sensitive and constructive manner would contribute to reconciliation. As such, Alliance have long favoured a comprehensive approach to the past. This includes assistance for individual victims in terms of the provision of services, opportunities for storytelling and acknowledgement, and the pursuit of justice and/or truth as means to achieve a degree of closure. Furthermore, it also requires societal-wide consideration of certain themes, acknowledgement, memorials, reflection, and, building upon these and other initiatives, the pursuit of reconciliation.

## Process of the Talks

Alliance had arguably a greater influence, both in terms of influencing the wording of the document and the insertion and shaping of certain aspects of the content of the final text (especially on the past), than other parties.

Most of the discussions involved the Haass team meeting with the parties separately to ask for ideas and testing proposals. Over the course of the final two weeks of the process, including the Christmas break, seven different texts of a proposed overall agreement were issued to the parties to solicit written comments and amendments, with the seventh text becoming the final proposed agreement.

At times, this process allowed certain proposals to be refined. However, it also led to swings in the nature and the balance of the document as different parties influenced thinking, and too frequently proposals were simply removed or difficult aspects not addressed as different parties essentially blocked further consideration.

## Outcome of the Talks

Overall, the Alliance team believes that genuine progress was made during the talks. However, the party was very disappointed that an overall agreement was not found.

The final product as a whole does not meet the ambitions of the Alliance Party and also wider society for these issues to be properly addressed as a precursor to a more cohesive, shared and integrated society, entrenching both peace and prosperity.

Nevertheless, the many proposals in the final text and related ideas should now form the basis for future discussions. Indeed, it is possible that some or even many of the proposals may be taken forward by the parties.

Alliance has provided an honest assessment across the three strands. While not giving the document as a whole an unqualified endorsement, the party will seek to work with the other parties and the two governments to finesse or finalise the proposals, and to facilitate implementation. Alliance will also give full scrutiny to any related legislation to be taken forward.

## Parades

Alliance has considerable reservations regarding the proposed way forward in this area. The Parades Commission is to be replaced by an Office for Parades, Select Commemorations and Related Protests, to handle the administration of applications to parade or counter-protest, and an Authority for Public Events Adjudication to make determinations on those parades or protests that receive objections and where mediation has not been successful. On a plus point, the potential for enhanced regulation of non-parade-related assemblies was resisted.

There is some stronger language regarding commitment to decisions and respect for the rule of law. However, Alliance has major concerns regarding the lack of accountability around parade and protest organisers, weaknesses in the code of conduct, and the criteria for the Adjudication Body in making determinations. While it is a strong feature that the Code of Conduct will apply to all parades, the final draft was actually weaker than in previous versions and it is probable that the Unionist parties, at the behest of the marching orders, may continue to reserve its general applicability to all parades. Alliance succeeded in including strong values-related language to be inserted in this section, changing the appointments process for the Adjudication Body to restrict the ability of OFMDFM to carve it up, and to make the Code of Conduct apply to all parades.

There is no certainty regarding changes in attitude or behaviour on the part of those who have caused difficulties recently.

## Flags

With respect to flags, there is no real agreement. The Unionist parties essentially refused to engage with any substantive proposals. The Nationalist parties largely acquiesced in this one. So in many respects, Alliance remained the only party willing to engage on this issue.

Instead, all issues were referred to another proposed Commission on Identity, Culture and Tradition. This would comprise seven political appointees, including one from Alliance, and eight others to be selected by OFMDFM through the public appointments process. Alliance did ensure that the public appointments process would be used for this rather than leaving the appointments to the direct political patronage of the First Minister and Deputy First Minister.

This commission would examine a range of issues, including the official and unofficial flying of flags, language issues and a Bill of Rights.

The party believed that the Haass Talks were the best opportunity to address problems relating to the flying of flags as all the main parties were involved and an international chair was in place. Alliance does not see the sense in passing this onto another process, in particular an inferior one. Nonetheless, the party has indicated that it would participate in this.

Ultimately, there is no agreement in this area, and the can has essentially been kicked down the road.

## Contending with the Past

Most progress was made on dealing with the past, despite the initial assessments of many commentators and politicians. In practice, the positions of the political parties are less fixed in this area than in others, and as a result, there was more room for flexibility.

The proposals extend to increased support for victims, space for acknowledgements, opportunities for storytelling, a new Historical Investigations Unit (replacing the Historical Enquiries Team and aspects of the Police Ombudsman), a new system for the recovery of information in relation to individual cases and the analysis of broad themes that capture a number of incidents. These latter tasks would be facilitated by the Independent Commission for Information Retrieval (ICIR). It is the last aspect that is most innovative, and a system of limited immunity preventing information provided in good faith from being used in prosecutions to incentivise disclosure.

Alliance heavily influenced the creation of a mechanism for truth recovery and the concept of limited immunity (in contrast to an amnesty) in relation to information provided in order to facilitate this process. The theme of opportunities for storytelling and the emphasis upon services for victims are also consistent with our approach.

The discussions couldn't provide a sufficient consensus on matters such as the definition of a victim, or how to create a Peace Centre or Museum, or to determine the future of the Maze Long Kesh site. There are also concerns about the willingness of paramilitaries, and the UK and Irish governments to play their full role in the disclosure of information, and over the willingness of the two governments to provide resources.

It is recognised that the range of mechanisms here will not address the needs of every victim. However, collectively they amount to a significant improvement upon an already very imperfect system and hold out the potential to bring assistance to a much greater number of victims.

## Implementation and Reconciliation Group

Finally, this group is proposed to be established to monitor implementation of the overall agreement and the delivery by the new structures to be created, to play an advisory role and to facilitate debate and conversation leading to reconciliation, and to identify themes for further investigation by the ICIR. In addition to a representative from each of the five Executive parties, it will have representation from civic society including victims.

This chair of the body will serve as an Oversight and Implementation Commissioner. The Commissioner post was a direct proposal from Alliance and the IRG itself was derived from an Alliance proposal for a Reconciliation Forum.

## Reaction of Other Parties, and their Potential Motivations

Sinn Féin – They have endorsed the document as a whole, but have expressed some scepticism around the parades section and questioned the wisdom of yet another process on flags. Their rush to endorse may reflect a calculation that the DUP will at best give qualified support and as such they may be trying to look good in terms of international opinion and to place the DUP on the defensive.

SDLP – They have also endorsed the document as a whole, though their language in doing so varies and at times this endorsement is a general one. Their prime motivation is to bank the progress made on dealing with the past. They have considerable reservations on parades.

UUP – They are taking the package to their Party Executive. Despite what Nesbitt has said about clear choices to be made, they are likely to be watchful of what the DUP did. They were arguably the least constructive and engaged party during the talks, and their positions were barely distinguishable from the DUP.

DUP – The party is also to consult internally, and with external stakeholders (in particular the marching orders). They have said that they support the broad architecture, but expressed serious concerns over some proposals and aspects of language. It is unlikely that the DUP will reject the document, but give qualified support and work to make changes.

## Next Steps

It is likely that the five Executive Parties will form a working group to explore if and how to implement aspects of the final text, and also to change or finesse certain aspects or to work them up further. Major parts of the text will require legislation either in Westminster or in the Assembly.

The final text of the talks process can be found on a the government website.[264]

## 2014 LOCAL GOVERNMENT ELECTIONS

These were elections to the new eleven councils reduced from the original twenty-six. The new councils would not be fully brought into effect till April 2015, so those elected were in 'shadow form'. The existing councils and their councillors continue in office till April 2015.

The Alliance Party approached the coming elections with some trepidation. The flags dispute had precipitated much antagonism towards Alliance in some quarters. However, in other quarters there was approval for the action taken. There was a dramatic increase in party membership, up by 113 in 2013. There were also good improvements in funding. The change in the structure of local government councils meant a corresponding decrease in the number of councillors from 582 to 462. Indeed there probably were too many councils, but perhaps fifteen councils would have been more appropriate, as with eleven councils the whole of the province is roughly split into a Nationalist south and west and a Unionist north and east. With these changes came many boundary changes resulting in quite different electoral areas, sometimes bringing in areas that sitting councillors were not familiar with or known in.

The election results were not as bad as might have been feared, but not as good as some might have hoped either.[265] Indeed the *Newsletter* gave some very positive comments: 'Among the stand out results over the week end was the news that the Alliance's Michael Long scored ahead of both his nearest DUP and UUP rivals in Lisnascarragh.'[266] An Alliance Party statement said:

> The story of this election is undoubtedly the sight of Long topping the poll in East Belfast – proving the name is seen by people as positive, hardworking and reliable for everyone in the City.
>
> The result has shown the predictions of gloom and doom by the soothsayers were wrong and voters want to see a non-tribal approach focussing on the key issues.
>
> The Alliance hailed gains it had made in North Belfast, Lisburn and Rowallane.
>
> The implosion in the Alliance Party's vote in the capital city which some had predicted simply did not materialise.
>
> DUP Leader Peter Robinson said that Mrs Long was 'on notice' that her seat was likely to change hands, pointing to the vote in the areas which make up the Westminster seat, but Alliance members pointed

to the different boundaries between Westminster and the local government areas and to the plethora of candidates.

Despite some opinion polls suggesting 13% support for Alliance, its share of the vote was down by 0.7% to 6.7%, resulting in thirty-two seats, down two. (An estimate had been made for all parties about how many seats in the eleven new councils would be expected compared to the seats held in 2011 in the old twenty-six councils.)[267]

The overall results suggest that there was perhaps some disillusionment with the parties in government at Stormont as all the main parties except UUP lost votes: the DUP was down 4.1% to 23.1% giving it 130 seats, a loss of fifteen; SDLP was down 1% to 13.6%. They still won sixty-six seats, a loss of one, though their leadership considered the result a disaster. Sinn Féin was down 0.7% to 24.1%, giving them 105 seats, a loss of ten, but surprisingly UUP was up 0.9% to 16.1%, giving them eighty-eight seats, a gain of eleven. Minor protest parties were the main gainers. TUV was up 2.5% to 4.5%, giving them thirteen seats; PUP was up by 1.4% to 2%, resulting in four seats, a gain of three; UKIP was up 1% to 1.4% (three seats, a gain of two). Strangely the Greens lost 0.2% to 0.8%, but won four seats, a gain of three, largely at the expense of Alliance. A new breakaway party from the UUP, called NI21, were lucky to win any seats as the leaders, Basil McCrea MLA and John McAlister MLA, had a major disagreement just coming up to the elections. But they got 1.83% of the vote and won a seat.

In an enlarged Belfast City Council, Alliance won two extra seats, giving them eight seats with 11.5% of the vote, still holding the balance of power. Unfortunately they probably put up too many candidates in some areas. Thus in Titanic Marie Hendron lost her seat to a new Alliance candidate, David Armitage, which was a pity as she was the proposer of the controversial vote about flags in Belfast City Council. In Botanic it was expected that Duncan Morrow, nephew of Addie Morrow, formerly CEO of the Community Relations Council and currently lecturer at the University of Ulster would easily win a seat. But he lost to another new Alliance candidate, Emmett McDonough-Brown. In Ormiston they won two seats, but fielded four candidates, allowing Ross Brown of the Greens to win a seat. Overall agent Jim Hendron considered[268] that his wife Máire would have topped the poll, if they had not put up two candidates. We noted in Chapter 4 the fickleness of the electorate in South Belfast, often preferring a new candidate to the sitting councillor, which was why Anna Lo was the only candidate in the 2011 Assembly elections (see earlier comment by Gordon Kennedy in

Chapter 7). The listing of the candidates on the ballot paper in alphabetical
order can also be a factor. The best results were that Michael Long (MP
Naomi's husband) topped the poll in Lisnaharragh and Nuala McAllister
won a new seat in Castle.

An interesting effect was that, because of the flags issue, Alliance candidates were getting fewer transfers from Unionists, but more transfers from
Nationalists, who no doubt respected the principled stand taken by Alliance.
So in South Down Councillor Patrick Clarke, coming sixth with 690 first-
preference votes (up from 565 in 2011), held his seat with transfers from the
SDLP, beating off a UUP candidate (the SDLP probably put up too many
candidates in this Slieve Croob area).

After pressure from Alliance Party headquarters, South Down Alliance
also put up Patrick Brown in the Rowallane area and Ciarán McIvor in the
Mourne area. Although Patrick Brown stood in 2011 and obtained a creditable 474 votes, this time he was away studying politics at Sheffield University.
However, to everyone's surprise he got 510 first-preference votes, coming
seventh, but with transfers from Sinn Féin, won a seat over a UUP candidate.
UUP's Danny Kennedy MLA publically complained that he was just a
paper candidate. Kennedy said, 'He did not put up any posters; he did not
canvass and did not attend the count'. (Patrick was handing in his thesis in
Sheffield.) Of course he was known in the area and all electors had received
Alliance Party leaflets about him. Éamon McEvoy got a creditable 260 votes,
coming 9th.

In Lisburn-Castlereagh Alliance did very well, winning seven seats with
12% of the vote, including one for Vasundhara Kamble, originally from India.
In North Down-Ards Alliance won seven seats with 13.4% of the vote.
It might have been more but the Greens won three seats in this area.

Elsewhere, Alliance candidates won three seats in East Antrim, one seat
in Causeway Coast and Glens and four seats in Antrim – Newtownabbey.
Despite six candidates being fielded and the party receiving 3.9% of the vote
in Armagh – Banbridge-Craigavon, Sheila McQuaid lost her seat and Harry
Hamilton missed out by two votes on the ninth count in his area.

Sadly a number of long-serving prominent Alliance councillors lost their
seats, especially women, including Máire Hendron (Belfast), Sheila McQuaid
(Banbridge), Lynne Frazer (Newtownabbey – first Alliance Mayor in 2006),
Yvonne Boyle (Coleraine), Jayne Dunlop (Ballymena). Long-standing councillors Pat McCudden (Newtownabbey) and Alan Lowther (Antrim) also lost
out. Thirteen councillors lost seats, but thirteen new councillors won seats.

As some compensation a number of these councillors were made Deputy

Mayor for the year, including Máire Hendron (Belfast), Yvonne Boyle (Coleraine), Pat McCudden (Newtownabbey) and Anne Wilson (North Down) – not standing again this time.

## EUROPEAN ELECTION 2014

The most successful election for Alliance was the European election, held on the same day as the local government elections. Anna Lo was the candidate as she had a high profile as an MLA and had international publicity as the first Chinese person to be elected to a European parliament. She campaigned widely and then gave a significant interview to the *Irish News*, which was featured on the front page.[269] Among the questions, she was asked her views about a United Ireland. Perhaps rather naively, she admitted having no problem with the idea of a united Ireland. She was reported by John Manley of the *Irish News* as follows: 'I think it is such a small place. To divide it up and the corner of Ireland to be part of the United Kingdom – it's very artificial.'

The South Belfast MLA describes herself as 'anti-colonial' but insists a thirty-two-county Ireland can only be achieved with the consent of the majority in the north and that it should maintain strong links with its nearest neighbour; nevertheless, she says a united Ireland would be 'better placed economically, socially and politically'.

Unification is unlikely during her lifetime, Ms Lo says, but both she and her party would support the removal of the border if that was the majority's wish.[270]

This raised a media furore and a commotion among the other parties as the Alliance Party was perceived to be a pro-union party! This point was debated widely in the media. So at the Alliance Party Annual Conference on 22 March in La Mon House Hotel, Anna Lo, as Alliance candidate for the EU elections, made a rousing speech, saying that Alliance Party members came from different backgrounds whereby they might favour the union with Great Britain or with Ireland. In fact Northern Ireland's constitutional future would be determined by its people. She declared that what motivated her was not a united Ireland but a united Northern Ireland. Unusually she was given a standing ovation, except that Alliance Councillor Geraldine Rice declined to stand up. Councillor Rice later said: 'I don't agree with what she said … but it is not Alliance's view, it is Anna's own personal view and everyone is entitled to their personal view.'

There may have been others who thought Anna's statement rather unwise, but she nevertheless received great support from the vast majority of Alliance

Party members, as shown by the standing ovation. She was backed by the party leader's speech, which also aimed at clarifying the situation, reiterating the official Alliance Party policy.[271] Later in the, *Belfast Telegraph*,[272] First Minister Peter Robinson said that in view of Anna's statement to the *Irish News*, Unionist voters should not give second-preference votes to Alliance Party candidates. Whether that affected the voting in the local government elections we can only speculate, but it clearly did no harm to Anna Lo's vote in the EU election. Reports of shameful verbal attacks on her, which could only be described as racist, probably also gained her some sympathy. Although she came out of nowhere to almost win a seat she obtained the highest vote ever for Alliance candidates in EU elections, with 44,432 votes (7.1%), compared with Oliver Napier's 39,026 votes (6.8%) in 1979.

## NEXT CHALLENGE

In 2015 Naomi Long will be defending her Westminster seat in East Belfast. It is going to be a difficult challenge as the Unionists are determined to defeat her, probably with a single, agreed Unionist candidate, if they can agree. They hope that the knock-on effect of the flag protests will turn people against Naomi. But that hope could be counterproductive, as there is much sympathy for the way she has stood up to the threats and violence, continuing to work for her constituents. She and her Alliance Party team will need to concentrate on the positive achievements she has made as an MP. Even so the tribal vote may prevail.

# 9

# Alliance Party principles and organisation

## INTRODUCTION

This chapter includes a discussion of party principles and their application, party organisation and the major policy areas.

## PARTY PRINCIPLES

The Alliance Party was founded on the basis of a number of party principles which were inviolable.

There are four main features of the party's founding principles concerned with:

1   The Alliance Party and the border
2   Alliance as a party of reconciliation
3   Economic approach and relation with other parties
4   The rule of law and security

From the beginning the Alliance Party was guided by a set of principles, from which more detailed policies were developed.[273] The first principle concerned a commitment to the union and to a devolved government. It said:

> We support the constitutional position of Northern Ireland as an integral part of the United Kingdom. We know that the overwhelming majority of our people share this belief and that provocative debate about it has been the primary cause of all our most fundamental troubles. The union

is in the best economic and social interest of all citizens of the state. It also implies British standards of democracy and social justice, which will be energetically secured and steadfastly upheld. We are firmly committed to the principle of devolved government and would not support any attempt to suspend or dissolve the Northern Ireland parliament.

In general, elections in Northern Ireland had been only about one thing – the border. They were largely a head count of those who supported the union with Great Britain (Unionists) and those who did not (Nationalists). This head count was roughly also a head count of Protestants and Catholics. Little attention was given to detailed everyday political policies.

The Alliance Party tried to shift the emphasis from the border controversy towards the crucial need to combat sectarian division. This principle stated the simple fact that a clear majority of the Northern Ireland electorate was in favour of Northern Ireland remaining part of the United Kingdom (something that was duly demonstrated in the Border Poll of 1973) and that there were practical benefits in this. Nationalists called Alliance 'a Unionist party with a small "u"', while Unionists said that Alliance was 'unsound on the border question'. The question of the Alliance Party's attitude to the union with Great Britain and the relationships with the Republic of Ireland has always figured strongly in the attempts by political opponents to combat its cross–community appeal. This issue is discussed at some length in Chapter 5. Despite efforts to discount it, the issue is always there as it is the central issue for Unionist and Nationalists. Undoubtedly this has been an impediment to progress over the years.

When put to the test, such as in the Border Poll campaign in 1973, Alliance had put forward the pragmatic majority view that the economic and social interests of the province are best served by maintaining the union with Great Britain. However, they have made it absolutely clear that the Northern Ireland community must have the right to make that basic decision. Northern Ireland must remain part of the United Kingdom as long as that is the will of the majority. If, however, at any time popular opinion switches to a preference for uniting with the Republic to form a united Ireland that must be accepted. The key factor is always 'consent'.

A survey of council members was carried out in 1988, which showed the range of views held by individual members. A members questionnaire conducted through the Party Council asked how members saw themselves in 'the Nationalist-Unionist Spectrum', on a rating of 0 to 10, 0 being the Nationalist end and 10 being the Unionist end, so 5 was the centre. Average scores were for self, 5.64, for the party, 5.71 and the ideal, 5.39. Thus the conclusion was that:

A plurality of party members sees themselves in the absolute centre of this spectrum. There is however a considerable number with mild Unionist leanings, but not a majority. Soft Nationalists are few in number.[274]

Ever since the formation of the Northern Ireland State a large measure of self-government was given to the province. Overall the Stormont Parliament was responsible to the British Parliament in Westminster. As we have seen, this Stormont Parliament was always controlled by the Unionist majority who frequently abused their powers, leading to the civil rights movement in 1968–1972. Despite the abuse of powers, Alliance considered that full participation by Northern Ireland people in addressing their own problems was a key factor in healing community divisions. For this reason the commitment of the party to devolved government has always been absolute. However, it was clear that a measure of devolved local government by people elected from Northern Ireland was the best way forward. A radically different form of government was needed in which power would be shared between the communities in Northern Ireland. In effect each section should have a veto on the overall decisions. 'Power sharing' became a major principle of the Alliance Party which came to be written into all the proposals for devolved government over the next thirty years. We can see how it operated, or failed to operate, in the chapters on the three Assemblies that were established over that time.

One important omission from the founding principles was the party's position on relations with the Republic of Ireland. This became known as 'the Irish Dimension' and soon took its place as a key issue in the developing political situation.

The second principle states that:

Our primary aim is to heal the bitter divisions in our community by ensuring:-

Equality of citizenship and of human dignity;

The rooting out of discrimination and injustices;

The elimination of prejudice by a just and liberal appreciation of the beliefs and fears of different members of the community;

Equality of social, economic and educational opportunities;

Highest standards of democracy at both parliamentary and local government levels;

Complete and effective participation in our political, governmental and public life at all levels by people drawn from both sides of our present religious divide.

This principle expressed the core of Alliance Party thinking – healing community division by ensuring equality, justice and participation. This is dealt with at length in Chapter 11, which includes discussion of sectarianism, religion and identity.

The third principle relates to 'economic dogma', in which Alliance declared it would not follow the traditional left–right economic principles of the Labour and Conservative parties in Great Britain. It said:

> Our economic policies will not be shackled by any economic dogmas, whether socialist or conservative. The Alliance Party will never accept any such socio-economic allegiance. Nor is there any intention or desire whatsoever to affiliate with any other party.

In effect this was a declaration of support for a mixed economy – not tied to socialism or private enterprise entirely. In practice the economic policies of the party tended to be social democratic in nature, encouraging private enterprise in many areas, but having State control on others such as health and education. Although not formally linked to the Liberal Party (which continues to exist in Northern Ireland), its economic policies are very similar to those of the British Liberal Party (now the Liberal Democrats, following a merger in 1988 between the Liberal Party and the Social Democrat Party, which broke away from the Labour Party in 1981).

The fourth principle is 'universal respect for the law':

> We firmly believe that without universal respect for the law of the land and the authorities appointed to enforce it, there can be no measurable progress. We, therefore, intend to secure the rapid achievement of such respect and the absolutely equal enforcement of the law without fear or favour, in every part of the state. Equal justice will be guaranteed to all citizens regardless of their political or religious persuasion.

Unique among the political parties in Northern Ireland, Alliance has adhered to the principle of respect for and obedience to the law. Adherence does not, however, mean acceptance that the existing laws are sacrosanct. Indeed Oliver Napier's main commitment as Minister for Law Reform in the 1973/74 Executive was to seek amendment of inappropriate laws.

On the Nationalist side there was always reluctance to accept laws laid down by a Stormont Parliament whose legitimacy they challenged. However, ever since the signing of the Ulster Covenant in 1912, Unionists also have given themselves permission to act against the law when they claimed it was in their interests to do so. Clearly, this was exercised during the Ulster Workers' Council Strike in 1974, in the opposition to the AIA in the late 1980s and more recently in response to determinations by the Parades Commission.

One might say that when the DUP continued to oppose the 1998 Belfast Agreement it was opposed to the law, as this agreement was made into an International Agreement between Great Britain, Northern Ireland and the Republic of Ireland! The SDLP refused to recognise the official police force, the RUC, which since its foundation had failed to be accorded legitimacy by the Nationalist population for reasons and with consequences discussed earlier in Chapter 6. The SDLP now participates in the Policing Board, in the local policing partnerships and encourage more Catholics to join the Police Service. In 2007 Sinn Féin finally agreed to be represented on the Policing Board and on the policing partnerships. Sinn Féin's absence from these bodies had been one of the major obstacles to progress following the Belfast Agreement. In 2010, Alliance Party leader David Ford was appointed Minister for Policing and Justice, as described in Chapter 7.

## PARTY ORGANISATION AND COMMITTEES[275]

In order to understand how the party operates, it is necessary to explain the decision-making structure and levels. Key central groups are the party officers, the Party Council, and the Party Executive with its sub-committees.

The party officers are: the president, vice-presidents, chair, vice-chair, general secretary, two joint honorary treasurers, party leader, deputy leader, chief whip, party organiser. They are elected at the Party Council AGM, except the chief whip, who is appointed by the party leader. The leader has to be re-elected every year by STV voting at the AGM. Even if there is only one candidate a formal election is held.

The Party Council is the governing committee of the Alliance Party. It meets at least four times per year. Membership consists of all officers and executive members and vice-presidents, elected MEPs, MPs, MLAs and local district councillors. Up to ten representatives from each association are also members of Council. Additional members may attend as observers. Council decides all the policies of the party and its decisions are binding.

The Party Executive Committee is elected by Council once a year. It consists of the party leader and deputy leader, party chair and deputy chair, two party treasurers, the general secretary (now chief executive), the party organiser and up to fifteen elected executive members. It normally meets monthly. Its purpose is to execute the decisions made by Council and to run the party between council meetings. Within the Executive are a number of sub-committees, chaired by executive members, but also containing other members with particular interests or expertise.

The Finance and General Purposes Committee, as the title suggests, is key to the financing and general running of the party. The Political Organisation Committee, chaired by the political organiser, looks after everything to do with elections and preparation for elections. There is usually a Strategy Committee consisting of members of the Executive selected by the party leader, whose members consider day-to-day and week-to-week aspects of the overall political situation particularly those related to constitutional matters.

The Policy Committee is responsible for the development of more detailed policies on a range of issues via a number of policy sub-committees. These policies are developed over a period of time and are submitted via the Policy Committee to the Council for approval or amendment. There is also a Disciplinary Committee elected direct from Council, which fortunately needs to meet only rarely.

Originally an association corresponded to a Westminster constituency or an Assembly electoral area, which usually amounted to the same thing. Within each association there may be branches, corresponding to the local district council areas. These divisions had to be modified as time went by, due to changes in electoral boundaries and the increases in the number of Westminster constituencies.

Each association has an Executive Committee normally consisting of chair, vice-chair, secretary, treasurer and about six other members, elected at the annual general meeting of the association. In addition any members who are party officers, and those elected to public office are members of the association Executive Committee. The association nominates members for election to the Party Executive and nominates delegates to Council. It is responsible for raising funds for the party in accordance with an annual levy. Candidates for election to Westminster, Stormont or local government are normally selected by the Association Committee but must be approved by the Party Executive. An association may propose motions for debate at Council and Conference and may form one or more branches within that association, each of which will have its own committee.

The party holds an annual conference, open to all party members together with guests. The main feature is the party leader's speech. It also debates motions on policy proposed by Executive or by any association, or Branch, or affiliated organisation. The conference is organised by a Steering Committee elected by council, chaired by the party chair or vice-chair. The conference is chaired by the party president. In addition to the main debates there are fringe events on issues of special interest. A number of awards are presented at the conference to associations and individuals for meritorious service. These awards include the Rose Bowl and the Howard Johnson Cup and Shield.

Representatives of the press are present, including the BBC and Ulster Television. Press releases are given to them and they focus on the party leader's speech in particular. Guest speakers are often included from other political parties, particularly the Liberal Democrats and often from the Republic of Ireland or appropriate organisations, from within or outside Northern Ireland. Motions approved at the conference do not automatically become party policy but may be referred to Council and Executive for development into policy statements.

Alliance, in company with other political parties, obviously needs a head-quarters with office accommodation. Initially David Cook allowed the party to use his house in Cromwell Road. Later, premises were rented elsewhere in Cromwell Road, but after a bomb attack and as greater space became needed the party acquired a building at 88 University Street, Belfast, which they still occupy. The premises are formally owned by Lagan Properties, the share-holders being a range of Alliance party members.

The day-to-day operation of the party revolves around the chief executive (formally known as the general secretary). Grace Wilson was the first general secretary, appointed in 1970. She was followed by Bob Cooper until he was elected to the Assembly and then the Convention. John Cushnahan, Susan Edgar, Eileen Bell, David Ford, Allan Leonard, Stephen Farry, Gerry Lynch, Stephen Douglas have all served as general secretaries and Sharon Lowry is the present incumbent.

Duties carried out by a general secretary give the office holder a compre-hensive insight into the workings of the party and many contacts with the media and people in other parties as well as local businesses. The position has provided an effective platform for becoming an elected councillor or Assembly member. As we shall see, John Cushnahan was elected to Belfast City Council, then to the Prior Assembly and became party leader. Eileen Bell was a North Down councillor also elected to the Good Friday Agreement Assembly. She became deputy leader and for a time Speaker at the Assembly. David Ford struggled to get elected for Antrim Council, but did so and was also elected to the Assembly and became party leader. He was followed by Stephen Farry who was a North Down councillor and Mayor of North

Down. When he was elected to the Assembly to replace Eileen Bell. Allan Leonard acted as a temporary general secretary. It was necessary to have other people acting as support staff helping at headquarters, as assistant secretaries, for example. Occasionally a student intern was employed on particular tasks.

Funding these posts is a major and essential concern for the party. Occasionally grants are obtained through the EU Peace funds and from the Rowntree Foundation. Most of the money comes from members' contributions, raised as a levy on each Association, together with contributions from MLAs and local councillors and special fundraising events.

## ALLIANCE PARTY POLICIES[276]

The Alliance Party has always tried to have a well-developed set of policies on all major issues. In conjunction with these policies there have always been party spokespersons, appointed by the party leader to answer questions on issues of policy. These people are from among the Assembly members when there is an Assembly in operation, otherwise from elected local councillors. Alliance was probably more organised and advanced in this regard than most other Northern Ireland political parties. In recent years there has also been a paid Policy Officer to facilitate the developments of policy matters.

Within this structure, policy sub-groups are set up to study and produce working papers on different policy areas. These papers are developed into policy papers and following approval by the Policy Committee, chaired by the Policy Convenor, are submitted to the overall governing body, the Party Council, which normally meets quarterly. The papers are debated in Council and approved, rejected or sent back for further discussion, after which they are made available to party members and to the public. They are generally used in the production of election manifestos. The 2011 Assembly version describes policies in considerable detail over ninety-five pages.[277, 278] Newer versions were prepared for the local government elections 2014[279] and for the European elections 2014.[280] Occasionally a list of policy summaries is issued,[281] particularly for the information of new members. The most up-to-date information about Alliance Party policies can be found on the party's website,[282] which includes policies on: Shared Future, education, the economy, health, poverty and social exclusion, environment, democracy, farming and rural areas, transport, culture, arts and leisure, employment and learning, and justice.

'Many of the ideas put forward by Alliance have been taken up by government, reflecting the high calibre of Alliance representatives.'[283]

## POLICY PAPERS

Policy papers exist on all the following areas and are regularly updated. Salient points of some of the main Alliance Party policies are presented below:

### Democracy

Some of the areas covered include proposals for reforming the Agreement, an example being 'Agenda for Democracy', aimed at breaking the political deadlock in 2003–2006. It aimed to bridge the gaps and to create space for political movement with compromise proposals.

### Shared Future

Largely through strenuous efforts made by Alliance, in 2004 the government produced a paper called 'A Shared Future', which is a major part of Alliance policy. The publication followed a consultation report by Dr Jeremy Harbison in 2003 which said:

> Our vision for Northern Ireland is of a peaceful society in which everyone can freely and fully participate, achieve their full potential, and live free from poverty. We want a fair and effective system of government, underpinned by rights that are guaranteed for all, and responsibilities that all must share. We wish to support dialogue, and to foster mutual understanding and respect for diversity.[284]

The final document was published in the House of Commons in March 2005.

Alliance has made many meaningful suggestions about how public expenditure in Northern Ireland can be reduced to save some of the wasted £1 to £1.5 billion per year, as referred to on page 133.

### Policing and Justice

This is now devolved, with the Alliance party leader David Ford acting as Minister for Policing and Justice, as described in Chapter 7. Alliance supports Community Restorative Justice. Chapter 6 includes an account of Policing in Northern Ireland and the Alliance Party's involvement. In Chapter 12 is an account of party leader David Ford's work as Justice Minister.

Alliance has successfully pushed for more effective enforcement of terrorist laws against paramilitary flags. It is now a criminal offence to display them in public, though this is rarely enforced. The party has secured for Northern Ireland the most comprehensive set of 'Hate Crime' laws in the UK against racial, sectarian and homophobic attacks.

## Constitution and Governance

Governing must be by consent with a devolved power-sharing executive. The NI Assembly should be reduced in size. Voting should be by weighted majority free from communal designations.[285] See discussion by Farry and Neeson in Chapter 6.

## Community Relations and a Shared Future

This will involve desegregation and integration. There should be a reformed Community Relations Council. Much emphasis has been placed on this fundamentally important topic above and it will be addressed again in Chapter 12.

## Equality

Alliance supports the Single Equality Act and Fair Employment, avoiding discrimination on grounds of age, sex or religion.

This area involves issues of considerable controversy. While the party remains neutral on the issue of abortion rights (believing this to be a matter for the individual conscience of members), the Justice Minister is hoping to clarify the existing rules under which abortion might be permitted. Currently an Act dating back to the nineteenth century forbids abortion except to save the life of the mother. Many people travel to England from Northern Ireland at their own expense for abortions.

The other issue is legal rights for lesbian, gay, bisexual people and transgender people (LGBT). Initially provision was brought in for Civil Partnerships supported by then deputy leader Eileen Bell MLA in 2005, though the decision caused some internal tensions.[286] Since Prime Minister David Cameron pushed through a Bill allowing same-sex marriage in England and Wales, against much opposition particularly from Churches and from some members of his own party, there has been pressure to extend the legislation to Northern Ireland. When the debate in Westminster was in progress, Alliance MP Naomi Long wanted to know the party's position so she could decide how to vote. She put the pros and cons to a Party Council meeting in Newcastle on 9 June 2012.[287] Several prominent actively gay members including former chief executive, Gerry Lynch, and North Down councillor Andrew Muir spoke in favour of same-sex marriage as 'an equality right'. Other people were reluctant to express a contrary opinion, perhaps from fear of being considered homophobic. At a further Party Council in September 2012 the matter was formally debated and a policy decision made to support same-sex marriage by about 80% in favour, and 20% against. Party leader David Ford had decided to stand down from being an Elder in the Presbyterian Church, as the party's decision would inevitably be in conflict with his Church's official policy. Subsequently, on two occasions Alliance supported attempts to introduce legislation in the Assembly proposed by Sinn Féin MLA Catriona Ruane, but opposition from both DUP and UUP ensured that it was defeated.

The question remains: was it sensible to establish party policy on this issue? Arguably it could have been left as a matter of conscience, as with the abortion issue.

## Human Rights

Basic human rights should be enshrined in a Bill of Rights. In 2001 Alliance Party member Professor Bryce Dickson was appointed as Commissioner of Human Rights.[288]

## Victims

Alliance seeks the creation of a public forum to allow victims (self defined) to tell their stories, which would be placed on an official record. Alliance would investigate the needs of carers who look after victims and survivors and ensure that adequate funding is put in place for victims' organisations. Exiles should be included as victims of the troubles and Alliance will lobby for meaningful legislation responses and sentences in regards to the seriousness of the crime and the human rights abuse associated with exiling.[289]

## Economy

Alliance supports a high-growth, high-tech, dynamic and sustainable business economy integrated into the European and global economy.

The economy needs to be rebalanced with more development of private industry, and decreased dependence on the public sector. The party encourages more research and development and improving the skills level, especially of young people, including more apprenticeship schemes. Alliance continues to call for tax-varying powers, especially to cut the rate of corporation tax to 12.5%

## Finance

Alliance would seek some local tax-raising powers, including a regional income tax to replace the regional rate. Water charges should be based on ability to pay.

## Education

Alliance supports the formation of a single education authority and the amalgamation of existing schools by consent. The target set was that integrated schools should constitute at least 10% of the total by 2010. Despite public demand of over 80%,[290] the level was only 7% in 2014. The Sinn Féin Minister for Education has not encouraged more integrated schools. A pupil profile should be used to replace selection tests for 11 year olds, which should be abolished. Apart from Sinn Féin, the other parties have been reluctant to abolish selection tests. Many grammar schools supported by parents continue selection and conduct their own tests. Alliance supports the need for nursery places for every child, and adequate resources for vocational, technical and academic education choices. Since becoming Minister of Employment and Learning, Dr Stephen Farry has continued to address these issues, as described in the account of his ministerial stewardship in Chapter 12. He has addressed teacher training, university places, FE colleges and apprenticeships

## Health and Social Services

The main Alliance proposal is for free personal care for those in nursing or care homes, as well as free eye and dental checks and free digital hearing aids. Alliance supports the proposals in the Compton report.[291] There should be greater focus on prevention, care should be closer to home, primary care needs re-designing and hospitals need reshaping. Health care should be focussing on patient need, rather than artificial targets, to ensure that healthcare, such as that provided in A&E, is provided to the people who need it the most.

## Environment and Transport

The Alliance Party has major policies on protecting the environment, at least as strong as measures proposed by the Green Party. The party supports the implementation of the Kyoto and Rio treaties on combating global warming. Adequate infrastructures should be in place before planning new housing developments. Pollution and resources depletion should be taxed, including a levy on plastic bags. The use of recycled products should be rewarded.

Alliance is an environmentalist party. They believe that climate change is happening, that humanity is responsible, but also that we have the capacity to address this very serious danger. They support a sustainable Northern Ireland, as part of a sustainable world. Alliance has been a consistent and vocal advocate for the environment.

Importantly, they know that failing to tackle climate change will hurt our economy. The Stern Report proved that waiting before tackling climate change could cost us twenty times the cost of doing it now.

Alliance supports tackling climate change and protecting the environment by: establishing a Green New Deal to stimulate investment in renewable energy and energy efficiency; helping to tackle climate change and creating thousands of jobs in hi-tech industries; investing in renewable energy rather than fracking; creating a public-sector-wide Sustainable Development Strategy so that the environment is at the heart of our government. Alliance supports global efforts to protect the environment. It aims for legislation for a target to reduce our emission by 80% by 2050.

Alliance would prefer an independent Environmental Protection Agency, separate from the Northern Ireland Environment Agency under the Department of the Environment, common with those in the rest of the UK and in the Republic of Ireland. Flood prevention measures should be simplified. Our natural landscape should be protected by setting higher targets for woodland creation.

## Transport

Investment should be rebalanced away from roads and into public services. Public transport should be integrated by creating links between the bus and rail network, car users, ports and airports. Alliance encourages cycling by increasing the number of cycle lanes in Northern Ireland and including cycling proficiency in the physical education curriculum.

## Energy

Alliance supports an all-Ireland energy network. Northern Ireland should aim for 20% renewable forms of energy by 2020 and 50% by 2050. There needs to be more capital investment for less developed renewable technologies, such as tidal power and photovoltaic (solar panel) power.

Solar water heating is encouraged, the use of geothermal energy is supported where available and the development of biogas from waste. There could be further use of biomass and energy crops on surplus land.

Alliance is opposed to the use of lignite and of nuclear fuel.

The party encourages domestic energy-saving including cavity wall insulation, double glazing, loft insulation, use of long-life lightbulbs, high-efficiency boilers. People are recommended to use 'A'-rated white goods – fridges, freezers, washing machines, dishwashers.

Alliance would require landlords to provide energy-efficient housing.

Fuel-poor households should be identified and encouraged to access the Warm Homes Scheme.

Both environmental degradation and fuel poverty need to be addressed.

## Social Development

Alliance would seek better funding for the Citizens' Advice Bureau. Adequate housing must be available to break the pattern of homelessness, with links to and between employment, health and social services.

Alliance encourages more mixed housing to break down the community apartheid, which blocks the possibilities for sharing.

## Agriculture and Rural Development

Alliance proposes a 10% production subsidy for environmental schemes. There should be improved relations between suppliers and retailers. Organic food production should be encouraged. Alliance would extend the compulsory country-of-origin labelling. CAP must be reformed to make sure that there is a financially sustainable future for farmers in Northern Ireland which reflects the unique situation in Northern Ireland.

## Culture, Arts and Leisure

Cultural tourism should be integrated. The arts should be used to explore and heal both past and current conflicts. Alliance supports the appreciation of Cantonese, Irish and Ulster-Scots languages. The library service should be enhanced. The Football Offences Act (1991) should be extended to Northern Ireland. Alliance supports a new national stadium for football, rugby, GAA and other major sports to be at the site of the Maze/Long Kesh prison. After much wrangling, this proposal has been ruled out by other parties, especially the DUP and new finance has been shared with the existing sports facilities: Windsor Park for soccer, Ravenhill Road for rugby and Casement Park for Gaelic sports. There is still a proposal to have a peace memorial on the Maze site, originally approved by everybody including the DUP, who then rejected it after a Sinn Féin commemoration of an IRA activist in Castlederg took place. The site is now also used for the agricultural show, formerly at Balmoral in South Belfast.

## International Affairs

Alliance is a pro-European and internationalist party and members of European Democratic and Reform Party (ELDR) and of Liberal International. They support entry into the eurozone as soon as this is practicable and in the interests of the UK. The UK Government and others must meet the 0.7% of GDP for overseas aid. Alliance supports the Make Poverty History campaign.

## Women's Issues

Alliance supports the Convention on the Elimination of all Forms of Discrimination against Women (CEDAW) and UN Security Resolution 1325 on Women, Peace, and Security.

Alliance would seek statutory funding to increase women's participation at leadership levels, including a government review of how better to accommodate female advancement in the civil service.

Alliance policy also includes family-friendly working practices such as career breaks for the family, better childcare facilities, opportunities to continue education at home and re-enter employment, as well as concern for welfare and benefits needs and refuge support for women who have suffered domestic abuse.

# 10

# The party leadership

## INTRODUCTION

A good leader needs a range of qualities, including a tension between power and authority versus a degree of humility and willingness to serve. A leader needs to have a strong personality that attracts others. She or he needs a degree of self-confidence combined with a willingness to listen to others and seriously consider their contributions. But in the end he/she needs to be decisive.

Politics is about power. One may have excellent ideas and policies, but without access to power they can rarely be implemented. In politics a leader needs to be able to project themselves, not only to their party faithful but also through the media to the wider community. But one does need an understanding of how society works, what needs changing, and imagination to produce new ideas.

## ALLIANCE PARTY LEADERS

In accordance with the rules of the new Alliance Party, the leader was to be the leader of the Parliamentary Party at Stormont. Thus when Phelim O'Neill switched from the Unionist Party to the Alliance Party he became the party's first leader. When he failed to win an Assembly seat in the 1973 elections, Oliver Napier, who had won an Assembly seat, became leader. Subsequently when there was no Stormont Assembly the Party Council elected the party leader every year, using the STV voting system, even if there was only one candidate.

During the Prior Assembly Oliver Napier resigned from the leadership, having been leader for eleven years. Also he had been offered a new responsible legal post. John Cushnahan took over without a contest. After the demise of that Assembly, John Cushnahan was without a job so he had move to the Republic of Ireland where he became an MEP for the Fine Gael party. John Alderdice then took over as leader. He continued until after the Good Friday Agreement when he resigned to become Speaker and Seán Neeson became leader. After a rather uncomfortable period in office he resigned and there was a contest between Eileen Bell (the deputy leader) and David Ford (then general secretary) that was won by David Ford.

# RIGHT HONOURABLE PHELIM O'NEILL (LORD RATHCAVAN)[292]

Phelim O'Neill was born on 2 November 1909. He was educated at Eton College and served in the Royal Artillery during the Second World War, rising to the rank of major. He was a member of the United Kingdom Parliament for North Antrim from the by-election of 27 October 1952 to the general election of 1959 when he stood down. An Ulster Unionist member of the Stormont Parliament for North Antrim from the general election of 1958 until the prorogation of the Parliament in 1972 he acted as Minister of Education from 12 March 1969 to 3 May 1969. He served as Minister of Agriculture from 3 May 1969 to 23 March after being appointed a Privy Councillor in 1969.

Phelim O'Neill became the first party leader. He joined the Alliance Party in February 1972 and became leader of the Parliamentary Party until after the Stormont Parliament was prorogued in 1972. He was leader of the Alliance Party delegation to the Darlington Conference of 1972 and while carrying out this role he gave stirring addresses to party conferences held in the Ulster Hall. His long experience as a parliamentarian on the 'liberal wing' of the Unionist Party was highly valuable to Alliance during that period.

Though O'Neill contested North Antrim in the 1973 elections to the Northern Ireland Assembly, he was not successful. Dr Hugh Wilson won a seat for Alliance in the same constituency on that occasion. So Oliver Napier took over as leader. He had won a seat in East Belfast and had been one of the main founders of the party.

Phelim O'Neill subsequently succeeded his father to a peerage as 2nd Baron Rathcavan on 28 November 1982. He died on 20 December 1994.

## SIR OLIVER NAPIER[293, 294]

Oliver Napier was born on 11 July 1935, the eldest son of Belfast solicitor James Napier and Sheila Bready. He was educated at St Malachy's College, Belfast and Queen's University Belfast, following which he became a solicitor and entered his father's law practice, Napier and Sons, Solicitors. His first political involvement was with the ULP. He was married to Lady Briege and had nine children and twenty-three grandchildren. He died on 2 July 2011 after a long illness.

As we have seen in Chapter 1, it was Oliver Napier who first 'dreamed the dream' which became the Alliance Party and, with others, brought it to fruition. As Joint Political Chairmen in the initial organisation Oliver Napier and Bob Cooper were the most prominent policymakers and spokespersons but it was Napier who was the natural choice as leader to succeed Phelim O'Neill. His leadership lasted 11 years – from 1973 until 1984

He was Minister of Law Reform in the power-sharing Executive of the 1973 Northern Ireland Assembly. He came close to winning a Westminster seat in 1979 when he was less than 1,000 votes behind Peter Robinson's total for East Belfast. Oliver was a member of Belfast City Council from 1973 until he retired in 1989, when he was awarded a knighthood. He was the first Alliance Party candidate for the European elections in 1979. He also won a seat in East Belfast to the Prior Assembly in 1982. In 1984 he stepped down from the party leadership but stayed in active politics.

He came back to fight a by-election in North Down in 1995 and again at the general election in 1997. In 1996 he was elected to the Northern Ireland Peace Forum for North Down. He served on the Board of Governors of the first integrated school in Northern Ireland, Lagan College.

Sir Oliver Napier was a shrewd politician and a profound political thinker with the imagination to see new ways forward for Northern Ireland. He had great confidence and charisma when addressing party members, but was rather reticent when interviewed on radio or TV. He was very much a family man and a committed Catholic. He showed great courage when his home was attacked by loyalists in 1977, when he was opposing Ian Paisley's unsuccessful attempt to foment another 'workers' strike'. He rarely talked about this episode.

Tributes to him were many and heartfelt. Lord Alderdice said:

> Oliver Napier was possessed of a steely courage, sharp political acumen, unflinching integrity and an absolute commitment to liberal values and

the cause of peace in Ireland ... Northern Ireland was fortunate indeed to have had Oliver Napier, especially in the darkest days of the Troubles, when he pointed the way to a better future, and gave real leadership along that difficult road.

The current Alliance leader, Northern Ireland Minister for Justice David Ford, said his legacy could be seen at the heart of the party.

Oliver embodied the spirit of Alliance and he was the man who inspired me to join the party. [He] was a statesman and a visionary. His vision was of a united Northern Ireland and he put his heart and soul into bringing that about. He was ahead of his time but the vision he had is demonstrated in all the excellent work being done to improve community relations in Northern Ireland.

Tánaiste and Labour Party leader Éamon Gilmore said Sir Oliver had a vision of a society in Northern Ireland that is reconciled and integrated – a vision only now being realised.

Interviewed in 1999 by Allan Leonard, an MA student at University College Dublin and former general secretary of the Alliance Party who is now director of Northern Ireland Foundation, an independent non-profit organisation based in Belfast, Sir Oliver said he saw the Alliance Party helping create a liberal democracy in Northern Ireland. Asked how this might come about, he replied:

Ireland, North and South, is going through a catharsis from a peasant society on the fringe of Europe to one more at the heart of Europe and becoming a liberal democracy ... One that stops whingeing and solves its own problems ... Northern Ireland is on the verge of changes that are as dramatic – the old shibboleths will be shouted louder and louder by fewer and fewer people. Alliance will be the party hopefully leading into the new, radical liberal democracy of the future.

## JOHN CUSHNAHAN[295]

John Walls Cushnahan was born on 23 July 1948. He was educated at St Mary's Christian Brothers Grammer School, Belfast and Queen's University, Belfast, where he obtained a Bachelor of Education degree. He was also a member of the Institute of Public Relations. He is married to Alice and has five children.

John Cushnahan worked as a teacher before going into politics. He was general secretary of the Alliance Party from 1974 until 1982 and was chief whip from 1982 to 1984. He was a member of Belfast City Coucil between 1977 and 1985.

In 1982 he was elected to the Prior Assembly for North Down, where he served as chairman of the Education Committee and was involved in the merger of the Ulster Polytechnic with the New University of Ulster to form the University of Ulster. His role was purely advisory as there was no devolution to that Assembly and all power continued to be exercised by the direct rule ministers. Thus it was Nicholas Scott MP who actually made the merger decision after a study by Lord Chilver.

Two years later, in 1984, he became the new leader of Alliance, succeeding Oliver Napier. During his tenure as leader he sought to strengthen the party's links with the British Liberal Party. The AIA was signed during this period and Cushnahan led the party towards supporting it against the united opposition of the Unionist parties. When the Assembly was dissolved in 1986 Cushnahan found it financially difficult to remain in politics, though he worked as a lobbyist in Washington DC, USA, for a while. He stood down as leader in 1987 to be succeeded by John Alderdice.

In 1989 Cushnahan made a surprise political comeback when he moved to the Republic of Ireland and stood as a Fine Gael candidate in the 1989 election to the European Parliament, winning a seat in the Munster constituency. He was an MEP for fifteen years before retiring at the 2004 elections.

During this time he enjoyed an active and varied career as vice president of the Regional Policy Committee (1992-1994); European Parliament specialist in cross-border and interregional co-operation (1989-1994), European Parliament Rapporteur on China/Hong Kong from 1996; vice-president of the Foreign Affairs Committee (1997-1999). Appointed Head of Mission of a seventy-seven-member EU Electoral Observation Team in Sri Lanka in September to October 2000 and again in November to December 2001, he was a member of the European Convention 2002 and European Parliament Rapporteur on Pakistan 2002.

As party leader John Cushnahan was an ebullient character with an outgoing personality, which came across well on the media and as a platform speaker. He was a determined politician, pushing for action as distinct from imaginative thinking. His background as a teacher and general secretary of the party gave him good experience of people.

# LORD JOHN ALDERDICE[296]

John Thomas Alderdice was born on 28 March 1955. He was educated at
Ballymena Academy and Queen's University Belfast, where he graduated in
medicine. He specialised in psychiatry and psychotherapy and was appointed
Ireland's first consultant psychotherapist in 1988. He is a fellow and honorary
fellow of the Royal College of Psychiatrists, an honorary fellow of the Royal
College of Physicians of Ireland, an honorary professor in the University of
San Marcos in Lima, Peru, a visiting professor at the University of Virginia and
an honorary affiliate of the British Psychoanalytical Society. He is married
and has three children. He is an elder in the Presbyterian Church of Ireland.

John Alderdice joined the Alliance Party in 1978. He was elected to the
Executive Committee in 1984 and became chair of the Policy Committee in
1985. During this time he and Eggins, accompanied by Paul Maguire, attended
the annual meeting of the ELDR in Brussels, where they met David Steel,
then leader of the British Liberal Party. John Alderdice became vice-chair
of the party in 1987. In October of that year, he was elected Alliance Party
leader, against a challenge from Seamus Close. At that time he had never been
elected to any public office but in June 1989 he was elected to Belfast City
Council, topping the poll in the Victoria area of East Belfast. In 1993 he was
re-elected to Belfast City Council with the largest vote of any candidate in
Northern Ireland in that election. During this Council term (1993–97) he
was also a member of the Belfast Education and Library Board, and a trustee
of the Ulster Museum.

In the 1987 general election he contested Belfast East for the party.
He received 32.0% of the vote, the highest percentage ever achieved by
Alliance in an individual seat in a Westminster election, until Naomi Long
won the seat in 2010 with 37%. He lost to Peter Robinson, while still firmly
establishing Alliance on the political map. Alderdice again contested Belfast
East in the 1992 general election when he obtained 10,650 votes (29.9%),
again coming second to Peter Robinson.

In 1988 John Alderdice suggested a qualified majority vote to form a
devolved power sharing Assembly with a voluntary coalition in the Alliance
key document, 'Governing with Consent'.

From 1991 to 1998 John Alderdice led the Alliance delegations at the
various inter-party and inter-governmental talks in Belfast, London and
Dublin on the future of Northern Ireland. In 1994, after the ceasefires, he led
Alliance into the Forum for Peace and Reconciliation, established by the Irish
Government at Dublin Castle. This action was particularly significant since

Alliance was the only non-Nationalist party there. He was also the first non-Nationalist party leader to attend the White House for the annual St Patrick's Day celebrations in 1995, and since then has continued, in frequent visits to Washington, to contribute to US/NI relationships.

In 1996 he was elected to the new Northern Ireland Forum and led the Alliance delegation there and in the multi-party talks chaired by Senator George Mitchell. He played a significant role in the Irish Peace Process, being one of the key negotiators of the Good Friday Agreement. He was subsequently elected a member of the new Northern Ireland Assembly in June 1998.

However, he surprised everybody when he decided to stand down as Alliance leader after eleven years in that position, and was immediately appointed Speaker of the Assembly, a post he held until retiring in February 2004.

In 2003 he was appointed to serve on the four-person Independent Monitoring Commission charged by the British and Irish Governments with monitoring paramilitary activity and security normalisation in Northern Ireland. He was elected an Executive Member of the Federation of European Liberal, Democrat and Reform Parties (ELDR) in 1987. He was treasurer and then vice-president of ELDR between 1995 and 2003.

John Alderdice was created a life peer in 1996, as Baron Alderdice of Knock in the City of Belfast. He sits in the House of Lords as a Liberal Democrat. Lord Alderdice was vice-president of Liberal International from 1992, the worldwide federation of liberal political parties. He was chairman of the Human Rights Committee from 1996 to 2005, and deputy president from 2000. He became president of Liberal International in May 2005. He was also joint chairman of the Critical Incident Analysis Group and the chairman of the World Federation of Scientists Permanent Monitoring Panel on Motivations for Terrorism.

Lord Alderdice has been awarded several honours: the John F. Kennedy Profiles in Courage Award in 1998; the W. Averell Harriman Democracy Award in 1998; the Silver Medal of Congress of Peru in 1999 and 2004; the Medal of Honour, College of Medicine of Peru in 1999 and the Freedom of the City of Baltimore in 1991.

Fergus Pyle, writing in *The Irish Times*,[297] noted that he made 'no secret of his [religious] affiliations'. His father was a Presbyterian minister. Pyle hints that maybe that was why he attracted a higher vote than Catholic Oliver Napier.

Former Secretary of State Mo Mowlam described him as follows:[298]

The Alliance Leader, John Alderdice, I found amiable. He was bright and probably one of the more articulate party leaders around. Much to his party's disgust he left it to become speaker of the new assembly in July 1998. He was a good leader for a non-aligned, moral high-ground sort of party. John was a psychiatrist by trade, which certainly gives him a very well-developed sense of self. I'm not one to criticise that – his self-confidence was a plus in a process where the battle involved such titanic egos as Ian Paisley's. You needed to be tough to get a word in edgeways, and John always managed.

## SEÁN NEESON[299]

Seán Neeson was born in Belfast on 6 February 1946. His education was at St Malachy's College and then Queen's University Belfast, where he obtained a BA degree. This was followed by a Diploma in Education from St Joseph's College of Education. From 1968 to 1984 he taught in St Comgall's High School, Larne. He is married and has four children. After the collapse of the Prior Assembly in 1986 he took a marketing diploma at the University of Ulster (Jordanstown), which led to him setting up Neeson Marketing Enterprises, which he ran from 1989 to 1998.

He was elected as an Alliance Councillor to Carrickfergus Council in 1977 where he continued until his retirement in 2013.[300] He is a Catholic who became mayor of this largely Protestant borough in 1993.

In 1982 he was elected to the Prior Assembly where he was appointed deputy speaker. In 1983 he was a candidate for East Antrim in the Westminster general election, coming third. He fought the 1986 Westminster by-election, coming second and was again second in both the 1987 and 1992 general elections. He dropped to third in the 1997 general election but was back to second in 2005. On several occasions his vote was the highest of any Alliance Party candidate in Westminster elections

In 1996 has was elected to the Northern Ireland Peace Forum and then to the new Assembly in 1998 as an MLA, a seat he held in 2003 and 2007. He became the major spokesman for the Alliance Party and in 1998 was elected as leader when John Alderdice stood down to become Speaker of the Assembly.

Despite their role in the negotiations of the Good Friday Agreement, Alliance won a disappointing 6.5% of the vote in the Assembly elections, giving them just six seats. They lost at least one seat to the Northern Ireland Women's Coalition who won two seats. New thinking was clearly needed

to stop further decline in the party's fortunes. As leader, Seán Neeson set up
The President's Review, carried out by Phillip McGarry. With Stephen Farry
he wrote a detailed and predictive analysis of the Good Friday Agreement.[301]
He promoted the Patten Review of policing in 1999, except that he opposed
the 50:50 recruitment aims.

In 1999 he fought in the European election, obtaining only 2.1% of the vote,
so in 2001 he was deselected as the Westminster candidate for East Antrim
after a failed attempt to broker an electoral pact with the Ulster Unionists.
In September 2001 Seán Neeson resigned from the leadership, which was
then won by David Ford. He continued as a councillor for Carrickfergus and
as an MLA.

Seán Neeson served on the Police Authority from 1991 to 1997. He is a
board member of the National Museums and Galleries of Northern Ireland,
and represents Northern Ireland on UK National Historic Ships Committee.
He is a member of the Northern Ireland Museums Council.


## DAVID FORD[302]


David Ford was born in Orpington, Kent, on 24 February 1951. His education
began at Warren Street Primary School and Dulwich College, London.
Having spent summer holidays in Gortin, County Tyrone, he moved to
Northern Ireland in 1969 to study economics at Queen's University Belfast.
He then worked for a year as a volunteer at the Corrymeela Community at
Ballycastle. In 1973 he began a career as a social worker. He is married and
has four children.

He joined the university branch of the Alliance Party while at Queen's.
In 1989 he became general secretary of the party and stood, unsuccessfully,
for Antrim Borough Council. Antrim was a difficult Council for Alliance, but
in 1993 David Ford was elected as a councillor, and again in 1997 and 2005.
He failed to win a seat in the 1996 Peace Forum, but in 1997 he obtained 12%
of the vote in the Westminster general election in South Antrim. In 1998 he
won a seat as an MLA for the Assembly, which he has held ever since.

When Seán Neeson resigned as party leader David Ford was elected to
that position on 5 September 2001, by 86 votes against 45 for then deputy
leader, Eileen Bell. Ford is considered as on the liberal international wing
of the party, being also a member of the Liberal Democrats. Eileen Bell was
considered to be a more traditional bridge-builder.

David Ford said:

I am keen to co-operate with other non-sectarian groups in Northern Ireland, including political parties that will stand against the tribal divide. Our links to the South are not as good as they should be, either with the PDs or with Fine Gael, where we have many natural allies. We must also recognise that Northern Ireland is not unique in the world. Our stand is not different in substance from those who work for peace and reconciliation in Cyprus, Palestine or Bosnia. We should learn from friends abroad. To suggest that 'our wee province' is unique is to do a disservice. There is little more objectionable than the sight of the political begging bowl being dragged out by sectional politicians.[303]

David needed to stabilise the Alliance Party after poor results in the 1990s. He was challenged in 2001 when there were not enough Unionist votes to re-elect David Trimble as First Minister, so Prime Minister Tony Blair persuaded three Alliance MLAs to temporarily re-designate as 'Unionists', to the disgust of Seamus Close. It was only a temporary fix as the Assembly collapsed in 2002.

In the 2003 Assembly elections Ford had a difficult fight to hold his seat against Martin Meehan of Sinn Féin. It was a very poor election for Alliance and they were fortunate to hold all six Assembly seats. His own vote increased from 8.6 to 9.1%, but Meehan's vote was up to 11.5% from 7.3%. However, due to favourable transfers Meehan lost out to Ford by 180 votes with SDLP's Thomas Burns fourteen votes ahead of Ford, also being elected.

For the 2004 European elections David Ford persuaded three other groups (the Conservatives, the Women's Coalition and the Workers' Party) to join with Alliance in putting up a joint candidate, John Gilliland, President of the Ulster farmers Union, to stand as an independent. He won 6.6% of the vote, the best result for a centre party since Oliver Napier's 6.8% in 1979.

Following the St Andrews Agreement in 2007, Alliance had much improved results in the Assembly elections, holding the existing six seats and winning a new seat for Anna Lo in South Belfast. David Ford won 13% of the vote in South Antrim, coming third.

In 2011, after much discussion within the Alliance Party, David Ford accepted the post of Minister of Policing and Justice. He was elected by a cross-community vote in the Assembly after nominees from SDLP and UUP were rejected. His pre-condition was that the Alliance Party Policing and Justice policy programme, written by Dr Stephen Farry, MLA would be accepted and that the Shared Future document 'Cohesion, Sharing and Integration' would be published. This document was in many ways unsatisfactory. Some

Alliance Party Executive members thought that accepting this ministerial post would be a 'poisoned chalice', but in fact he has been remarkably successful, with very few criticisms.

## DEPUTY LEADERS

During Oliver Napier's time as leader there were successively three deputy leaders.

## SIR ROBERT COOPER[304, 305]

Robert George Cooper was born in 1936 in a mainly Protestant part of Donegal, close to the border. Sir Robert's mother was a schoolteacher and the family tradition was Unionist. He attended Foyle College in Londonderry, then Queen's University, where he took an LLB and was chairman of the Young Unionists. Sir Robert died peacefully in his County Down home on Tuesday, 18 November 2004. He is survived by his wife and two children.

In 1970, Bob Cooper was one of the leading founders of the Alliance Party. He was elected for West Belfast to the 1973 Assembly and again to the Constitutional Convention in 1975. He served as Minister for Manpower Services in the 1974 power-sharing Executive and was the first joint political chairman of the Alliance Party with Sir Oliver Napier.

He was the first deputy leader, serving from 1974 until 1976, when he was appointed chairman of the new Fair Employment Agency, later the Fair Employment Commission, which meant that he had to retire from party politics, though his wife, Lady Patricia, continued as an active member of the party.

During his twenty-three years at the helm of combating discriminations in employment, Bob Cooper had to endure relentless criticism. There were Unionists who believed that the Fair Employment Agency which he headed, later to be replaced by the Fair Employment Commission, was not interested in discrimination against Protestants. There were Nationalists who felt that anti-discrimination measures were not aggressive enough. At the time of Cooper's 1976 appointment as head of the FEA, aged 39, a Unionist politician is said to have remarked that was typical of the British Government's 'cunning' to appoint someone who was so thick-skinned.

Some critics observed that, as a Presbyterian southerner married to a Catholic, Sir Robert's personal curriculum vitae fitted the bill for his role in fighting discrimination. Some pointed to the imbalance in FEC staff in favour of Catholics. 'In any body such as this, you will always see a preponderance of those vulnerable,' Sir Robert explained. 'You see it in England, where blacks or women are concerned. The important thing is we make it clear that Protestants are welcome.'

Robert Cooper was given an honorary degree by Queen's University, Belfast, where he had studied law and also awarded a CBE. After retiring as chairman of the FEC for Northern Ireland in 1999, Sir Robert served as the chairman of the Integrated Education Fund, until early in 2004, when he took over the development campaign to increase the number of integrated school places available to children in Northern Ireland.

He was a member of the Secretary of State's Standing Advisory Commission on Human Rights from 1976 to 1999. In 1998 Robert George Cooper, CBE, received a knighthood for services to equal opportunities.

## BASIL GLASS[306]

John Caldwell Basil Glass was born on 21 April 1926 at Drumshambo in County Leitrim, the son of a Methodist minister. He studied law at Queen's University, Belfast, and became a solicitor in 1950. He was married and had four sons and two stepsons. He died in November 2005.

At the time of the formation of the New Ulster Movement in February 1969 Basil Glass was already a household name in the legal profession. He was elected joint treasurer of the New Ulster Movement with Oliver Napier in 1969. He was a founder member of the Alliance Party, of which he was the first chairman. In those early days the task of organising the party was enormous and the work fell heavily on the chairman. Basil was working by day in his law office and by night for the Alliance, helping to set up branches east and west of the Bann. He was part of the Alliance Party's negotiating team during the 1970s, at the Stormont Castle talks and at Sunningdale, where the principle of power sharing was firmly established. The Alliance negotiating team both in Stormont Castle talks and at Sunningdale consisted of Basil, Oliver Napier and Bob Cooper and they made a formidable team.

Those negotiations in the autumn and winter of 1972 are part of history. First were the talks between Alliance, the SDLP and the UUP on the formation of a future power-sharing administration. Basil was a good negotiator – diplomatic but very firm. He genuinely liked his political opponents but he was not prepared to sell his own position short and in spite of enormous political differences of background and culture agreement was reached. When they went to Sunningdale, where the two governments joined the negotiation, Basil was again deeply involved in the negotiations. Again agreement was reached after days of tough and continuous negotiation.

He became president of the party in 1973 and in the same year was elected as an Assemblyman for South Belfast. He was made chief whip of the Alliance Party group.

He stood for Westminster in the October 1974 general election, coming second with 24% of the vote. He, along with Jim Hendron, was elected to the Constitutional Convention in May 1975 for South Belfast.

Basil Glass became deputy leader of the party from 1976 to 1980, after Bob Cooper's appointment to the Fair Employment Agency.

He was elected to Belfast City Council in 1977, a post he held till 1980. He stood again for Westminster in the 1979 general election, improving his vote to 25%. But he failed to win a seat in the 1982 Prior Assembly election.

In 1987, he was appointed to the High Court bench as Bankruptcy and Companies Master of the High Court – in effect the judge sitting in virtually all insolvency cases.

Just before he died on 30 September 2005 he was talking to the Revd Harold Good about his role in the recent decommissioning of IRA arms to which Harold was a witness. Basil said that he was so glad to have lived to see the day when all Republican arms were put beyond use. Harold said, 'Basil, I was only finishing off what you started'.[307]


## DAVID COOK[308]


David Cook was educated at Campbell College, Belfast, and Pembroke College, Cambridge. He is married and has five children.

David Cook was a founder member of the Alliance Party, and had the distinction of providing the first party office in his Belfast home. He was elected to the Party's Central Executive in 1971 and to Belfast City Council in 1973, a position he held until 1985. In 1978, he became the first non-Unionist Lord Mayor of Belfast since Partition. He stood for Alliance in Belfast South in the February 1974 general election, taking just under 10% of the vote. He improved this to 27% of the vote at the Belfast South by-election, 1982. In the same year he won a seat on the Prior Assembly for Belfast South. He consistently won over 20% of the vote in South Belfast in the 1983 general election, the 1986 by-election and the 1987 general election. He also stood for Alliance in the European Parliament election, but took only 5% of the vote, coming fifth behind Danny Morrison of Sinn Féin.

From 1980 until 1984, Cook served as the deputy leader of the Alliance Party. In 1994, Cook was appointed chairman of the Police Authority of Northern Ireland, but he was sacked from this role in 1996 after losing a vote of confidence. After a critical account of his role appeared in the Report of the Policing Authority to the Patten Review in 1998 he undertook a lengthy libel case, ultimately settled out of court to his satisfaction.[309] He subsequently sat on the Craigavon Health and Social Services Trust. David Cook works as a solicitor, eventually becoming a senior partner at Sheldon and Stewart Solicitors.

## ADDIE MORROW[310]

Addie was born in July 1928 on a farm in County Down and became a leading member of the Northern Ireland farming community. He was an early member of the ecumenical Corrymeela Community (later led by his brother John) and of the New Ulster Movement and Alliance Party. Addie Morrow died in 2012. He is survived by his wife and three children.

He was elected to Castlereagh Borough Council in 1973, holding his seat at each subsequent election, until standing down in 1989. He was very frustrated by the negative attitude of DUP councillors on that council.

In 1982, Morrow was elected to the Prior Assembly representing East Belfast. At the 1983 general election, he stood unsuccessfully in Strangford, taking 15% of the vote. When John Cushnahan took over as party leader in 1984, Addie became deputy leader until 1987.

At the 1987 general election, Morrow increased his share of the vote in Strangford to 20%. For the 1992 general election, he switched to contest North Down, taking just under 15%. Morrow became party chair, but stood down in 1993, citing disappointment at the failure of other parties to use the Brooke-Mayhew Talks to reach agreement. Addie Morrow later became party president.

## GORDON MAWHINNEY[311]

Gordon Mawhinney was born on 4 January 1943. He is married and has two children. He works in property development.

Gordon first stood for election in Area C of Newtownabbey in 1981, but was not elected. The following year he was elected to the Prior Assembly for South Antrim. In 1983 he obtained 11.9% of the vote at the Westminster election in South Antrim. He increased his share of the vote to 16% in the 1987 general election, coming second in the poll. Gordon Mawhinney took over as a deputy party leader from 1987 until 1991. He won a seat on Newtownabbey Council in 1989 in the new Manse Road area. In 1993 he switched to the university area and again won a seat, but did not stand again in 1997. He instituted the mobile advice centre, using a caravan, also shared by Will Glendinning in the Falls Road area. Gordon was particularly keen to expose the activities of the Loyalist UDA and was given special security protection at his house.


## SEAMUS CLOSE[312]

Seamus Close was born on 12 August 1947. He is married to Deirdre and they have three sons and one daughter. Like Sir Oliver Napier and Seán Neeson, he was educated at St Malachy's College and the College of Business Studies. He is a company secretary and company director. He was awarded an OBE in 1997.

Seamus was involved with the Alliance Party from its early stages. He was elected to Lisburn Council in 1973 and continued to hold a seat until 2011. He became Mayor of Lisburn in 1993. Seamus Close will have been one of only two councillors to have served the full length of the council itself, since 1973.

In August 1981 he was the Alliance candidate for the second Fermanagh and South Tyrone by-election, following the death of hunger striker, Bobby Sands. Since 1983 he has contested all elections for Lagan Valley apart from the 1986 by-election called in protest against the AIA, when the local Alliance branch decided not to contest the seat as they considered the by-election to be a political stunt. He came second in Lagan Valley in the last four Westminster elections. In the 2001 general election he obtained the highest vote share of any Alliance candidate and in that year was nominated for Parliamentarian of the Year.

In 1982 he won a seat in the Prior Assembly for South Antrim. He failed to win a seat in the 1996 elections for the Northern Ireland Forum, so he was also included on the province-wide list. As the most senior Alliance member not to be elected locally, he got one of Alliance's two seats. He went on to top the poll in the 1998 election for the new Northern Ireland Assembly and held that seat in the 2003 Assembly election. In the first of those Assemblies he was a member of Assembly Public Accounts Committee and of the Finance and Personnel Committee.

Seamus served in many roles for the Alliance Party. He was party chair from 1981 to 1982 and often a member of the key Alliance delegations in successive talks about the future of the province, culminating in the Belfast Agreement of 1998. He was a member of the Atkins Conference in 1980, of the Alliance Talks Team at Brooke-Mayhew Talks in 1991, of the Dublin Forum for Peace and Reconciliation in 1994, of the Northern Ireland Forum for Political Dialogue, 1996-1998 and of Alliance Talks Team at Castle Buildings Talks, 1996–1998.

Seamus became deputy leader from 1991 to 2001. Sadly he resigned from that post in June 2001, citing differences with the leadership of Seán Neeson. He now works as a political commentator for BBC Northern Ireland.


## EILEEN BELL[313]

Eileen Bell was born on 15 August 1943 at Dromara in County Down and grew up in West Belfast. She was educated at Dominican College, Belfast, and later at the University of Ulster, where she obtained an honours degree in History and Politics. She worked as a civil servant until 1973 and thereafter in the personnel department of Marks and Spencer, 1974-1978. She was also Welfare Officer for the Community of the People.

In 1986 Eileen Bell became general secretary of the Alliance Party. She was elected to North Down Council in 1993.

She was a member of the Alliance Talks Team at the Brooke-Mayhew Talks 1991-1992 and of the Dublin Forum for Peace and Reconciliation 1994-1996. In 1996 she was elected to the Northern Ireland Forum for Political Dialogue and was a member of Alliance Talks Team at Castle Buildings Talks, 1996-1998. Elected to the new Northern Ireland Assembly in 1998, she retained her seat in the 2003 Assembly elections. Eileen Bell acted as the Speaker of the Assembly established by the Northern Ireland Act 2006 and of the Transitional Assembly established by the Northern Ireland (St Andrews Agreement) Act 2006. On 8 May 2007 she was appointed Speaker of the Northern Ireland Assembly (which had been suspended since 2002) but was replaced that same day by William Hay of the DUP. She did not stand in the next Assembly elections in 2007.

In June 2001 Eileen Bell was appointed deputy leader of the Alliance by Seán Neeson, following the resignation of Seamus Close over disagreements on the party's direction. Eileen Bell stood for the leadership as a traditionalist bridge-building candidate, against David Ford who was on the more consciously liberal, internationalist wing of the party. At the party's Council Bell received forty-five votes to Ford's eighty-six and she remained the party's deputy leader until 2005, when she stood down.

Eileen was also a member of the Northern Ireland Probation Board, from 1997 to present, and the North Down Partnership, 1996–2001. She was on the Local Government Research Consortium at Warwick University.

She was made a CBE in the 2008 New Year Honours.


## NAOMI LONG[314]

Naomi Long (*née* Naomi Rachel Johnston) was born in East Belfast on 13 December 1971. She was educated at Mersey Street Primary School and Bloomfield Collegiate School, and then attended Queen's University, Belfast, graduating in 1994 with an MEng in Civil Engineering (with Distinction). She worked as a consultant in structural engineering and later in environmental and hydraulic engineering. She is a committee member of Bloomfield Presbyterian Church, a Girl Guide Senior Section Guider, and a governor of Victoria Park Primary School. She is married to Councillor Michael Long.[315]

Naomi Long was elected to Belfast City Council for Belfast Victoria in 2001 and held the seat in 2005. She was elected as an Assembly member for Belfast East in 2003, taking over from John Alderdice and re-elected in 2007 when she more than doubled the Alliance vote to 18.8%, a higher vote than Alderdice obtained in 1998. She came in second ahead of Sir Reg Empey, leader of the UUP.

She has been appointed to a number of Assembly posts in 2007: deputy chair of the Committee of the Office of First Minister and Deputy First Minister (OFMDFM); secretary of the All Party Assembly Group on Roads Safety; secretary of the All Party Assembly Group on Children & Young People; Member of the All Party Group on International Development.

In the Alliance Party she was Alliance Education Spokesperson (1999–2006) and Alliance Regional Development Spokesperson (appointed 2007). When Eileen Bell stood down, Naomi Long was elected deputy leader of the Alliance Party in 2005.

Alliance leader David Ford announced in the Assembly that party deputy leader Naomi Long would take up the post of deputy chair of the Assembly Committee of the Centre.

David Ford stressed the importance of the role as follows:

I am extremely pleased to announce that Naomi Long will become Deputy Chair of the Committee of the Centre. I believe that Naomi is the right person to hold the First Minister and the Deputy First Minister to account.

This is a very important role. This Committee has the responsibility for the creation of a genuinely shared future. Alliance is the only party that has plans to deliver an end to segregation. We will also be pressing the Executive to make the right decisions even if they are tough decisions.[316]

Alliance deputy leader Naomi Long MLA commented:[317]

I am very much looking forward to taking up this post. There is much work to be done to deliver the real shared future that the people of Northern Ireland deserve. The tribal parties in the last Executive failed to make progress on this matter and we will hold them to account to ensure that they get working to end segregation.

It is essential that we build a united and stable community. OFMDFM will play a critical role in this, both in terms of policy and how the First and Deputy First Ministers personally develop their leadership function within that Department.

We also want to see the legacy of the past addressed properly. Last October, we published a document on this issue, and we will apply pressure on the Executive to implement it. Victims and survivors must have a voice and we want to ensure that they are heard.

She was chair of East Belfast sub-group of the District Policing Partnership (2004-2005) and a member of East Belfast Area Youth Project Steering Panel. In 2010 Naomi was elected Lord Mayor of Belfast City Council, a role she carried out with great aplomb and success. Elected as the Alliance Party's first elected MP for Westminster in 2010, she defeated sitting MP Peter Robinson who was also leader of the DUP and First Minister of the Assembly. She decided to resign her seat in the Assembly to be replaced by Chris Lyttle and also on Belfast City Council to concentrate on duties as a full-time Member of Parliament. She continues as deputy leader.

# 11

# 'A party of reconciliation'?
# Religion and identity

Previous chapters have presented a chronological analysis of the origins and development of the Alliance Party during thirty years dominated by community violence and followed by fifteen years of attempts to implement the Belfast Agreement and to promote mutual tolerance in a devolved parliament. Applications of the d'Hondt model of consocation means that the two parties representing extreme ends of the political system theoretically share power, but in practice share out power. The principles on which the Alliance Party was built and the policies operated by its leaders and other senior members at various points in time have been presented and critiqued.

The focus of this chapter will be on the strengths of the party's plan to be the party of reconciliation, occupying the centre ground between two blocs of confessional parties who identify with different states. Let us consider some definitions of and comments on the word 'reconciliation' garnered from people inside and outside the party before examining the Alliance Party's record in attempting to promote it.

The Oxford Dictionary defines reconciliation as 'make friendly again after an estrangement'.[318] A better summary definition might be, 're-establishing a relationship in which both sides accept that despite recognised differences they belong together'.[319] It is thus a process, not an event. As historian Joe Liechty says, it involves 'a set of interlocking dynamics'.[320] Liechty expresses it as the bringing together of four elements: 'forgiving', 'repenting', 'truth seeking' and 'justice seeking'.[321]

Reconciliation is often presented in theological terms.[322] However, it has to be applied in many situations and is not specifically religious. Theologian John D'Arcy May recognises that reconciliation is 'at the same time personal and political'.[323] South African peacemaker Wilhelm Verwoerd, grandson of

Hendrik Verwoerd, who initiated apartheid, considers that reconciliation in the political sphere might be considered either as friendship, or as tolerance.[324] Some might consider this definition rather weak, though tolerance might be a stage in the process. Liechty and Clegg suggest that 'Tolerance is a useful tool for resisting sectarianism, but not sufficient on its own'.[325]

The Alliance Party has consistently seen itself as a party of reconciliation since its beginnings. Though the word is not used in the party principles,[326] they spell out aims that are about reconciliation: for example, the principles speak of 'healing divisions', 'eliminating prejudice' and 'appreciating the beliefs and fears of others'. In 1972 an Alliance Party member William McComish, writing in *Alliance News*, refers to Alliance as 'the party of reconciliation'.[327] The leading article in *Alliance News* October 1979[328] is headed 'Reconciliation is the Word' and favourably compares statements made by Pope John-Paul II on his visit to Drogheda[329] with Alliance Party principles. His Holiness said:

> Never think you are betraying your own community by seeking to understand and respect and accept those of a different tradition. You will serve your own tradition best by working for reconciliation with others.[330]

In 1984 Charles Kinahan, a party president, in a letter to *Alliance News*, said, 'RECONCILIATION [his capitals], that one big word epitomises the Alliance message'.[331] Nearly twenty years later, in the document 'Building a United Community',[332] the party sees the need for reconciliation as a Community Relations initiative.[333] The document goes on to say:

> Individual citizens are of equal worth. [They] have different needs, individuals need to have a shared sense of identity and values, plus a common sense of belonging and destiny. Society needs to be cohesive as well as respectful of diversity.
>
> Section 3.3.1 refers to an open and free society, where we are all equal citizens: not a society where we merely tolerate difference, but rather a society where we celebrate diversity and cherish individuality.[334]

There are dangers in claiming the high moral ground of being 'the party of reconciliation'. For some it smacks of arrogance. In an interview in 2003 with former deputy leader Addie Morrow[335] he agreed that McComish went too far when he said, 'I believe that the Alliance Party embodies the Christian message of reconciliation' and 'that the Alliance Party, the party of reconciliation is the only political party which can be supported by anyone calling himself

"Christian"'.[336] It is acceptable for him to make such a statement as an individual on his own behalf, but his blanket application to all Christians must be construed as a sectarian remark that is contrary to the spirit of reconciliation.

Rather than just take prima facie statements by individuals within the Alliance Party that it is a party of reconciliation, we should analyse how the Alliance Party stands up in practice to the various elements of reconciliation. If we consider Liechty's four limbs of reconciliation – 'forgiving', 'repenting', 'truth seeking' and 'justice seeking'[337] – we can apply four 'tests' and then see whether the 'fruits of reconciliation' – 'peace, trust, hope, confidence and togetherness' – are evident.

Is Alliance a forgiving party? Unfortunately forgiveness is not generally much in evidence between opposing political parties. Whitley Stokes, writing in 1799, said, 'the only hope for peace in Ireland is mutual forgiveness'.[338] However, while recognising the wrongs done by others to society, Alliance has in effect expressed a de facto forgiveness in that they continue to work together with members of all other parties, including former paramilitaries within Sinn Féin to forward the political process. Alliance, Sinn Féin and the SDLP have clearly acted in this way by becoming involved with their political opponents in power-sharing exercises. Arguably, an example of such an event by the Alliance Party was a decision by the three Belfast city councillors representing Alliance to vote for Sinn Féin Councillor Alex Maskey as Lord Mayor.[339] That act of forgiveness took a great deal of courage and heart-searching and did not have the approval of all the party members outside the city council.[340]

When it comes to repentance, political parties are generally very slow to admit to their mistakes. They are too ready to blame others. There have certainly been moves from members of Sinn Féin to apologise, such as a statement by Martin McGuinness[341] and another from the IRA in their May 2003 statement.[342] At the time of the formation of the Alliance Party, those who left either the Unionist Party or a Nationalist Party to join Alliance were in effect admitting the wrongs inflicted by the Unionists in the old Stormont Government, or realising that there is a better way forward than working exclusively for Nationalist aims. Those pioneers of the New Ulster Movement and founders of the Alliance Party were clearly expressing remorse for past wrongs and aiming to make restitution for them. In a radically new party they were changing their attitudes and behaviour. New members, by adopting those attitudes, are embracing those acts of repentance.

The Alliance Party would certainly approve of truth seeking at every level. It is also totally behind the pursuit of justice (now demonstrated by David Ford as Minister for Policing and Justice) (Principle no. 4[343]), though it is not clear how they define justice. The party's attitude to justice can be demonstrated from the party leader's speech to Conference in April 2003.[344] While talking about how to deal with 'On the Runs' (OTRs) – 'fugitives from justice', who are wanted by the police for prosecution for terrorist activities and persons already convicted who have escaped from custody – David Ford said that they should be treated in the same way as those prisoners who were released under the terms of the Belfast Agreement.[345] Justice must be seen to be done and in any resolution the OTRs might be released on licence rather than given amnesty. In addition, the concerns of the victims should be taken into account as should those who have been exiled by paramilitary threats. These threats should be lifted. These principles of justice in action show an even-handed approach to justice applicable to all, including the 'legitimate forces of the state [who] must obey the law themselves'. In the South African 'Truth and Reconciliation Commission', the search for truth was often balanced against the application of retributive justice. Currently the Alliance Party is sceptical about applying a similar process in Northern Ireland.[346]

Reconciling attitudes and acts can also be judged by their ultimate 'fruits', to use a word from scripture.[347] Does the party aim to produce results such as 'peace, trust, hope, confidence and togetherness' indicated by Liechty[348] and Lederach[349] as fruits of reconciliation? Certainly Alliance has been involved in many peace processes. Many Alliance members and supporters demonstrated their sincerity by joining the peace marches initiated by Nobel Peace Prize winners Betty Williams and Mairead Corrigan in 1976/77.[350]

John Paul Lederach, a seminal figure in the field of conflict resolution, says, 'Trust' is the 'fruit' that is most lacking in 'statist' negotiations.[351] The Alliance Party appears to engender trust, as members have been appointed to important cross-community posts, as described in Chapter 3. The British Government certainly shows trust by making these appointments and their track records in post testify to the wisdom of doing so. However, Frank Wright suggests:

> The best service the British could do for the people in Ireland is to make it possible for the different national groups to recognise the validity of each other's mutual mistrust. Only when that is possible is it also possible to create trust.[352]

Perhaps the Alliance Party should take on this task themselves? Politicians and party members should be in a better position than people in Great Britain to understand the issues of mutual mistrust from within the State. Alliance is ever full of hope that its influence will lead to a peaceful State denuded of discrimination and inequality, as described in Principles 2 and 4.[353]

## PARTY PRINCIPLES AND POLICIES
## REGARDING SECTARIANISM

The Alliance Party was founded on the basis that, 'our primary objective is
to heal the bitter divisions in our community by ensuring: – (c) The elimination of prejudice by a just and liberal appreciation of the beliefs and fears of
different members of the community,'[354]

In an attitudes survey of about 300 party members carried out in 1998[355]
one question asks for their attitude to 'Buzz-words to describe Alliance' on a
scale of 1 to 5. The buzzwords 'Non-Sectarian', 'Anti-Sectarian' and 'Cross-
Community' had high ratings of 4.64, 4.43 and 4.43 respectively. These are
the highest rating of the twelve 'buzz-words' in that questionnaire. Clearly
most Alliance Party members consider themselves to be non-sectarian, and a
large majority say they are anti-sectarian. Many also consider themselves to
be 'cross-community'. There is a small but significant minority of respondents which rejects or is indifferent to these terms. Some respondents may, of
course, have fallen into a familiar trap of giving what they judged to a right
answer – rather than a totally honest one.

In their book, *Moving Beyond Sectarianism*, Joe Liechty and Cecelia Clegg
discuss definitions of sectarianism. In summary they say:

> Sectarianism is a system of attitudes, actions, beliefs and structures …
> at personal, communal and institutional levels … which always involves
> religion and typically involves a negative mixing of religion and
> politics … which arises as a distorted expression of positive, human
> needs especially for belonging, identity, and the free expression of
> difference … and is expressed in destructive patterns of overlooking
> others … belittling, dehumanising, or demonising others, justifying or
> collaborating in the domination of others.
>
> Physically or verbally intimidating or attacking others.[356]

Thus they consider that an act can be sectarian if presented in a certain
way. A factual statement of belief or membership of an organisation that
potentially promotes sectarian ideas need not be sectarian. Allan Leonard,
in his MA thesis about the Alliance Party, asks 'if anyone who supports the
Union or a united Ireland is sectarian'.[357] The answer must surely be that
they are sectarian, only if they act in a sectarian manner. Holding particular
political views is not itself sectarian.[358] After the Agreement Referendum and
Assembly elections, party leader Seán Neeson suggested, 'Moderate Unionism

and moderate Nationalism are enjoying a honeymoon, but they still represent sectarian politics and institutionalise a divided society'.[359]

The Alliance Party policy paper on Community Relations has a section on sectarianism.[360] Sectarianism is combined with racism and defined in this paper as 'Racism, sectarianism and other forms of prejudice are about institutionalising difference and putting people into boxes'.

The Alliance Party says that:

These differences are often imagined or constructed rather than real or substantive, and that they are present not only in working class communities or at interface areas but also in the leafy suburbs and down at the golf club. Rather sectarian attitudes are prevalent and persistent throughout Northern Ireland society.[361]

The document is strongly critical of the constant division of the people of Northern Ireland into 'two communities', thus ignoring cross-community relationships, 'you are identified by the community in to which you were born'.[362] The definition of sectarianism says that it always involves religion.[363]

Alliance tries to avoid emphasis on religion as politics should not be about religious differences. However, the issue cannot be entirely avoided, hence they refer in their fundamental principles in 2f: 'Complete and effective participation in our political governmental and public life at all levels by people, drawn from both sides of our present religious divide'. Then in 4 it says, 'Equal justice will be guaranteed to all citizens regardless of their political or religious persuasion'.

These were the original principles written in 1970. Perhaps in more recent times Alliance has been inclined to avoid the religious difference issue. On this theme it is interesting to consider the comments of Liechty and Clegg about non-sectarian and anti-sectarian categories:

Non-sectarianism judges sectarianism to be a problem and probably an evil. It responds by working around it. Certain topics in religion and politics are avoided in mixed settings. The weakness of this position shows up when a crisis makes sectarianism unavoidable. Cordial avoidance can become wary, suspicious avoidance.[364]

One cannot avoid asking at this point if sectarianism can be detected within the Alliance Party or between the Alliance Party and its members and those of other persuasions. In Alliance Party circles generally, it is noticeable that religion is rarely discussed. The perceived religious affiliation of most members is generally known by the usual signals. However, there is not usually a problem if people discuss their Church activities.

By searching carefully, exceptions to the rule often emerge. Addie Morrow told a story in which a senior member of the party, a lapsed Catholic, berated another senior party member who is a practising Catholic. The one said something to the effect that no enlightened person believes in religion in this day and age. The other was apparently quite upset. Perhaps the hostility felt was more powerful because it was intra-tribal.[365] This type of situation is well described by Liechty and Clegg as involving 'secular liberalism ... often antagonistic with the churches'.[366]

But one might ask how Alliance people cope in wider society when they encounter sectarianism. Generally the confident hope is that Alliance people will name and confront sectarianism in a positive manner, but maybe this is not always done. Liechty and Clegg also criticise anti-sectarianism,[367] in that, 'When sectarianism encounters difference, that encounter often runs in a sequence something like this: Encounter – judge – condemn – reject – demonise – separation/antagonism'.

When post-sectarianism encounters difference it should ideally go like this: encounter – listen – observe – accept – celebrate – togetherness/friendship. This is a sequence parallel to that for the dynamics of sectarianism. While this does not normally cause a problem within Alliance, it is likely that when others from sectarian groups encounter Alliance opposition to sectarianism (or even indifference) it creates an antagonism towards the Alliance Party and its members.[368] A major issue has been and still is about flags. In 2002 Councillor Stewart Dickson in Carrickfergus and Councillor Sara Duncan in Castlereagh complained about the flying of paramilitary flags in their respective areas, and both had their houses attacked.[369] But that response was mild compared with the events following the vote in Belfast City Council in December 2012 to restrict the flying of the Union Flag to designated days – analysed in detail in Chapter 8.

Such sectarian violence arises particularly in times of increased polarisation of political groups. If and when a process of reconciliation commences, acceptance of the others' right to hold their position is upheld, in spite of the hostile manner in which difference is expressed. The celebration is about rejoicing in the difference, and about accepting and befriending the other person with their differences. An early example of such acceptance can be found even in the eighteenth century, when Penal Laws oppressed Catholic and dissenters. The evangelist and originator of Methodism John Wesley in his 'Letter to a Roman Catholic' (1759)[370] states that 'even if we cannot as yet think alike in all things, at least we can love alike'.

# RELIGIOUS ATTITUDES IN THE ALLIANCE PARTY

The basic premise of the Alliance Party is that its members can be from any and all religious persuasions or none. This is shown in principles 2 (c) and 4.[371] Various opinion polls have estimated the religious breakdown of Alliance members and supporters, as summarised in the table below:[372]

Table 3 Religious affiliations of Alliance Party members compared with population.

|  | Moxon-Browne 1978 | Evans and Duffy 1992 | Bodilis 1993 | Eggins 2003 | Population Census 1991 |
|---|---|---|---|---|---|
| Protestant | 50.5 | 50.2 | 50.9 | 52.6 | 52.9 |
| Catholic | 40.5 | 31.2 | 25.5 | 18.4 | 38.4 |
| None | 9.0 | 18.7 | 23.5 | 28.9 | 14.0 |

For the Alliance Party there are 50.2% Protestant, 31.2% Catholic and 18.7% who state no religion (Evans and Duffy 1992), sample size not known. An earlier survey by Moxon-Browne in 1978[373] found 50.5% Protestant, 40.5% Catholic and 9.0% no religion (sample size 1,277). Bodilis, in his MA thesis of 1993 on a sample of fifty-one, gives figures of 50.9% Protestant, 25.5% Catholic and 23.5% no religion. The net proportion of Catholics would be 38% in Evans and Duffy's survey, compared with the 1991 Census figure of 38.4% (stated) or 41.5% (estimated),[374] which is perhaps surprising, as Alliance appears to draw most of its supporters from areas with a Protestant majority. Significantly in those areas the SDLP often did not field a candidate, and so Catholics, having no other party to vote for, tended to vote Alliance. However, since the emergence of Sinn Féin as an electoral force, the SDLP has fielded more candidates in these areas in addition to Sinn Féin, with a corresponding decline in Alliance votes presumably cast by Catholics.

It is interesting that the proportion of Alliance supporters giving 'No religion' is much higher than for any other named party. For UUP the 'No religion' proportion is 7.1%, for DUP, 10.4%, for Sinn Féin, 5.2% and for the SDLP, 2.9%. There is a category of 'Other', which registers 22.1% 'No religion'.[375] The breakdown of people into Catholics and Protestants in national census data has been criticised by Alliance, who would prefer there to be no mention of religion as they consider that one's religion should not be related to a particular state, country or area to define one's politics. One can argue that there is a territorial heresy, continuing from the time of Constantine[376] when he made Christianity the State religion in c. 313,[377] thus establishing 'Christendom'. Since then many counties have allied the state with the predominant religion. Thus since the time of King Henry VIII the established religion in England has been the Church of England. In their document 'Building a United Community' Alliance authors point out that in the 2001 census 14% of the population do not describe themselves as either Protestant or Catholic.[378] Alliance is critical of attempts by the census analysers to put some of these persons into a category, using other signals from other information in the census return.

Generally speaking religion is not an issue in Alliance. Many members are active churchgoers and workers, though some are not. In a survey of fifty-four Alliance Party election candidates, E. Bodilis found that twenty-four attended church once a week, eight more often, twelve less often, and ten never.

As far as we are aware, there was not usually any conscious decision to split Alliance Party Executive posts equally between Catholics and Protestants. However, there is a perception by some that in the leadership election in 1987, with Catholic (Seamus Close) and a Protestant (John Alderdice) candidates, voting Council members preferred the Protestant candidate because the previous two leaders had both been Catholics.[379] There have now been three Catholic party leaders and three Protestant. Generally the deputy leader chosen has come from the other religious persuasion, demonstrating a conscious effort to provide balance between cultural origins.

It was a perceived initial aim of the Alliance Party to negate the religious differences between Protestants and Catholics in politics. Thus for the 1973 local government and Assembly elections, Oliver Napier, a Catholic, stood in East Belfast (a largely Protestant area) and Robert Cooper, a Protestant, stood in West Belfast (a largely Catholic area – although it includes the Shankill, a predominantly Protestant enclave). Both were elected, though not easily, Napier on the eighteenth count and Cooper on the twelfth count.[380] Over time Oliver Napier gained a personal reputation and easily held the East Belfast seat. Cooper held West Belfast in the Convention election on the eighth count[381] and after he had taken on the Fair Employment post, Will Glendinning (another Protestant) held the seat in the 1982 Assembly election, again on the eighth count.[382] He also held a council seat for Lower Falls[383] – a very Catholic area. This evidence would seem to suggest that Alliance candidates tend to be selected according to personal attributes of integrity and fair-mindedness, rather than on a basis of religious affiliation.

Do Alliance people pay too little attention to religion, when it is such a defining issue for most other parties? Does their non-sectarian, non-religious stance offend or antagonise some people? Is the Alliance Party's claim to be 'the party of reconciliation' regarded by some as putting themselves on a pedestal, of being 'holier than thou'? Both Seamus Close and Philip McGarry during interviews agreed that this was probably the case.[384] People are generally emotionally alienated by such attitudes from people who claim to be 'born again Christians' suggesting that they are better than everyone else. They quickly call it hypocrisy. Could it be argued that setting oneself apart from others as being non-sectarian or anti-sectarian is itself a form of sectarianism? Joe Liechty, when discussing the problem of religion and conflict, suggests that there are three ways in which people deal with this problem. One is to ignore it, saying 'help! We're secular' and the 'world is becoming more secular: it will go away'. In any case the conflicts are really about something else.[385] Newly elected party leader John Alderdice stated that 'the real division is not between Protestant and Catholic or Unionists and Nationalist, but between those for and those against the democratic processes'.[386] The next is to 'suppress it, or at least control it;'[387] the third is to 'deny there is a problem'.

However, Orthodox Jewish Rabbi and conflict resolution practitioner Marc Gopin is clear that 'religion will not go away, it must be dealt with creatively'.[388] He suggests that two very different scenarios are possible 'from the human interaction with traditional religion'.

> Religion is one of the most salient phenomena that will cause massive violence in the next century ... [or] religion will play a critical role in constructing a global community of shared moral commitments and vision.[389]

He goes on to say:

> Never before in history have so many leaders [Ghandi, King, the Dalai Lama, Tutu] and adherents been inspired to work for a truly inclusive vision that is multicultural and multi-religious.
>
> If the world of thoughtful people is open to the infinite herme-neutic variability of religious traditions, one may discover, in the most surprising places of the religious world, the basis for a future that allows for co-existence between religious and secular people globally and even for a shared vision of a civil society.[390]

Marc Gopin gave a lecture in Belfast to a mixed audience and was amazed at the positive response.[391]

## ETHNIC AND ETATIC IDENTITIES

With historical power blocks in Northern Ireland being based on ethno-religious identity it is important to consider relevant aspects of the concept of identity in this discussion and to relate them to the Alliance agenda.

There are, according to Liechty[392] and Schöpflin,[393] two relevant identities: *ethnic* and *etatic*. With Liechty we define ethnicity not in terms of bloodlines, the myth of common decent, but in terms of 'reproduced culture'. The shared memories of family-like relationships and bonds must be taken seriously. Humans are 'hard-wired' to socially construct 'ethnic identities'. These identities are not rigid but can and will develop and change. The 'etatic identity' is the state to which we give allegiance. Schöpflin says: 'Usually the one dominant ethnic group imposes its ethnic vision on the state to create an etatic identity and this is then imposed in turn on all the ethnic groups in that territory.'[394] It is not easy to separate the two in the Northern Ireland situation.

Frank Wright considers Northern Ireland to be an 'ethnic frontier society'[395] in which the dominant metropolitan power has the legitimacy of government and a monopoly of violence and retribution. In his opinion the law is theirs and one should identify with law and State.

The Alliance Party does identify with law and state. Its fourth principle states that:

> We firmly believe that without universal respect for the law of the land and the authorities appointed to enforce it, there can be no measurable progress. Equal justice will be guaranteed to all citizens regardless of their political or religious persuasion.[396]

There are many examples of their adherence to this principle, such as their attitude to decommissioning[397] and support for the police service.[398]

However, in an 'ethnic frontier society' there will be those who deny the legitimacy of the State and therefore the legitimacy of the State's monopoly of violence. Sooner or later they will oppose that State legitimacy in order to try to establish what Schöpflin calls their own 'community of moral worth',[399] which is necessary for their own 'cultural reproduction'. There will be what René Girard calls 'mimetic rivalry' and 'mimetic desire',[400] leading to representative violence against so called 'legitimate targets'. In the view of Irish Republicans, the forces of the State and their agents become legitimate targets. Mimetically in parallel with the State forces, so called 'loyalist' paramilitary groups evolve to institute 'representative violence' in response. Their so-called 'legitimate targets' are Irish Catholics. Thus fear and suspicion spreads out of proportion to the actual violence. There are now what Wright calls 'mutual deterrence communities'. He describes a 'vortex of antagonism', which is very hard to break. 'The most significant in a vortex of antagonism are those who can both threaten violence and control the threat simultaneously.'[401]

Wright develops the internal logic of escalating violence thus: 'this process only looks irrational to someone at a distance from it. Seen from within, each escalation of rivalry generates excellent reasons for the next escalation. Violence always generates reasons for itself.'[402]

Moderates such as the Alliance Party must 'understand and respect those reasons, but never to take them at face value or as necessary and sufficient'.[403] The best that can be achieved is a 'tranquillity of mutual deterrence'. But this is not peace.

In Northern Ireland one of the most hopeful signs of getting out of this vortex of antagonism is the increasingly positive relationship between London and Dublin, which has grown out of the AIA of 1985. Britain takes both its historical quasi-colonial role and its current role seriously, including the role of Dublin as a rival metropolis.[404]

Leichty also considers that the role of Christianity has been a restraining one, despite the Churches' many alleged failures.[405] Wright argues the need to create political structures equidistant from the local situation, such as 'something approaching joint sovereignty of Britain and the Irish Republic', if legitimacy is to be accepted by all parties.[406] Though the Good Friday Agreement was fully endorsed by both the British and Irish governments, it did not attempt to establish joint sovereignty. There are established a North/South Ministerial Council and East/West British-Irish Council with a British-Irish intergovernmental conference to encourage co-operation.

Unfortunately a large section of the Unionist community and a small section of the Nationalist community, despite the referendum and elections, disputed the legitimacy of the Agreement until the St Andrews Agreement in 2007, when the DUP agreed to come into government along with Sinn Féin.

Within the Nationalist community Sinn Féin has been very slow to accept the legitimacy of the new Police Service of Northern Ireland (PSNI) as representing the 'monopoly of violence'. Since coming into government in 2007 and particularly after the devolution of Policing and Justice in 2010, this has changed and now Sinn Féin fully supports the PSNI. This tardy acceptance of the PSNI is not surprising, as policing has been a contentious issue in Ireland for almost 2 centuries.

Frantz Fanon made a similar general analysis in 1963. In a discussion of colonisation and decolonisation he noted that:

The colonial world is a Manichean world. It is not enough for the settler to delimit physically, that is to say with help of the army and the police force, the place of the native. As if to show the totalitarian character of colonial exploitation the settler paints the native as a sort of quintessence of evil.[407]

Thus we are trapped in a 'them and us' dichotomy. Those members of the two opposing religious groups who persist in divisive attitudes see the other as at least wrong, at worst evil. Ian Paisley[408] (following the Presbyterian Westminster Confession of Faith[409]) demonised the Pope as the 'anti-Christ' and with it the Roman Catholic Church. Members of the Orange Order must 'strenuously oppose the fatal errors and doctrines of the Church of Rome' to quote the standards of the Orange Order. Conversely extreme Irish Republicans demonise Britain as the evil coloniser who must be removed and regard Ulster Protestants as the agents of Britain.

A number of opinion polls have asked about identity. It would appear from the opinion polls in Table 3 (above) that there is little difference between the commitment of Nationalists to the identity 'Irish' and that of Unionists to the identity 'British'. In a survey of identities academics Karen Trew and Cate Cox[410] found that professional people in the Nationalist community tended to favour the identity 'Irish', of which they were 'very proud'[411] though 'not rewarded', whereas working-class people favoured the identity 'Catholic', of which they also were 'very proud' and 'rewarded'. They are united through the community of the Catholic Church. What seems clear is that Nationalists have least problem in defining their *ethnic* identity as 'Irish' – which usually means 'Irish Catholic' or just 'Catholic', though their perceived or stated *etatic* identity is more variable.

Table 4   *Etatic* (National) Identities[412]

| Identity | Protestant-Unionist | | | Catholic-Nationalist | | |
| | Rose[413] 1968 | Moxon-Browne[414] 1978 | Smith[415] 1986 | Rose 1968 | Moxon-Browne 1978 | Smith 1986 |
|---|---|---|---|---|---|---|
| Irish | 20 | 8 | 3 | 76 | 69 | 61 |
| British | 39 | 67 | 65 | 15 | 15 | 9 |
| Ulster | 32 | 20 | 14 | 5 | 6 | 1 |
| British/Irish | 6 | 3 | 4 | 6 | 8 | 7 |
| Northern Irish | N/A | N/A | 11 | N/A | N/A | 20 |

Trew and Cox found that only 27% of 'Protestants' said that religion was 'very important'. Sometimes they call themselves British, which is why they attach so much importance to the union with Britain, though they do not have the same high 'cognitive commitment' to being 'Protestant' as Irish Catholics do to being 'Catholics'. Sometimes they see themselves as 'Ulster', sometimes 'Northern Irish', occasionally even 'Irish'. The proliferation of Protestant religious denominations means that they do not have a fully unifying Church community. Unionists are more aware of what they are not. They are not part of the Irish Catholic community. They are 'Protestant', though 'Protestant' can mean just 'not Catholic', and may not even mean 'Christian' in the pure sense.

DUP and MP Gregory Campbell revealed an interesting insight into this problem when he attended, by invitation, the West Belfast Festival – a mainly Nationalist event. He remarked on the high self-confidence of the people there in contrast to the relatively low self-esteem of his own community, and doubted that the DUP would have the courage to invite a leading member of Sinn Féin to a similar event in his community.[416]

John Whyte provides an excellent account of national identities according to survey reports.[417] He gives in three tables the results of three surveys, so one can see the changes over time. I have combined these tables into one for comparison. In Smith's 1986 survey the option 'Northern Irish' was introduced. This identity appealed to 11% of Protestants and 20% of Catholics, in contrast to Trew who says that one-third of Catholics and one-third of Protestants favoured identification with 'Northern Irish'.

'Northern Irish' is also the identity preferred by the Alliance Party.[418] Interestingly Whyte shows in his Table 4.7[419] that the proportion of Protestants identifying with Alliance in 1978 was 13% and of Catholics, 21%, mirroring the numbers identifying with the identity 'Northern Irish' in 1986. There is considerable overlap in these preferences. The term 'Northern Irish' has an appeal to quite a section of both Protestants and Catholics.

Clearly Alliance people are Catholic, Protestant, another religion or of no religion. Within the party all are equally valid and acceptable. But following the Good Friday Agreement it is clear that for the foreseeable future there will continue to be a large number of Protestants who wish to be distinct from Catholics and vice-versa. In trying to establish its own identity, Alliance must respect the other divisions, and try to work with both of them. Its own identity is clearly 'Northern Irish' with emphasis on the acceptability of all religions or none.

The Alliance Party's identity is, therefore, much more in tune with the ideas of social transformation than of consocation. Rupert Taylor gives an excellent account of the contrast between these two approaches.[420] Introducing them he points out how the South African move from apartheid to multi-cultural democracy resulted from the 'innovative action of an ever-increasing network of progressive movements, institutions, non-governmental organisations and associations (churches, trade unions, civics, women's groups) engaged in a "war of position" against apartheid rule.'[421] They achieved 'consensual democracy' not 'consociational democracy'. The difference in Northern Ireland is that there is not yet enough groundswell to break down the religious apartheid. Hence consociational democracy is likely to continue for the time being.

An insightful review of the Good Friday Agreement was written by Seán Neeson and Stephen Farry in 1999 (see discussion in Chapter 5).[422] However, Taylor shows that 'outside the formal political arena … the number and quality of concrete cross-community contacts appears to be increasing'.[423] He points to mixed marriages up to 10% from 1% since the Second World War,[424] cross-community housing projects, inter-schools contacts.[425] He also points out that there were twenty-eight integrated schools in 1994[426] compared with ten in 1990 and that both universities are non-sectarian.

Taylor says that many sociologists ignore the presence of 5,000 voluntary and community groups, with a per annum turnover of £400 million, equivalent to 6% of the gross domestic product. There are 65,000 volunteers and 30,000 paid workers, representing 5% of the workforce. Taylor also refers to 'noteworthy bodies' such as Corrymeela and the Community Relations Council, the Opsahl Commission[427] and Democratic Dialogue.[428]

John McGarry discusses the concepts of 'Civic Nationalism',[429] concluding that there are three varieties of civic nationalism. The first is Civic (Irish) Nationalism, the second is Civic Unionism and the third is Social Transformation or 'Bottom-Up' Civic Nationalism. McGarry says, 'Transformers are sceptical of the integrating capabilities of political institutions, even those with consociational (power sharing) … are likely to be dominated by sectarian elites.'[430]

Social transformation is a prerequisite for social integration. It needs policies to promote social integration and increased public expenditure to tackle the material basis of sectarian identities. It 'is popular with bodies such as Alliance Party, Democratic Left, Northern Ireland Women's Coalition and the Labour Party'. McGarry says that 'neither the first or second version [of civic nationalism] have any cross-community appeal or is likely to develop one' and that 'both the first and second are unrealistic and unfair. The third is merely unrealistic'.[431] Yet transformation is what must be tried and the

Alliance Party has the vision to do it. As Seán Neeson said: 'This Party is not about managing Northern Ireland's problems; it is about transforming them.'[432] That transformation must involve cross-community politics and 'moving beyond sectarianism'.

## CONCLUSION

This chapter presents evidence that the Alliance Party is the party of reconciliation. After discussing definitions of 'reconciliation', evidence is presented for Alliance not only claiming but also qualifying for that role.

The Alliance Party always attempts to combat 'sectarianism', definitions of which are considered. The attitudes to sectarianism within the party are discussed. A significant political policy paper, 'Community Relations' produced in 2001, covers this topic extensively.

A major issue in Northern Ireland politics is religion, whether one is 'Protestant', 'Catholic' or of no religious preference. This has been analysed in numerous surveys and the results and their significance are discussed. In general about 50% of party members are perceived to be 'Protestant', 20-30% 'Catholic' and 15-20% having no religion. This latter tally for no religion is higher than in the population as a whole. The question is considered, do Alliance people pay too little attention to religion, when it is such a defining issue for most other parties? Does their non-sectarian stance irritate some people by appearing 'holier than thou'?

Attempts to maintain a religious balance among party officers and leaders are described. The concepts of identity both *etatic* (national) identity and *ethnic* identity are engaged with and there follows a discussion as to how different groups in Northern Ireland – including Alliance members – see themselves in relation to them. Results from various surveys are included.

Alliance is more in tune with the ideas of social transformation than of consociation, yet it is the latter on which the Good Friday Agreement is based. Comparison is made with the South African situation where they achieved 'consensual democracy' rather than 'consociational democracy'. The difference in Northern Ireland is that there is not yet enough groundswell to break down the religious division. The three concepts of civic nationalism are explained and the significance of many people being involved in cross-community voluntary work. In discussing how to combat sectarianism the works of Lederach and of Leichty and Clegg are heavily drawn upon.

The final chapter of this book will examine critically recent political events in Northern Ireland and the party's record of heading two ministries in Stormont and represented in Westminster by its deputy leader, Naomi Long. The party often appears to punch above its electoral weight. The authors will also speculate as to the party's future trajectory, following the unproductive outcome from the Haass–O'Sullivan talks of 2013.

# 12

# The way forward for
# the Alliance Party

## INTRODUCTION

In a great burst of enthusiasm the Alliance Party was formed in April 1970 with the mission of breaking down sectarian politics in Northern Ireland. If its founders had known then that forty-five years later, after an extended period of violent conflict, the party's mission would still not be completed they might have felt daunted. It is to the great credit of successive waves of activists that they have held the line through periods of relative success and disappointing setbacks. Particularly since the signing of the Good Friday Agreement there have been suggestions that the party's work is complete and that it will disappear or split between moderate Unionists and the SDLP. Alliance members think otherwise. They regard combating sectarianism and promoting cross-community politics very much as work in progress. Promoting the Shared Future option is a major task, which is being largely ignored by other parties. The role in the Assembly must include working to change the cross-community voting system that effectively disenfranchises centre parties such as Alliance. The party must consolidate its recent gains and build a platform for a further increase in the number of MLAs.

## DECLINE IN VOTES AND REVIVAL

The Alliance Party's initial electoral performance was perhaps more modest than the party expected.[433] There were early electoral successes of the 1970s when Alliance Party candidates received 13.7% in the 1973 local government elections and 14.4% in 1977. In Assembly elections they received 9.2% in 1973, 9.8% in 1975 and 9.3% in 1982. In the 1979 Westminster election Alliance won 11.9%. Then there was a general decline in electoral performance. There was a partial recovery when Alliance Party candidates received 10% in the Westminster election of 1987 and 8.7% in 1992. In the 1993 local government elections Alliance won 8% of the votes. After some poor election results in 1998, 2001, and 2005 there has been a substantial recovery in support for Alliance; currently up to 8% in both Assembly and local government elections. This is still much below the results achieved in the 1970s and 1982.

The decline started with the local government election in 1981, during the IRA hunger strikes. The vote dropped to 8.9%, giving thirty-eight seats.[434] Even so, at the Assembly elections in the following year the vote held up at 9.3%, and due to the vagaries of the STV system produced 10 Assembly seats.[435] From then on the vote in both local government and Assembly elections declined to between 5 and 7%.

It is instructive to look at opinion polls, mostly published in the *Belfast Telegraph* or in *Fortnight*, from time to time. Generally the opinion polls overestimate the likely Alliance Party vote. For example, in a survey conducted by Edward Moxon Browne[436] in 1979 in response to the question 'Which of the parties do you feel closest to?' Alliance received 19.5% (compared with 11.9% in the Westminster election that year). The effect is shown very well in John Whyte's book.[437] This phenomenon suggests that while many people are in principle in favour of a cross-community political party, the position at election times hardens. The people become more polarised – probably due to fear of what might happen if they desert their traditional political party, i.e. 'community loyalty'. In a questionnaire carried out by Eggins among Alliance Party members and others on the Reconciliation Studies MPhil course,[438] when asked to rate factors contributing to the decline in Alliance Party votes, 'community loyalty' received the highest response scores of from all respondents. Many of these situations depend on the political climate at the time and are beyond the control of the party.

The Bobby Sands by-election in 1981 signalled the entry of Sinn Féin into electoral politics. Frank Wright comments that: 'A more certain way [than the hunger strike issue] to polarise people round their own experiences of violence would be hard to devise'.[439] No doubt the SDLP felt threatened and the Alliance Party began to lose the support of some moderate Nationalists. From being abstentionist, more Nationalists and Republicans began to vote, and the electoral fortunes of both the SDLP and Sinn Féin were to rise. Despite a relatively high profile in the 1982 Prior Assembly, at the 1985 local government elections the Alliance vote fell further to 7.1%, giving them only thirty-four seats.

The next significant event was the AIA, signed in 1985. The Unionist parties combined in bitter opposition. So when the Unionist MPs all resigned to fight by-elections opposing the Agreement ('Ulster Says No') in January 1986, the Alliance vote dwindled to 32,095 votes, 5.5%.[440]

As the steam went out of the 'Ulster Says No' campaign, there was a partial recovery in Alliance fortunes, with general election votes up to 10% in 1987 and a recovery of local government seats up to forty-four in 1993 from 8.0% of votes.[441] Philip McGarry said that 'Alliance Party psephologists (those who do statistical analysis of elections[442]) think that moderate Unionists agreed with the Alliance Party's support for the AIA, and so the Alliance vote recovered'.[443]

Most interestingly, as negotiations developed towards the Good Friday Agreement, the shape of the Agreement was in many respects identical to the Alliance Party's 'Governing with Consent' document.[444] So why did the Alliance Party's vote not recover?

In fact the polarisation that had squeezed the Alliance Party still existed. There is evidence that, despite the Agreement, Catholics and Protestants were more divided than ever.[445] The SDLP were even more concerned about the threat to their vote from Sinn Féin and the Unionists were concerned about having their former enemies, Sinn Féin, sharing power in government with them. During the negotiations, while the Alliance Party negotiators did as much as they could to facilitate the production of an overall agreement, they did not have the electoral strength to negotiate a sound position for themselves within the Agreement.[446]

The Alliance Party vote continued to decline to 6.5% in the Assembly elections of 1998.[447] There was the disastrous 2.1% in the European elections of 1999,[448] followed by 5.1% in the 2001 local government elections yielding only twenty-eight seats.[449] Although there were only three Alliance councillors on Belfast City Council, they still had the balance of power. The 6.5% vote brought only six Assembly seats,[450] which was insufficient to obtain a place in the Executive. Had the STV transfers gone more favourably, as in 1982, there might have been enough votes to yield seven or eight seats out of 108. According to the d'Hondt method,[451] Alliance would have needed eight seats to obtain a place in the ten-member executive.

## WESTMINSTER REPRESENTATION

One major disappointment for the Alliance Party was their failure to win a seat in Westminster over a forty-year period. When asked in the questionnaire to rate the importance of the failure to win a Westminster seat to the decline of Alliance, both candidates and council members ranked this third. In 1972 after the Stormont Government was prorogued, one existing Unionist MP, Stratton Mills, switched to the Alliance Party. He stood down at the next general election in February 1974, however. Of more value to the party was the presence of Lord Henry Dunleath, a hereditary peer, in the House of Lords.

The closest the Alliance Party came to winning a seat in the Commons over the period up to 2010, was in 1979, when Oliver Napier came a close third.

After the death of Lord Henry Dunleath, Dr John Alderdice was made a life peer in 1996 at the instigation of the Liberal Democrat Party in Great Britain,[452] having come second with 29.8% of the vote in East Belfast in the 1992 general election.[453] His membership of the House of Lords helped to keep Alliance in touch with Westminster politics.

The election of Naomi Long to the East Belfast Seat, defeating sitting MP Peter Robinson, finally broke the log-jam and gave Alliance a strong voice in the House of Commons.

## TOO MIDDLE CLASS, POOR APPEAL IN NATIONALIST AREAS

The Alliance Party has suffered because it is often regarded as being too middle class.[454] This is well demonstrated in Moxon-Browne's survey.[455] Wright also refers to this middle-class issue.[456] Some councillors have been elected in working-class areas, but this support has usually diminished once those individuals have stood down, demonstrating the importance of their personal appeal. In Eggins' questionnaire[457] neither candidates nor council members ranked the middle-class problem very highly.

In the early days, before the SDLP became better organised, Alliance had a reasonable impact in Catholic areas, particularly in areas such as West Belfast. In East Antrim and East Belfast few Nationalist candidates stood. With the rise and success of Sinn Féin, the SDLP have been putting more candidates in these areas with an adverse effect on the Alliance vote. Many of the SDLP supporters, astutely perceiving increased educational opportunities as ladders leading to upward social mobility, have obtained professional jobs and many of them have moved into middle-class areas and threatened the Alliance vote there too. At the same time the SDLP vote has declined in some working-class areas of West Belfast, to be overtaken by Sinn Féin.

While the above factors have been outside the control of Alliance, one persistent problem has been the tendency for Alliance to be seen as a 'Unionist party with a small u'.[458] There is much evidence of this impression being held,[459] though in principle it is not intended.[460]

The Alliance Party leadership was more sympathetic to the Unionist Party's problems over the failure of the IRA to decommission its weapons than to the SDLP's standing up for the democratic rights of elected Sinn Féin members. For example, in 1995 the Alliance Party stated:

> The continued existence of illegal weapons undermines the peace process by perpetuating community fears of a return to violence, and casting doubt upon the real intentions of those who say that they have given up violence.[461]

Both candidates and Council members rated the problem of the decline in Nationalists' votes most highly, next to 'Loyalty to person's own community', which received the highest level of concern. Of course it is the aim of the Alliance Party to break down these community divisions, which makes it a chicken and egg situation.

## CHANGES IN UNIONIST PARTY POLICIES AND ALLIANCE PARTY POLICIES

Following the failure of the Sunningdale Agreement and the Constitutional Convention that followed, many Unionists turned their ideas away from a devolved parliament towards greater integration within the United Kingdom.[462] This innovation was driven largely by two Unionist MPs, Unionist Party leader James Molyneux[463] and Enoch Powell, who came to Northern Ireland from the Conservative Party and won the Westminster seat in South Down as a Unionist in the October 1974 election.[464] In 1987 Unionist thought swung back towards devolution and integrationist QC Robert McCartney was expelled from the Unionist Party in 1987, whereupon he set up his own UK Unionist Party and held the Westminster seat of North Down from 1995–2001. He lost the seat to Lady Sylvia Hermon (helped by the absence of an Alliance Party candidate). He opposed the Good Friday Agreement and his party won five Assembly seats in the 1998 elections. He stood in the 1999 European elections and won 2.9% of the votes. He opposed the St Andrews Agreement in 2007 then lost his Assembly seat in North Down in the 2007 elections. The only effect of this policy change within Unionism was to slow down moves towards another attempt at devolution. In fact this was probably as much to do with Unionist disenchantment with the AIA as with policy changes.

It might be considered that the Alliance Party's reluctant support for the AIA, signed in 1985 by British Prime Minister Margaret Thatcher and the Irish Taoiseach Garret Fitzgerald without any consultation with the people or parties in Northern Ireland would have damaged moderate Unionists' support for Alliance. In fact the Alliance vote made a partial recovery, so that in the 1987 Westminster election Alliance polled 10% (compared with 8% in 1983) and then in the 1993 local government election they polled 7.6% and gained forty-four council seats compared with thirty-four in 1985. Former party president and Belfast City Councillor Philip McGarry[465] suggested that moderate Unionists disapproved of the abstentionist behaviour of Unionists, following the AIA. In fact some Alliance councillors, particularly Addie Morrow in Castlereagh, Seamus Close in Lisburn and David Cook in Belfast, took successful court action against the Unionists and forced them to resume normal operations of local councils.[466]

There is some ambivalence in the Alliance Party's own policies that has not helped its relationship with other parties, which is described in Allan Leonard's thesis.[467] Leonard discusses two alternative models that Alliance people have for their party. These he calls 'civic liberalism' and 'bridge building'. Civic liberalism appears to be equated with a 'third tradition' model, whose political aim is to integrate Northern Ireland as a single community with a grand coalition government with weighted majority voting (as proposed in the 2001 Alliance 'Review of Assembly Designation and Voting System').[468] It represents the views of Sir Oliver Napier who commented: 'As peace begins slowly to emerge, the third tradition will begin to show the authentic voice of Northern Ireland'.[469]

Addie Morrow had similar views. He followed the tradition of the United Irishmen: 'My background was never Unionist. [It] comes from Home Rule'.[470]

Des Keenan said of the two traditional factional communities: 'It is better to forget them and to remember only the third tradition, that of decent Irishmen, Catholic and Protestant, who worked together for their mutual benefit'.[471]

Civic liberalism deems 'unionism and nationalism as incompatible ethno-nationalisms, and therefore ultimately irreconcilable', but 'moderate Unionists and moderate Nationalists do not see themselves as sectarian'.[472]

The alternative 'bridge building' approach accepts the continued existence of the two communities and a need to accommodate both. 'Alliance bridge builders are those who are more inclined to assist Unionist and Nationalist politicians to find common ground.'[473] The Alliance Party is, therefore, what Horowitz calls a multi-ethnic party.[474] As discussed in Chapters 3 and 5, this is largely the role Alliance has been playing in negotiations. The resulting problem Allan Leonard considers being that 'there is no guarantee that the electorate will sufficiently endorse such a reconciliation project'. He goes on to say, 'the danger to both "civic liberalism" and "bridge building" is power sharing with segmental autonomy, under which neither a "bridge building" nor a "civic liberal" party is required'. The implications are discussed further by Allan Leonard and in Chapter 5.[475]

## MEDIA PRESENTATION

In the twentieth and twenty-first centuries mass communication – newspapers, radio, television and social media have become very important modes of communication, compared with speeches to an audience, posters, leaflets and door knocking. It follows that the purveyors of the media have much control and hence much responsibility for the content and quality of what is presented. They often think of themselves as having to provide entertainment, rather than information and education. Items they cover have to be interesting and novel, so they tend to concentrate on the negative rather than the positive, on controversy rather than relevance/orthodoxy. This tendency, one might argue, plays into the hands of extremist politicians and especially terrorists. The media assume that their audience would prefer to hear about a murder or a riot than to hear about worthy actions. Experience suggests that a party that has a paramilitary wing makes better news copy than a moderate party presenting good sense.

When Ian Paisley threw snowballs at the visiting Irish Taoiseach's car, that was news.[476] When he was sent to jail for 'unlawful assembly', that was news.[477] It is difficult for a moderate person or party to present their views in a way that appeals to the primitive emotions. Yet this appears to be the way many people (especially Unionists) vote – out of the primitive instinct of fear. Often political parties present their more extreme views at election time, thus polarising the community even further, squeezing out the moderate view. Even some books by reputable journalists, such as the readable *Endgame in Ireland*,[478] hardly mention the Alliance Party, though others, such as Whyte's *Interpreting Northern Ireland*,[479] McGarry's *Northern Ireland and the Divided World*[480] and Wright's *Northern Ireland: A Comparative Analysis*,[481] give fair coverage of the contribution of the Alliance Party.

Too often interviewers are intimidated by extremist politicians and are not prepared to face them down and challenge them hard enough. In interviews with moderate politicians it is often the politician who is intimidated by the interviewer, because he/she is too polite. An example in spring of 2003 was on BBC TV's *Hearts and Minds*.[482] The presenter, Noel Thompson was interviewing Councillors Jim Rodgers and David Alderdice about Sinn Féin's first Lord Mayor, Alex Maskey, whose term of office was to end the following week. Rodgers, whose Unionist Party had refused to endorse Maskey as Lord Mayor, was unrepentant and aggressive whereas Alderdice was mild and almost repentant, being aware of the controversy within the Alliance Party over their decision to support Maskey. Rodgers said that the Alliance Party would suffer for it at the next election. Alderdice, already aware of this possibility, trod very carefully. As explained, the more extreme person came over more powerfully than the moderate person. In order to become newsworthy and be interviewed someone must have something different or, better still, radical to present.

In 1976 and 1977 the marches by the Peace People was newsworthy, made good TV coverage and hence gave a platform for moderate opinions.[483] Views expressing opposition to another group's opinions or activities can be newsworthy. It is hard for moderates to make the vitriolic attacks on others that make the headlines – if they do they lose their credibility as moderates. The Alliance Party seeks to present real policies about real bread and butter issues.

So what does the Alliance Party have to do to make news? Naomi Long received very good publicity as Lord Mayor of Belfast City, and since David Ford and then Stephen Farry obtained ministerial positions in the Executive, there has been plenty of publicity for Alliance, most of it good. The flags issue generated much publicity, not all of it quite as favourable.

The Alliance Party deluges the media with press releases.[484] Unfortunately many of them are ignored, as they do not make exciting news! In favourable times very hard-working Alliance Party councillors do make a personal impact[485] – though that generates votes primarily for the person, rather than the party.

One can trace this tendency of ignoring moderates through history. Frank Wright described some moderate groups, such as James McKnight and Charles Gavan Duffy and the Young Irelanders, who tried 'to make a trans-sectarian alliance work', in the nineteenth century.[486] Wright points out those groups such as this rarely receive a mention in mainstream history books. In an article commenting on Wright's work, historian Joe Liechty makes reference to another little known moderate, Whitley Stokes, who, writing in 1799 after the failure of the 1798 United Irishmen's rebellion, said that 'the only hope for peace in Ireland is mutual forgiveness'[487] (see also Chapter 11).

There was one period, in the 1950s, when the BBC was following a policy of bringing both sides together, which meant that the positive aspects of community relations were emphasised and the negative underplayed'.[488] Perhaps if this policy had operated during the later 'Troubles', the Alliance Party would have received more media coverage.

## COMBATING SECTARIANISM

In Eggins' questionnaire,[489] when asked about the priorities for the Alliance Party, 'combating sectarianism' was the second major choice for Protestants and the first choice for Catholics and first equal for those expressing no religious preference (none). Council members rated it second, but candidates ranked it as first choice. Similarly ISE students rated it their second priority. The differences are insignificant.

Sectarianism is widely agreed to be the biggest plague in our communities in Northern Ireland, poisoning relationships with others. Until it is overcome there will not be permanent peace and harmony in this statelet. Combating sectarianism is a major, slow process. It needs to begin by more people becoming educated about the nature of sectarianism. This problem has not been systematically addressed until relatively recently (2001). The book *Moving Beyond Sectarianism – Religion, Conflict, and Reconciliation in Northern Ireland* by Liechty and Clegg, published in 2001, is a seminal work in this area and has been briefly discussed in Chapter 11.[490] It has resulted in a series of spin-off workbooks aimed at different age groups.[491] Alliance members and public representatives could benefit from becoming more familiar with this material. They could liaise with people working in these areas at the Irish School of Ecumenics or the Community Relations Council. Sectarian issues can only be countered by personal encounters, which involve working in groups with people from other parties. Well-read and trained Alliance Party members would be competent to lead these dialogue groups since their membership of the party indicates that they are likely to be further along the road towards reconciliation than many others. It is an educational process that involves people changing their perceptions of each other. One cannot change people by preaching at them. They need to be allowed to see for themselves that there is a better way of relating to people with different views, particularly religious views. It is or should be a major concern of the Assembly. Combating sectarianism is a major aspect of 'conflict transformation'. John Paul Lederach describes

'Conflict transformation' in his various publications, particularly in *Building Peace – Sustainable Reconciliation in Divided Societies*.[492] He suggests in his introduction that, 'I believe that the natures and characteristics of contemporary conflict suggest the need for a set of concepts and approaches that go beyond the traditional statist diplomacy'.[493]

Lederach's idea is that rather than just addressing problems of conflict to resolve them, one must address the relationships between the protagonists. The resulting change in relational attitudes may lead people to view the problem in different ways and hence perhaps circumvent the conflict. It requires a willingness of the people involved to change their attitudes.

## CROSS-COMMUNITY POLITICS

One of the major suggestions from respondents to Eggins' questionnaire was that the Alliance Party should engage in cross-community politics. The Council members and ISE students made this their first choice, whereas candidates made it their fourth choice. Looking at party members only across the religious divide a similar picture was observed. Protestants and 'None' categories of respondents put it first and for Catholics it was second. There is no statistically significant difference between these responses.

The basic principle of the Alliance Party was to include people of both the Catholic and Protestant community and of other religions, or of no religion.[494] It was considered to be sufficient to obtain equal rights and opportunities for both Catholics and Protestants within the United Kingdom.[495] The party has been largely sensitive to the pro-union political position, partly for pragmatic economic reasons but also because Unionists are deemed to have greater difficulty than Nationalists in embracing power-sharing as they often show a siege mentality. The Alliance Party formerly attracted votes from Catholics who were sympathetic to the cross-community dimension or who had no Nationalist candidate to vote for.[496] Scant attention was given to the deeper aspirations of the Catholic community for Irish unity. Even increased relations with the Republic were played down,[497] because Alliance knew that it would not go down well with the Unionists. The Alliance Party needs to appreciate much more the aspirations of Nationalists and understand the overall benefits to all the people of Ireland of strong north-south relations. More sensitivity and more study and appreciation of Irish culture would place the party in a better position to explain those advantages to Unionists from a centrist neutral viewpoint.

The Alliance Party must stand fast in offering an alternative to sectarian voting. It has played a valuable part in bringing the Northern Ireland people to negotiate their own future and has played a crucial if unsung part in obtaining the Belfast Agreement.

If the other 'pro-Agreement' parties and the two governments are serious about implementing the spirit of the Agreement, they should be prepared to encourage those who would wish to vote for a non-sectarian party. If the arrangements for strengthening the influence of the 'Other' bloc's votes, as suggested in the next section, are made it will act as an incentive to moderate people to vote for parties in the 'Other' group. A strong representation from such parties would act as a catalyst[498] to promote the aims of the Agreement.

Church of Ireland priest, Revd Timothy Kinahan,[499] suggested that the Alliance Party's strength is in local councils and interacting with 'grass roots' people where councillors and their workers can actively work across the communities and practise 'moving beyond sectarianism'.[500] Lederach's model for building peace involves the interaction of people at all levels of society, not just the top echelon involved in statist diplomacy, but also the grass-roots community workers and especially the middle-range (profes-sional) leadership people.[501] Journalist Peter Walker confirmed this when he wrote in *Fortnight*:

> Real peace needs people based initiatives designed to promote peace. ... It can only be realised when diversity is respected. ... Localised problem solving efforts, involving ordinary people, are more likely to lead to genuine improvements in community relations than imposed solutions coming top-down from an outside elite.[502]

Another mode of operation suggested by Allan Leonard for the Alliance Party is for it to act as a 'bridge' between the other parties.[503] In 1992 the Alliance Party had its logo redesigned and the result was that the form of the 'A' was deliberately in the form of a bridge.[504] This option was not particularly favoured in the ques-tionnaire. Candidates ranked the idea of Alliance as a 'bridge party' as their fifth preference, compared with Alliance being a 'third party' (see earlier reference to 'civic liberalism' as the third party tradition' mentioned by Oliver Napier, Des Keenan and Allan Leonard) as third preference. Council members ranked it sixth with the 'third party' option as fourth. Of course during the Forum negotiations, Alliance's major role was to act as a bridge between the parties.[505]

Alliance would need to be a bridge in order to carry out a role combating sectarianism. A party must however have sufficient electoral strength as a stand-alone party before it has the opportunity to act as a bridge. Back in 2001 an editorial in the Belfast *Newsletter*[506] said: 'It is difficult to escape the conclusion that Alliance is in irreversible decline whichever way things go'.

One should contrast this comment with a more recent positive comment in the same newspaper (already quoted in Chapter 8), 'Among the stand out results over the week end was the news that the Alliance's Michael Long scored ahead of both his nearest DUP and UUP rivals in Lisnascarragh'.[507]

An Alliance Party statement said:

> The story of this election is undoubtedly the sight of Long topping the poll in East Belfast – proving the name is seen by people as positive, hardworking and reliable for everyone in the City.
>
> The result has shown the predictions of gloom and doom by the soothsayers were wrong and voters want to see a non-tribal approach focussing on the key issues.
>
> The Alliance hailed gains it had made in North Belfast, Lisburn and Rowallane.
>
> The implosion in the Alliance Party's vote in the capital city which some had predicted simply did not materialise.

The party will still have a meaningful role in local government, and it is vital that it attempts to enhance its appeal for the next Assembly elections in 2016 and seeks to increase its representation.

## A FUTURE ROLE IN THE ASSEMBLY

During the negotiating period for the Belfast Agreement up to 1998 the Alliance Party was so busy helping everybody else to reach an agreement that they gave insufficient attention to their own position.[508] They agreed to a system in which 'sufficient consensus' was required on certain issues but only between the Unionist and Nationalist blocks. The only contribution the centre parties had in voting was to the total vote.[509]

Alliance has been trying to have this situation rectified. At the Alliance Party Annual Conference in April 2000 an emergency motion that 'Conference calls upon the government to amend those sections of the Northern Ireland Act 1998 that discriminate against designated "other" in the assembly' was proposed by deputy leader Seamus Close, who said:

The cross community voting in the Assembly should be amended so that a majority of Nationalists plus others and a majority of Unionists plus others is required. This would not only be good for Alliance, but it would also be good for the whole country as the vote of extremists on each side would be minimised.[510]

The motion was passed, but the government did not respond, so, as we recalled in Chapter 6, in November 2001, when a vote was needed to restore Trimble and Mallon as First and Deputy First Ministers, three Alliance MLAs were pressured by the prime minister into redesignating briefly as 'Unionists'.

Immediately after this the party had a detailed review of the voting procedure.[511] This showed that if a weighted majority of 65% had been used it would have made little difference to the results of thirty-nine votes in the Assembly, apart from five to do with standing orders and three others. The review considers various other options. It rejects Close's idea[512] that votes of 'Others' should be counted with both 'Unionists' and 'Nationalists' and the idea that 'Others' should be a distinct block on a par with 'Unionists' and 'Nationalists', as this would make the votes of 'Others' of more value than the rest. This latter idea is briefly mentioned by John McGarry[513] who qualifies it in a footnote, that, 'there would have to be appropriate safeguards here to prevent rejectionist Unionists or Nationalists registering as 'Others' in order to prevent the passage of legislation'.[514]

Whatever is decided, the votes of 'Others' should count as much as the votes of 'Unionists' and 'Nationalists' and the 'Others' block should have the same status as these groups, perhaps even a guaranteed Executive seat.

Alliance has tried, so far unsuccessfully, to have the requirement for cross-community voting procedure modified, though at one point Peter Robinson of the DUP suggested that voting by weighted majority would be preferable. Currently the Nationalist parties do not agree. It should not disadvantage them, though perhaps they are afraid of being excluded unless there is a specifically Nationalist vote.

Alliance must work to increase its representation in the Assembly. David Ford suggested that they might have won three extra seats in 2011.[515] They did win one extra in East Belfast, reflecting the increase in votes overall, but it was still only 8%. They just lost out for an extra seat in North Down and were well short in East Antrim and North Belfast. The increase in numbers of young members is a very hopeful sign, as they do not have the baggage of political loyalty that so many of their elders have. The difficulties are in getting people to change their voting habits. This problem was discussed in an article in *Alliance News* which said:

If we are so trusted, why do not more people vote Alliance?

It is all about 'hearts and minds'. When we present Alliance Party policies and candidates, people seem to be favourably disposed, with their conscious, rational 'minds'. They accept our arguments. But the main driving force for actions is their unconscious emotions, or their 'hearts'. A dominant personality trait among Northern Irish people is their perceived identity. Whatever we say, their emotions tell them to vote traditionally for their 'community' candidates. This has been reinforced over years by inculcating fear of the other side.

There is also our 'spiritual intelligence' which aims to integrate the rational and emotional intelligences. Taoists liken this to the 'emptiness' at the hub of a wheel, neuroscientists call it the 'quantum vacuum' and theologians call it the 'ground of our being', or God. Because it is the spiritual dimension it is much directed by people's religion – protestant or catholic, hence tying in with their 'community' identity.

How do we counteract this effect? We have to get through to people's inner wants and needs, as well as arguing our case intellectually. Alliance are doing that by appealing to their pockets with the cost of segregation. The party also appeal through their concerns for integrated education. What are their 'hearts' desires' when it comes to elections? That is what we have to touch.[516]

There has been much discussion about whether the Alliance Party should be an opposition party or should seek to win ministerial office. Experience shows that they gain much more media coverage by having ministerial office, but under the current system they often have to accept majority decisions of the Executive coalition, which do not always match up with party policy. In recent times we have seen other parties, both the SDLP and the UUP, contradicting themselves by having ministries, and hence being part of the governing coalition and then trying to express opposition opinions. It is a difficult tightrope to walk, and is a consequence of the current system

## A SHARED FUTURE

A major concern has long been the need to share resources throughout all communities. As we saw in Chapter 7, the failure to share is costing Northern Ireland up to £1.5 billion per year, though such sharing has been an Alliance Party commitment for many years. When David Ford was being asked to take on the Ministry of Policing and Justice, the Alliance Party made it a precondition that the Executive should release its document on this issue, entitled 'Cohesion, Sharing and Integration' (CSI). It was a great disappointment and much criticised. Unfortunately, with the Alliance Party now in government and part of the Executive, there was much work to do in the areas of Policing and Justice and Employment and Learning. Although not always happy with some aspects of the Executive's proposals for the plans for government, after making their points the Alliance Ministers felt obliged to accept the majority decisions of the Executive.

The problem is that it is in the political interests of the other sectarian parties to maintain the differences between their communities, in order to maximise their share of votes. Little has been heard about CSI or a Shared Future in recent months. It is essential for the Alliance Party to continue to press for real progress in these areas, for the good of all the communities, to reduce sectarianism as well as to realise the financial benefit to everyone.


## PROMOTION OF POLICIES

The Alliance Party is probably unique in Northern Ireland in having a detailed range of policies on most issues, on which to base its campaigns. Other parties rely on the tribal vote and do not seem to need such detailed policies. The party has an excellent range of policy documents on all major issues, which are regularly updated by the appropriate policy groups and confirmed by the Party Council. However, it is not clear how many of the general public outside the party (or even within the party membership outside Council members) are aware of these policies. There are excellent documents about them on the website, and they need to be promoted very much more to the party membership and then to the public.

Party associations and branches frequently and rightly carry out surveys of local opinion and distribute focus leaflets to obtain feedback on people's opinions and reactions. A new, 'How to Build an Effective Campaign', was produced in 2014 by the Policy Officer, Sam Nelson.[517] This was distributed to all Association Committee members and included information and advice about surveys and focus leaflets. These are mostly about local issues, such as waste collection, dog waste and local planning situations. There is an almost total lack of promotion of most party policies. As referred to in Chapter 9, there is an excellent summary of party polices which is given to new members and potential new members.[518] No doubt it needs updating since it was published in 2006.

Probably most people (maybe not all) are aware of the Alliance Party emphasis on the Shared Future and what is needed to achieve it, as it has been frequently discussed and referred to in the media. People will know that the Alliance Party is foremost in promoting integrated education. Many people are probably aware of some of the activities of the two ministers and the Member of Parliament, though even this information needs to be more widely promulgated.

How many people are aware of the extensive environmental policies, which more than match those of the Green Party? How many know about Alliance polices on green energy, health and welfare, transport, farming and rural development and other key issues? If the party wishes to rely on its policies to attract voters, it needs to do a great deal more to publicise them to everyone.

This chapter concludes with a brief summary of the activities of MP, Naomi Long, Justice Minister David Ford and Minister of Employment and Learning, Stephen Farry.

## WESTMINSTER REPORT – NAOMI LONG MP[519, 520]

The Alliance Party Member of Parliament, Naomi Long, has been very active at Westminster:

> In September 2013 the government backed her amendment to increase transparency around political donations in Northern Ireland. Her addition to the Northern Ireland (Miscellaneous Provisions) Bill means the removal of the permanent anonymity for single donors of £7,500 or over to political parties in Northern Ireland. As a result, all donations of that size from January 2014 will be published as soon as the Secretary of State ends the local exemption due to be renewed in October of 2014.[521]
>
> She voted on Bills including the Finance Bill and the Consumer Rights Bill. She supported the Infrastructure Bill and the Modern Slavery Bill. She has in particular worked on the issue of freedom of (and from) religion as Vice-Chair of the All Party Parliamentary Group (APPG) for Freedom of Religion. She highlighted the plight of Christians and other religious minorities in Syria and Pakistan, during questions to the Foreign Secretary. She held a well-attended debate on religious freedom that received a positive response from the Foreign and Commonwealth Minister who was present. Naomi was very active in the campaign to free Meriam Yahia Ibrahim Ishag and her

two children who were imprisoned in Sudan on apostasy and adultery charges. She tabled an Early Day Motion calling for Meriam's release, which was well supported. Naomi is an active member of the Northern Ireland Affairs Committee and the Speaker's Committee on Electoral Reform. She has tabled several EDMs on Tackling Warzone Rape in Congo and beyond; unlicensed advertising of puppies; Religious Liberty in the Arab World; Lesbian, Gay, Bisexual, Transgender and Questioning (LGBTQ) people in Uganda and Nigeria.

Naomi has addressed many issues in correspondence, including climate change and recent flooding, fair fuel, event tourism (events as a motivation for tourism), armed forces memorials, multiple births, Haass, pancreatic cancer, ovarian cancer, diabetes, free votes in parliament, guide dogs.[522]

## MINISTERIAL ACTIVITIES

Similarly the two Alliance Party ministers have been equally active at Stormont. There follows an account of their activities.

### Achievements of the Policing and Justice Ministry[523]

As Minister of Policing and Justice, David Ford has made considerable achievements including a comprehensive reform of the Northern Ireland prison system, establishment of Policing and Community safety partnerships. He has ended the construction of new 'peace walls' and has begun a process to remove some existing ones. He has introduced alternatives to prosecution for young offenders and alternatives to prison custody. He has brought in new sports laws, including measures to tackle racist and sectarian chanting, and to create football banning orders. The criminal legal aid system has been reformed to bring it within budget, while maintaining access to justice. The law dealing with sex offenders has been tightened. David Ford has delivered a range of measures to improve the experience of victims and witnesses in criminal cases, and introduced a new offender levy to fund services for victims of crime.

### Achievements at the Department of Employment and Learning[524, 525]

Dr Stephen Farry as Minister for Employment and Learning has focused particularly on major reviews of apprenticeships and associated youth training, which were reported in December 2013 and early 2014 respectively.

In higher education he has frozen Tuition Fees for Local Students at NI Higher Education Institutions. The key was to ensure a package of funding for HEIs to address the shortfalls. This should be presented as an Executive decision, driven by Alliance leadership. Two other packages have to be agreed for the 2015–2016 and 2016–2020 period. These should be in place before next Assembly election.

There has been an increase of 1,350 undergraduate places in Science, Technology, Engineering, and Mathematics (STEM) subjects and a 60% increase in the number of publicly funded PhDs. There is a commitment to double these by 2020 from about 500 to about 1,000 places. As Northern Ireland has the highest level of hidden Economic Inactivity in the UK (27.4%), Stephen has worked at job creation with a programme called Assured Skills offered to inward investors. A new strategy, the first of its kind in these islands, is being developed to deal with economic inactivity. An existing Pathways to Success (NEETs[526] Strategy) is now a very dynamic and well-regarded strategy, with new projects and £25m budget.

Stephen has introduced legislation to improve shared parental leave and greater access to flexible working, particularly to maximise opportunities for women to access employment and to progress in their careers. He has worked to get more children from poorer backgrounds into university. He has introduced a Youth Unemployment Strategy with work experience and wages subsidies available, with £30m resources over three years.

In addition Stephen has introduced a Single Arbitration Scheme for Employment Disputes and produced a LGTBQ workplace strategy.

## CONCLUSION

It is clear that there is a continuing role for the Alliance Party. Alliance now has an MP, eight MLAs, two ministers and hence much greater media coverage. Despite recent successes, following a time of decline, there is great need to win more MLAs to combat continued sectarianism, and to develop cross-community politics. Many of the problems leading to the decline have been solved, except the cross-community voting system in the Assembly. The current momentum resulting in many new members, particularly young people and some defections from other parties is an encouraging sign. The Alliance Party needs to make more people aware of the content of many of its important policies. It needs to inform in order to persuade.

I will leave the final word on the future of the Alliance Party to Denis Loretto, one of the sixteen party founders. He says:

Look at education. The integrated education movement accepts that 'shared schooling', whereby segregated schools co-operate to some extent, is better than nothing. But they know that only when the great majority of Protestant and Catholic children go together to the same schools will their job be done. It's the same with politics. Until Catholics and Protestants working together across a range of political parties becomes the norm in Northern Ireland there will always be an important role for the Alliance Party.

# Notes

1  Dervla Murphy, *A Place Apart* (London: John Murray, 1978)

2  W.S. Gilbert and Arthur Sullivan, *Iolanthe or The Peer and the Peri* (1882)

3  J.L. McCracken, 'Northern Ireland' in T.W Moody and F.X. Martin (eds) *The Course of Irish History* (Cork: The Mercier Press, 1967), p. 317

4  *www.newadvent.org* › Catholic Encyclopaedia Penal Laws

5  R.R. McDowell, 'The Protestant Nation (1775–1800) in T.W. Moody and F.X. Martin (eds), *The Course of Irish History*, pp. 232-247.

6  http://en.wikipedia.org/wiki/Great_Famine_(Ireland)

7  Senia Paseta, Ibid., pp. 34–37

8  www.catholicculture.org/culture/library/dictionary/index.cfm?id=35103

9  Searle, G.R., *A New England? Peace and War 1886–1918* (Oxford: Clarendon Press, 2005), p. 142

10  www.1914-1918.net/36div.htm

11  www.taoiseach.gov.ie/eng/Historical_Information/1916_Commemorations/Irish_Soldiers_in_the_First_World_War.html

12  Patrick Lynch, 'Ireland since the treaty' in T.W. Moody and F.X. Martin (eds), *The Course of Irish History*, pp. 324-341.

13  Sir James Craig (Lord Craigavon), quoted in John D. Brewer with Gareth I. Higgins, *Anti-Catholicism in Northern Ireland, 1600-1998: The Mote and the Beam* (Basingstoke, Hants: Macmillan, 1998) p. 93

14  Richard Rose quoted in Ian Adamson, *The Ulster People* (Bangor, Northern Ireland: Pretani Press, 1991), p. 101

15  Brewer and Higgins, p. 90.

16  J L McCracken 'Northern Ireland', T.W. Moody and F.X. Martin (eds), *The Course of Irish History*, p. 312

17  *The Holy Bible: New International Version* (Guildford, Surrey; International Bible Society, 1984), Luke 20:25

18  Marva Down, *Powers, Weakness and the Tabernacling of God* (Ill.: Eedrmanns Publishing Co. 2002), p. 83

19  Anthony J. Gettins, *A Presence that Disturbs* (Liguori, Missouri: Liguori Publications, 2002), pp. 94–95

20  John D. Brewer and Gareth I. Higgins, *Anti-Catholicism in Northern Ireland. 1600–1998 the Mote and the Beam* (Basingstoke: Macmillan, 1998) pp. 98 and 101

21  David Ford quoted by Ian Butler, 'Party Conference 2010', *Alliance News*, January–March 2010

22  F. Eugene Scott, *Western Journal of Communication,* 40(4), 1976, pp. 249–259, quoted in www.informaworld.com/index/912228234.pdf

23  Quoted in *Ulster* (Harmondsworth, Middx. Sunday Times Insight Team, 1972), pp.30–31,

24  http://Cain.ulst.ac.uk/hmso/spa1922.htm

25  Terence O'Neill, quoted in http://cain.ulst.co.uk/issues/politics/docs/uup/uup69.htm

26  Denis Loretto, *Alliance, Liberals and the SDP, 1971–1985*, a personal memoir

27  Ibid., *Journal of Liberal Democrat History* 2001–2002, Issue 33, pp. 33–38

28  Personal letter from Sir Oliver Napier, 2009

29  New Ulster Movement, *The Reform of Stormont* (Belfast, June 1971) http://cain.ulst.ac.uk/othelem/organ/num/num71a.htm; New Ulster Movement, *A commentary on the Programme of Reforms for Northern Ireland* (Belfast, August? 1971), August 1971. http://cain.ulst.ac.uk/othelem/organ/num/num71b.htm; New Ulster Movement, *The Way Forward [in Northern Ireland]* (Belfast, November 1971); New Ulster Movement, http://cain.ulst.ac.uk/othelem/organ/num/num71.htm; New Ulster Movement, *New Ulster Movement Annual Report, 1970-71* (Belfast, December 1971) [PDF File; 41KB]; New Ulster Movement, *Northern Ireland and the Common Market* (January 1972); New Ulster Movement, *Two Irelands or One?* (Belfast, May 1972) http://cain.ulst.ac.uk/othelem/organ/num/num72a.htm; New Ulster Movement, http://cain.ulst.ac.uk/othelem/organ/num/num72b.htm; New Ulster Movement, *Violence and Northern Ireland* (Belfast, June 1972) http://cain.ulst.ac.uk/othelem/organ/num/num72b.htm;New Ulster Movement, http://cain.ulst.ac.uk/othelem/organ/num/num72e.htm;New Ulster Movement, *A New Constitution for Northern Ireland* (Belfast,August 1972);New Ulster Movement, *CAIN Politics,* http://cain.ulst.ac.uk/othelem/organ/num/num72d.htm; New Ulster Movement, *New Ulster Movement Annual Report, 1971-72* (Belfast, December? 1972) [PDF File; 44KB]; New Ulster Movement, http://cain.ulst.ac.uk/othelem/organ/num/num221.htm; New Ulster Movement, http://cain.ulst.ac.uk/othelem/organ/num/num71a.htm

30  Many of these papers are accessible through the internet

31  Jim Hendron, *Personal Memoirs*, personal letter, 21 July 2009

32  New Ulster Movement, *The Reform of Stormont*

33  New Ulster Movement, *The Way Forward*

34  New Ulster Movement, *Commentary on the programme of reforms for Northern Ireland*

35  New Ulster Movement, *Two Irelands or One?*

36  New Ulster Movement, *Violence in Northern Ireland*

37  New Ulster Movement, *Tribalism and Christianity* (NUM Publication, 1973)
    (not available on the WEB)

38  Mary Gethins, *Catholic police officers in Northern Ireland – Voices Out of Silence*
    (Manchester: Manchester University Press, 2011), p. 17

39  Quoted by Blair in Introduction to Tony Wright and Matt Carter,
    *The People's Party: The History of the Labour Party*

40  J. McGarry and B. O'Leary, *The Northern Ireland Conflict: Consociational
    Engagements* (Oxford: Oxford University Press, 2004), p. 181

41  Aaron Edwards, *A History of the Northern Ireland Labour Party: Democratic
    Socialism and Sectarianism* (Manchester: Manchester University Press, 2009).

42  blogs.lse.ac.uk/politicsandpolicy/
    book-review-a-history-of-the-northern-Ireland-labour-party

43  Berkley Farr, 'Liberalism in Unionist Northern Ireland 1921–1971', *Journal of
    Liberal Democrat History* 2001–2002, Issue 33, pp. 29–32

44  *Manchester Guardian*, 'Ulster Liberals', 1 March 1928, p. 8

45  ULP Papers, PRONI

46  Gordon Gillespie, *Albert McElroy: the Radical Minister 1915–1945* (Albert
    McElroy memorial Fund, 1985), p. 21

47  Constance Rynder, *Journal of Liberal History* 71 (Summer 2011), p. 16

48  Sir Oliver Napier, Ibid.

49  Denis Loretto, Ibid.

50  Ibid.

51  Jim Hendron, *Personal Memoirs*, 2004.

52  Sir Oliver Napier, Ibid.

53  John Hume, *John Hume: Personal Views: Politics, Peace and Reconciliation in
    Ireland.* (Dublin: Town House and Country House, 1996), p. 13.

54  Ibid., pp. 47–59 and 149–150

55  Denis Loretto, Ibid.

56  NUM Annual Report 1970/1971, http;//cain.ulst.ac.uk/othelem/organ/num/
    num221.htm

57  Electoral Reform Society, www.electoral-reform.org.uk/ers/history.htm
    accessed on 26 May 2003

58  J. Knight and N. Baxter-Moore, *Northern Ireland Elections of the Twenties*
    (The Arthur McDougal Fund, 1972), pp. 13–15

59  Horrowitz, 'The Northern Ireland Agreement: Clear Consociational and
    Risky', pp. 98–100

60  Ibid., pp. 92–95

61  *Alliance News*, February 1975, p. 1

62  Ibid., November 1976, p. 1

63  Ibid., February 1979, p. 8

64  Data was obtained from issues of *Alliance News* over this period

65  Sir Oliver Napier, speech at 40th Anniversary Dinner, Stormont Hotel,
    4 June 2010

66  Nicholas Whyte, www.ark.ac.uk/elections/

67  Quoted in Paul Bew and Gordon Gillespie, *Northern Ireland 1968–1999*:
    *A Chronology of the Troubles* (Dublin: Gill and Macmillan, 1999), p. 71

68  Bew and Gillespie, p. 76.

69  'Ulster Army Council', CAIN website Abstracts of Organisations,
    www.cain.ulster.co.uk

70  Government White Paper on *The Northern Ireland Constitution 1974*,
    http://cain.ulst.ac.uk/hmso/cmd5675.htm

71  David Alexander Butler, www.irishcentral.com

72  Sidney Elliott and William D. Flackes, *Northern Ireland Political Directory,
    1968–2000* (Belfast: Blackstaff Press, 2001), p. 216

73  Bew and Gillespie, p. 216

74  D. Murray, *Worlds Apart: Segregated schools in Northern Ireland* (Belfast; Appletree
    Press, 1985), Introduction

75  Bill Barbour, 'Integrated Education', *Alliance*, September 1973, p. 7; follow-up
    articles in October, p. 7 and a letter from Cecilia Linehan about a workshop
    on integrated education in November, p. 2

76  *Alliance News*, August 1974, p. 2

77  Eric Gallagher and Stanley Worrall, *Christians in Ulster 1968–1980* (Oxford:
    Oxford University Press, 1982), p. 162

78  Patricia Mallon, interviewed by Eggins, 30 May 2003

79  Gallagher and Worrall, *Christians in Ulster,* p. 162 and *Alliance News,* June 1977, p. 8

80  Bew and Gillespie, p. 156

81  NICIE Statement of principles, www.nicie.org/wp-content/
    uploads/2012/08/Statement-of-Principles1.pdf

82  Ian McMorris, chair, Board of Governors, NICIE, Annual Report, 2012–2013

83  Noreen Campbell, *Belfast Telegraph*

84  McMorris, Annual Report, 2012–2013

85  Oliver Napier, interviewed by Eggins, [month?] 2004

86  Nicholas Whyte, www.ark.ac.uk/elections

87  Ibid.

88  James Knight quoted in Nicholas Whyte

89  Ibid.

90  http://cain.ulst.ac.uk/events/assembly1982/summary.htm

91  Sydney Elliott, www.agendani.co/priors-assembly-attempt/

92  Tom Campbell, 'Assembly Report' in *Alliance News,* January 1985, p.8.

93  Cornelious O'Leary, Sydney Elliott and R.A. Wilford, *The Northern Ireland
    Assembly 1982–1986* (London: C Hurst and Co. Publishers, 1988). Extracts in
    htttp://cain.ulst.ac.uk/events/assembly/1982

94  *Alliance News*, 5 (6) (July 1975), p. 6.

95  Sidney Elliot and William D. Flackes, 'Election Results' in *Northern Ireland
    Political Directory, 1968–2000* (Belfast: Blackstaff Press, 2001), pp. 523–604

96  Colin Knox and Padraig Quirk, '"Responsibility Sharing" in Northern Ireland
    Local Government', http://wwww.ccruni.gov.uk/research/uu/knox94.htm

97  *Alliance News*, 4 (10) (July 1974), p. 4

98  Ibid., p. 1

99  Ibid.

100  Ibid., p.7

101  This can be seen in the 'level of education' and 'occupational status' tables in Moxon-Browne's survey comparing Alliance Party supporters with all respondents in Edward Moxon-Browne, *Nation, Class and Creed in Northern Ireland* (Aldershot: Gower Publishing Company, 1983), p. 47

102  McKenna and Melaugh, *The Northern Ireland Conflict Archive*, http://cain.ulst.ac.uk/election/rd1997, accessed on 26 May 2003

103  Bew and Gillespie, p. 342

104  Ibid., p. 366

105  *Alliance News,* (May/August 1999), p. 10

106  McKenna and Melaugh, *The Northern Ireland Conflict Archive*, http://cain.ulst.ac.uk/issues/politics/election/rd2001.htm, accessed on 26 May 2003

107  Philip McGarry thought that Alliance should have acted sooner to facilitate a Sinn Féin Lord Mayor, interviewed by Eggins, 20 June 2003

108  McKenna and Melaugh, *The Northern Ireland Conflict Archive,* http://cain.ulst. ac.uk/events/peace/ira231001.htm, accessed on 26 May 2003

109  'Alliance Backs Sinn Féin for Lord Mayor', *Alliance News* (May/June 2000), p. 2 and 'Maskey is Lord Mayor', *Alliance News* (May/August 2002), pp. 4–5

110  Barry McCaffrey, *Irish News* (3 June 2003), p. 1

111  Life and Times surveys

112  *Alliance News* (July 1977), p. 1

113  *Alliance News* (August 1985), p. 1

114  Northern Ireland Information Service, Birthday Honours List 1998, www. nics.gov.uk/nio/press/1998/, accessed 12 August 2003

115  Elliott and Flackes, *Northern Ireland Political Directory*, p. 207

116  Ibid., p. 155; Bew and Gillespie, p. 332

117  *Alliance News* (December 1985), p. 5

118  *Alliance News* (November 1985), p. 7

119  Northern Ireland Information Service, Birthday Honours List 1999, www.nics.gov.uk/nio/press/1998/, accessed 12 August 2003

120  Bew and Gillespie, p. 179.

121  Ibid. p. 185; http://cain.ulst.ac.uk/issues/politics/nifr.htm).

122  Bew and Gillespie, p. 170

123  John McGarry and Brendan O'Leary 'Consociational Theory, Northern Ireland's Conflict, and its Agreement Part 1: What Consociationalists Can Learn from Northern Ireland', *Government and Opposition*, 41 (2) (2006), pp. 249–277; www.poisci.upenn.edu/ppec/PPEC%people/Brenadn%20/

124  Desmond Fennell, *The Revision of Irish Nationalism* (Dublin; Open Air, 1989), pp. 48–52

125  *Alliance News*, December 1985, pp. 1, 3

126  Bew and Gillespie, pp. 189–194

127  Ibid., p. 199

128  Addie Morrow, personal comments at Alliance Party Council Meeting on
     13 September 2009

129  *Belfast Telegraph*, 1987

130  *The Guardian*, 20 May, 2011

131  Gordon Kennedy, personal discussion February 2014

132  Alliance Party, 'Governing with Consent' (Belfast, 1988)

133  Ibid., Section 3.15, p. 11

134  Ibid., Section 3.16, p. 12

135  Ibid., Section 4.5, p. 17

136  Peter Brooke Speech 1989, *cain.ulst.ac.uk/events/peace/pp8893.htm*

137  Peter Brooke speech 1990, Ibid.

138  Peter Brooke speech 1991, Ibid.

139  Alliance Party, 'Governing with Consent' (1988)

140  UUP change of heart 1 July 1992, cain.ulst.ac.uk/events/peace/pp8893.htm

141  David Ford quoted in Allan Leonard, *The Alliance Party of Northern Ireland and Power
     Sharing in a Divided Society* (MA thesis University College Dublin, 1999), p. 42

142  Gordon Mawhinney, quoted in Leonard thesis 1999, p. 42

143  David Ford, quoted in Leonard thesis p. 43

144  Andy Pollock (ed.), '*A Citizens' Enquiry': The Opsahl Report on Northern
     Ireland* (Dublin: The Lilliput Press and Initiative '92, 1993)

145  Ibid.

146  Laure Laroche, Essay: 'How far did the evolution of the international situation
     influence the peace process in Northern Ireland' (University College Dublin,
     17 October 2008)

147  Breen, Suzanne '"Traitors" — Martin Galvin's Rap for "Sell Out" by Sinn
     Féin', *Sunday World*, 19 June 2011; Jump up 'Republican rebels gain strength',
     *Observer*, 24 June 2000

148  Providing a Leading Voice for Human Rights and Democracy around the
     Globe, TedKennedy.org

149  British and Irish Governments, *Joint Communiqué (1995)*, paragraph 4

150  Ibid., paragraph 5

151  Jeson Ingraham 'The Irish Peace Process';
     http://cain.ulster.ac.uk/events/peace/talks.htm

152  http://Tedkennedy.org/ownwords

153  Hume Adams talks: cain.ulst.ac.uk/events/peace/talks.htm

154  O'Brien (1995), p. 290

155  Jeson Ingraham, '*The Irish Peace Process*', reported in CAIN WEB Service

156  http://en.wikipedia.org/wiki/
     Mitchell_Principles - cite_note-Indep-0#cite_note-Indep-0

157  Alliance Party, 'Governing with Consent' (Belfast: Alliance Party of Northern
     Ireland, 1988)

158  The DUP did not sign as they refused to participate in the negotiations with
     Sinn Féin

159  Allan Leonard, MA thesis, *The Alliance Party of Northern Ireland and Power Sharing in a Divided Society*, (Dublin: University College Dublin, 1999), pp. 50–59

160  Allan Leonard, MA thesis, pp. 53–54

161  Ibid., p. 53

162  Ibid., pp. 54–55

163  Ibid., p. 55

164  Ibid., pp. 55–56

165  Ibid., pp. 56–58

166  Ibid., p. 51

167  *The Agreement*, Strand One, Democratic Institutions in Northern Ireland, paragraphs 5 and 6

168  There was an attempt to modify this situation through a motion passed at an Alliance Party Council Meeting, but it was not accepted; see *Review of Assembly Designation and Voting System* (Belfast: Alliance Party, November 2001)

169  This weighted majority voting of 65% has recently been proposed by the DUP, but vigorously opposed by Sinn Féin

170  Leonard, Ibid., p. 54

171  Henry MacDonald and Patrick Wintour, 'The Long Good Friday', *Observer*, 12 April 1998, www.theguardian.com/uk/1998/apr/12/northernireland

172  McDonald and Lintour

173  Leonard, p. 57.

174  Ibid., p. 56.

175  The Good Friday Agreement, *The Agreement* (Belfast, HM Government, 10 April 1998), www.nio.gov.uk/aghrement.pdf

176  'An Alliance Party Perspective upon the Belfast Agreement', *Fordham International Law Journal*, 22(4) (1999), pp. 1221–1249

177  *The Agreement*, p.36.

178  Bew and Gillespie, pp. 369–370.

179  Elliott and Flackes, p. 155.

180  Nicholas Whyte, www.ark.ac.uk/elections/fa98.atm

181  Elliott and Flackes, p. 156.

182  Martina Purdy, *Room 21 – Stormont Behind Closed Doors* (Belfast; Brehon Press, 2005), p. 24

183  Seamus Close, interviewed by Eggins [date needed]

184  Purdy, Ibid.

185  Tom Kelly, 'Glad to hear Mallon go on the record', *Irish News*, Monday, 31 March 2014, p. 20

186  Eileen Bell, interviewed by Eggins, Stormont, 26 August 2003

187  Eileen Bell, MLA, Press Release, 13 November 2001

188  Eileen Bell, MLA, Press Release 24 September 2002

189  Eileen Bell, interviewed by Eggins, Stormont, 26 August 2003

190  A. Jocelyn, J. Evans and Jonathan Tonge, 'The Future of the radical centre in Northern Ireland after the Good Friday Agreement', *Political Studies*, Vol. 51 (2003), pp. 26–50, A Survey of Alliance Party members, 2001

191  Martina Purdy, *Room 21 Stormont Behind Closed Doors* (Belfast; The Brehon Press, 2005), p. 67

192  Stephen Farry and Seán Neeson, 'Beyond the 'band-aid' approach: An Alliance Party Perspective upon the Belfast Agreement', *Fordham International Law Journal*, 22(4) (1999), pp. 1221–1249

193  Colin Irwin, 'In Search of a Settlement: Summary Tables of Principal Statistical Results', 11-12 January 1998 (unpublished opinion poll on file with the *Fordham International Law Journal*)

194  John Whyte, personal opinion quoted in John Doyle, *Policing the Narrow Ground* (Dublin; Royal Irish Academy, 2010), p. 181

195  Timothy D. Sisk, *Power Sharing and International Mediation in Ethnic Conflicts* (1996). See Paul Dixon, 'Consociationalism and the Northern Ireland Peace Process: The Glass Half Full or Half Empty?' 3 *Nationalism and Ethnic Politics*, 23 (1997)

196  T. Fennell, *The Royal Irish Constabulary: A History and Personal Memoir* (Dublin: University College Dublin Press, 2003)

197  Mary Gethins, *Catholic Police Officers in Northern Ireland – Voices out of Silence* (Manchester; Manchester University Press, 2011), p. 17

198  *Alliance Party Principles*: 'The fourth principle is "universal respect for the law". We firmly believe that without universal respect for the law of the land and the authorities appointed to enforce it, there can be no measurable progress. We, therefore, intend to secure the rapid achievement of such respect and the absolutely equal enforcement of the law without fear or favour, in every part of the state. Equal justice will be guaranteed to all citizens regardless of their political or religious persuasion'

199  *Alliance News*, September 1984. Quoted in John Doyle (ed.), *Policing the Narrow Ground – Lessons from the transformation of policing in Northern Ireland* (Dublin, Royal Irish Academy, 2010), p. 180

200  Gethins, p. 22.

201  *Alliance News*, December 1974; Doyle, pp. 177 and 205

202  Ibid, March 1980

203  Ibid, May 1982

204  D.J. Cushnahan, *Northern Ireland Assembly*, Vol. 16, 29 June 1983, p. 1024; Doyle, p. 205

205. *Alliance News*, May 1986 and May 1987; Doyle, p. 205

206  *Sunday Tribune*, 10 May 1987; Doyle, p. 205

207  *Alliance News*, January 1987; Doyle, p. 177

208  John Alderdice, *Irish Times*, 10 January 1995; Doyle, p. 187

209  *Alliance Party of Northern Ireland Election Manifesto* (Belfast; APNI, 1997)

210  Alliance Party, *Continuity and change: an Alliance Party submission to the Committee on Policing*, 15 October 1998; Doyle, p. 187

211  *The Agreement* (Northern Ireland Office 1998), p. 22

212  Robert McGinty, 'Policing and the NI Peace Process' in John P Harrington (ed.), *Politics and Performance in NI* (Amhurst, Mass. University of Massachusets Press, American Congress of Irish Studies, 1999), p. 110

213  *Alliance News*, September/October 1999

214  Ibid., November/December 1999

215  Ibid., January/February 2000

216  Reported in 'Alliance Action on the Police Bill', *Alliance News*, July/
     August 2000, p. 6

217  Martina Purdy, *Room 21, Stormont – Behind Closed* Doors (Belfast: The Brehon
     Press, 2005), pp. 70, 71

218  Mo Mowlam, *Momentum: The Struggle for Peace, Politics and the People* (London:
     Hodder and Stoughton, 2002)

219  http://en.wikipedia.org/wiki/David_Ford

220  Seamus Close, interviewed by Eggins, 24 June 2003, verbatim from tape recording

221  Martina Purdy, p. 301

222  Evans and Tonge

223  Evans and Tonge

224  Arendt Lijphart, *British Journal of Political Science*, 5 (1975), pp. 83, 106

225  John McGarry and Brendan O'Leary, 'Consociational Theory, Northern
     Ireland's Conflict, and its Agreement Part 1: What Consociationalists Can
     Learn from Northern Ireland', *Government and Opposition*, 41 (2) (2006),
     pp. 249–277; www.poisci.upenn.edu/ppec/PPEC%people/Brenadn%20/

226  Ibid.

227  Ian Paisley, *The Revivalist*, April 1981, quoted in David Gordon, *The Fall of the
     House of Paisley* (Dublin, Gill and Macmillan, 2010, p. 23

228  Alliance Party, *A Review of the Assembly Designations and Voting Systems*,
     November 2002

229  Philip McGarry, *The President's Review* (Alliance Party, December 1998)

230  Alliance Party Council Minutes, June 1998

231  *The Alliance Party's Strategic Plan 2000–2002* (Alliance Party, June 1999)

232  Alliance Party, *Building a United Community*, January 2003

233  A. Jocelyn, J. Evans and Jonathan Tonge, 'The Future of the radical centre in
     Northern Ireland after the Good Friday Agreement', *Political Studies*, Vol. 51
     (2003), pp. 26–50, A Survey of Alliance Party members, 2001

234  Stephen Martin, *Alliance News*, November 2007–January 2008, p. 8

235  St Andrews Agreement, www.nio.gov.uk/st_andrews_agreement.pdf

236  David Ford, *The St Andrews Agreement*, nistandrewsbill161106.pdf

237  S. Bruce, *Paisley* (Oxford; Oxford University Press, 2007); Quoted in John
     D. Brewer, Gareth Higgins and Francis Teeney, *Religion, Civil Society and Peace
     in Northern Ireland*, (Oxford; Oxford University press, 2011), p. 78

238  Northern Ireland Official Report, 12 November 2007, quoted in David Morgan,
     *The Fall of the House of Paisley* (Dublin, Gill and Macmillan, 2010), p. 111

239  Ibid., Chapter 12; *Surprise in Dromore*, pp.169–181

240  Ibid., p. 187

241  Ibid., p. 206

242  John D. Brewer and Gareth Higgins, *Anti-Catholicism in Northern Ireland 1600–1998:
     the Mote and the Beam* (Basingstoke, Hants: Macmillan, 1998), pp. 108–115

243 Alliance Party, *Building a United Community* (Alliance Party, January 2003)

244 *A Shared Future – a Consultation Paper on Improving Relations in Northern Ireland* (Community Relations Unit, OFMDFM, 2003)

245 Northern Ireland Office, *Devolving Policing and Justice in Northern Ireland: A Discussion Paper* (Belfast: Northern Ireland Office, 2005)

246 *Road Map for Devolution of Policing and Justice:* www.nio.gov.uk/devolution_doc_pdf.pdf

247 The Patten Report: Independent Commission on Policing for Northern Ireland, a New Beginning; Policing in Northern Ireland: the Report of the Independent Commission on Policing for Northern Ireland (Belfast: HMSO, 1999)

248 Liam Clarke, 'Devolved policing is best way out of mess: policing needs the long arm of Alliance', *Sunday Times*, 2008

249 *www.belfasttelegraph.co.uk/…away…shared-future-plans-16163206.html*

250 David Ford, 'Alliance Says No?', *Alliance News,* July–August 2008, p. 3

251 Alliance Party, *Alliance Party Proposals for a Programme for Policing and Justice*, http://www.allianceparty.org/pages/justice.html (8 February 2010)

252 Quoted in Mary Gethins, Ibid., p. 218

253 allianceparty.org/document/latest/alliance-response-to-ni-draft…

254 www.community-relations.org.uk/fs/doc/CRC_Submission_to_CSI.pdf

255 Revd Dr Norman Hamilton, Address to Newry District Inter-Church Forum Inaugural Meeting, Sean Holywood Arts Centre, Newry, 21 November 2010

256 www.wikepedia.org/wiki/John_Larkin_(Northern_ Ireland)

257 James McClure, *Alliance News*, April–September 2010, pp. 4–5

258 Gordon Kennedy, personal discussion 27 February 2014

259 http://cain.ulst.ac.uk/issues/identity/flag-2012.htm

260 Naomi Long, 'Compromise will be necessary', Special Feature article, *Alliance News*, October-December 2013, pp. 20–22

261 Stephen Farry and Seán Neeson, 'Beyond the 'band-aid' approach. An Alliance Party Perspective upon the Belfast Agreement', *Fordham International Law Journal*, 22(4) (1999), pp. 1221–1249

262 Alliance Party, *For Everyone*, February 2014.

263 Alliance Party, *Briefing for Party Members on the Haass Talks and their outcome*, 2014

264 www.northernireland.gov.uk/haass.pdf

265 www.bbc.co.uk/news/events/vote2014/ni-council-election-results

266 Sam McBride Political Correspondent, *Belfast Newsletter, 26th May, 2014 Newsletter Election Special*

267 Nicholas Whyte, http://sluggerotoole.com/2014/04/06/the-11-new-district-councils/

268 Jim Hendron, personal conversation, May 2014

269 John Manley, interview with Anna Lo MLA, *Irish News*, 20 March 2014

270 Ibid.

271 Alliance Party Conference, 2014

272 *Belfast Telegraph*, April 2014

273  Alliance Party, 'Statement of Principles upon which the Alliance Party was founded on April 21 1970' in *Constitution and Rules* (1970), p. 20

274  Alliance Party, *Members Questionnaire: Council Report* (Belfast: Alliance Party, 1998)

275  Alliance Party, *Alliance Party of Northern Ireland Constitution and Rules,* as amended December 2001

276  Alliance Party, *Policy Handbook,* September 1991

277  Alliance Party, *Alliance Party Manifesto: Assembly Election 2011*

278  http://allianceparty.org/document/manifesto Manifesto Summary, Assembly Election 2011

279  Ibid., Local Government 2014 Manifesto

280  Ibid., European Manifesto 2014

281  Alliance Party, *Alliance Policy Summaries,* June 2006

282  http://allianceparty.org/

283  See for example in Chapter 3

284  http:/www.asharedfutureni.gov.uk/

285  Farry and Neeson article and review proposals

286  Quoted in, *Party Council Document on Same Sex Civil Marriage;* Alliance Party, 9 June 2012

287  Quoted in, Party Council Document on Same Sex Civil Marriage; Alliance Party, 9 June 2012.

288  Commissioner for Human Rights

289  Alliance Party, *Alliance Policy Summaries,* June 2006

290  Life and Times Survey

291  www.dhsspsni.gov.uk/transforming-your-care-review-of-hsc-ni-final-report.pdf

292  Phelim O'Neill, en.wikipedia.org/wiki/Phelim_O'Neill,_2nd_Baron_Rathcavan

293  Sir Oliver Napier, en.wikipedia.org/wiki/Oliver_Napier

294  Sir Oliver Napier, www.absoluteastronomy.com/topics/Oliver_Napier

295  John Cushnahan, en.wikipedia.org/wiki/John_Cushnahan

296  Lord John Alderdice, www.parliament.uk/biographies/john-alderdice/26850

297  Fergus Pyle, *Irish Times,* 5 October 1987.

298  Mo Mowlam, *Momentum, The struggle for Peace, Politics and the People* (London; Hodder and Stoughton, 2002), pp. 145, 146

299  http://archive.niassembly.gov.uk/members/biogs_03/neeson_s.htm

300  www.belfasttelegraph.co.uk/news/politics/exalliance-chief-sean-neeson-bows-out-after-36-years-29553474.html

301  Stephen Farry and Seán Neeson, *Beyond the 'band-aid' approach. An Alliance Party Perspective upon the Belfast Agreement,* Fordham International Law Journal, 22(4) 1999, pp.1221 – 1249

302  David Ford, en.wikipedia.org/wiki/David_Ford

303  David Ford, www.davidford.org

304  Sir Robert Cooper, en.wikipedia.org/wiki/Bob_Cooper_(politician)

305  Sir Robert Cooper, www.belfasttelegraph.co.uk/imported/

obituary-sir-robert-bob-cooper-13682092.html

306  Basil Glass, en.wikipedia.org/wiki/Basil_Glass

307  Basil Glass memorial service, Lisburn Methodist Church in 2005

308  David Cook, en.wikipedia.org/wiki/David_Cook_(politician)

309  Robert McGinty, 'Policing and the NI Peace Process' in John P. Harrington
     (ed.) *Politics and Performance in NI* (Amhurst, Mass. University of Massachusets
     Press, American Congress of Irish Studies, 1999) p.110,

310  Addie Morrow, en.wikipedia.org/wiki/Addie_Morrow

311  Gordon Mawhinney, en.wikipedia.org/wiki/Gordon_Mawhinney

312  Seamus Close, en.wikipedia.org/wiki/Seamus_Close

313  Eileen Bell, en.wikipedia.org/wiki/Eileen_Bell

314  Naomi Long, news.bbc.co.uk/2/hi/uk_news/northern_ireland/8666703.stm

315  http://allianceparty.org/contact/belfast-east-naomi-long-mp

316  Naomi Long, www.naomilong.com

317  Ibid.

318  H.W. Fowler and F.G. Fowler (eds), *The Concise Oxford Dictionary* (Oxford:
     The Clarendon Press, 1958), p. 1015

319  Based on Byron Bland's definition in Revd Byron Bland, 'The Post-troubles
     Troubles: The Politics of Reconciliation in Northern Ireland', unpublished
     paper, 2001

320  Joe Liechty, ISE Lecture, 'Theology and Dynamics of Reconciliation', session
     IV, 24 October 2001

321  Ibid.

322  For example, 2 Corinthians 5: 17–19 (all Biblical quotations are taken from
     the *The Holy Bible. New International Version* (London: Hodder and Stoughton
     1988))

323  John D'Arcy May, 'A Rationale for Reconciliation', *Uniting Church Studies,* 7
     (1) (2001), pp. 1-13.

324  Wilhelm J. Verwoerd, 'Towards the Truth about the TRC: A Response
     to Key Moral Criticisms of the South African Truth and Reconciliation
     Commission', *Religion and Theology,* 6 (1999), pp. 303–324.

325  Joe Liechty and Cecelia Clegg, *Moving Beyond Sectarianism* (Dublin: Columba
     Press, 2001), p. 158.

326  Alliance Party of Northern Ireland, 'Statement of Principles upon which the
     Alliance Party was founded on April 21, 1970' in *Alliance Party Constitution
     and Rules* (Belfast: Alliance Party of Northern Ireland, 1970, revised 1974 and
     1995), p. 20

327  William A McComish, 'Christianity and Alliance', *Alliance News* (July 1972), p. 5

328  *Alliance News* (October 1979), pp. 1, 3

329  'Address of Pope John Paul II at Drogheda, 29 September 1979' in *The Pope
     in Ireland – Addresses and Homilies* (Dublin: Veritas, 1979), pp. 16–25

330  Ibid., p. 23

331  Charles Kinahan, 'Letter to editor', *Alliance News* (May 1984), p. 5.

332  Alliance Party, *Building a United Community*, p. 10

333  Gillian Robinson, *Northern Ireland Social Attitudes Survey 1989–1996* (Belfast:
     CCRU, 1998), www.ccruni.gov.uk/research/nisas/robinson.htm, quoted in
     *Building a United Community*, p. 10

334  Alliance Party, *Building a United Community*, p. 12

335  Addie Morrow, interviewed by Eggins, 30 May 2003

336  McComish, 'Christianity and Alliance', *Alliance News* (May 1984), p. 5

337  Liechty, ISE Lecture, 'Theology and Dynamics of Reconciliation', session IV,
     24 October 2001

338  Whitley Stokes, *Projects for Re-establishing the Internal Peace and Tranquillity
     of Ireland* (Dublin, 1799), p. 44, quoted in Joe Liechty, 'History and
     Reconciliation: Frank Wright, Whitley Stokes, and the Vortex of Antagonism'
     in Alan D. Falconer and Joe Liechty, *Reconciling Memories*, (Dublin: Columba
     Press, 2nd edition 1998), p. 160

339  Belfast City Council, www.belfastcity.gov.uk/alexmaskey.htm, accessed on
     3 June 2003

340  Addie Morrow confirmed that there had been a small number of resignations
     from the party over this issue (Addie Morrow interviewed by Eggins,
     30 May 2003)

341  Referring to the Enniskillen Remembrance Day Bomb, Martin McGuinness
     admitted that 'they [Unionists] have been hurt by me and they have been hurt
     by republicans down the years. There is no question … it is time to bring it all
     to an end', Radio 5 interview reported in *Sunday Times* (5 August 2001)

342  'IRA Statement of May 6' *Irish News* (7 May 2003), p. 6

343  Alliance Party, 'Statement of Principles', p. 20

344  David Ford, 'Party Leader's Speech to Conference 2003', *Alliance* (March and
     April 2003), pp. 8–9

345  *The Agreement* (Belfast: The Governments of the United Kingdom and
     Northern Ireland of Ireland, 1998), p. 25

346  *A Truth Commission for Northern Ireland?* ITV 'Insight' programme, 11 April 2002

347  'You will know them by their fruits', Matthew 7: 20

348  Liechty, ISE Lecture, 'Theology and Dynamics of Reconciliation', session IV,
     24 October 2001

349  John Paul Lederach, *Building Peace*, xvi

350  Eric Gallagher and Stanley Worrall, *Christians in Ulster 1968–1980*
     (Oxford: Oxford University Press, 1982), pp. 177–181

351  Lederach, *Building Peace*, p. xvi

352  Frank Wright, 'Reconciling the Histories of Protestants and Catholics in
     Northern Ireland' in Falconer, Alan D., and Liechty, Joe, *Reconciling Memories*
     (Dublin: Columba Press, 2nd edition 1998), p. 136

353  Alliance Party, *Statement of principles*, p. 20

354  Ibid. p. 20

355  Alliance Party, *Members Questionnaire – Council Report* (1998)

356  Liechty and Clegg, 'What is Sectarianism? A working definition', in *Moving
     Beyond Sectarianism*, pp. 102–147

357  Allan Leonard, *The Alliance Party of Northern Ireland and Power Sharing in a Divided Society* (MA thesis: University College Dublin, 1999), p. 1

358  Liechty and Clegg, pp. 149–150

359  Seán Neeson, *Alliance News* (September/November 1998)

360  Alliance Party, *Community Relations*, p. 5

361  Ibid.

362  Ibid.

363  Leichty and Clegg, pp. 28–29

364  Ibid., pp. 24–26

365  Addie Morrow, interviewed by Eggins, 30 May 2003

366  Leichty and Clegg, pp. 24–26

367  Ibid.

368  An example in August 2003 is that two Alliance Councillors had windows broken because they publicly opposed sectarian paramilitary flags and emblems see Stephen Farry, 'Blowing in the Wind – the search for an answer to flags', *Alliance News* (July/August 2003), pp. 4–5

369  Ibid., Editorial, p. 2

370  Burch, Samuel and Reynolds, Gerry (eds), *John Wesley: A Letter to a Roman Catholic* (Belfast: Cornerstone Community and Clonard Monastery, 1987), p. 8

371  Alliance Party, 'Statement of Principles', p. 20

372  G. Evans and M. Duffy, 'Beyond the Sectarian Divide: The Social Bases and Political Consequences of Nationalist and Unionist Party Competition in Northern Ireland', *British Journal of Political Science*, 27 (1997) pp. 47–81, Quoted in Michael Keating, 'Northern Ireland and the Basque Country' in John McGarry (ed.), *Northern Ireland and the Divided World* (Oxford: Oxford University Press, 2001), p. 189

373  Edward Moxon-Browne, *Nation, Class and Creed in Northern Ireland* (Aldershot, Hants: Gower Publishing Company Ltd, 1983), p.65

374  Conflict Archive on the Internet Project, http://cain.ulst.ac.uk/ni/popul.htm#cath

375  Evans and Duffy, G. Evans and M. Duffy, 'Beyond the Sectarian Divide: The Social Bases and Political Consequences of Nationalist and Unionist Party Competition in Northern Ireland', *British Journal of Political Science*, 27 (1997), pp. 47–81

376  Brian Eggins, 'The Territorial Heresy', unpublished essay as contribution to ISE Reconciliation Studies Course

377  Hans Kung, *The Catholic Church* (London: Phoenix Press, 2001), p. 42

378  www.ons.gov.uk/ons/guide-method/census/2011/census-data/2001-census-data/index.html

379  Seamus Close, interviewed by Eggins, 24 June 2003

380  Fionnuala McKenna and Martin Melaugh, 'The Northern Ireland Conflict Archive', http://cain.ulst.ac.uk/election/ra1973, accessed on 26 May 2003

381  Ibid., http://cain.ulst.ac.uk/election/rcc1975, accessed on 26 May 2003

382  Ibid., http://cain.ulst.ac.uk/election/ra1982, accessed on 26 May 2003

383  Elliott and Flackes, *Northern Ireland Political Directory*, pp. 266–267

384  Seamus Close, interviewed by Eggins, 24 June 2003; Philip McGarry,

interviewed by Eggins, 20 June 2003

385  Joe Liechty, 'Religion and Conflict: The Work of Marc Gopin', ISE Lecture
     notes 12 February 2003

386  Fergus Pyle, *Irish Times*, 5 October 1987

387  Liechty, 'Religion and Conflict', 12 February 2003, p. 1

388  Ibid.

389  Marc Gopin, 'Alternative Global Futures in the Balance' in *Between Eden and
     Armageddon: The Future of World Religions, Violence and Peacemaking* (New York:
     Oxford University Press, 2000), p. 4

390  Ibid.

391  Ibid., p. 7

392  Joe Liechty, ISE Lecture notes, 'Conflict and Corporate Identity' session 3,
     Belfast, 22 January 2003, 1

393  George Schöpflin, 'Civil Society, Ethnicity and the State: a threefold
     relationship', Paper delivered to Conference, 'Civil Society in Austria', Vienna,
     20–21 June 1997, www.ssees.ac.uk/index.htm, accessed on 14 August 2003

394  Schöpflin, 'Civil Society, Ethnicity and the State', www.ssees.ac.uk/index.htm,
     accessed on 17 August 2003

395  Frank Wright, *Northern Ireland: A Comparative Analysis* (Dublin: Gill and
     McMillan, 1987), pp. 1–20

396  Alliance Party of Northern Ireland, 'Statement of Principles upon which the
     Alliance Party was founded on April 21 1970' in *Alliance Party of Northern
     Ireland: Constitution and Rules* (Belfast: Alliance Part, 1970), p. 20

397  Alliance Party, *Submission to the International Body on Decommissioning* (Belfast:
     Alliance Party Headquarters, December 1995), p. 3, quoted in Kirsten
     E. Schulze, 'Northern Ireland and Lebanon' in McGarry (ed.), *Northern Ireland
     and the Divided World*, pp. 259–260

398  Allan Leonard, MA thesis, p. 53

399  Schöpflin, 'Civil Society, Ethnicity and the State', www.ssees.ac.uk/index.htm,
     accessed on 14 August 2003

400  René Girard, *Violence and the Sacred* (Baltimore and London, 1981), pp. 13–25,
     quoted from Wright, *Northern Ireland: A Comparative Analysis*, pp. 20–22

401  Frank Wright, 'Reconciling Memories' in Alan D. Falconer and Joe Liechty
     (eds), *Reconciling Memories* (Dublin: Columba Press, 2nd edition, 1998), p. 131,
     quoted in Liechty 'Conflict and Corporate Identity' session 3, 7

402  Wright, *Northern Ireland: A Comparative Analysis*, p. 121

403  Liechty, 'Conflict and Corporate Identity', session 3, 5

404  Wright *Northern Ireland: A Comparative Analysis*, p. 20

405  Liechty, 'Conflict and Corporate Identity', session 3, 9

406  Wright, 'Reconciling Memories', p. 133, quoted in Liechty, 'Conflict and
     Corporate Identity' session 3, 8

407  Frantz Fanon, *The Wretched of the Earth* (trans. by Constance Farrington)
     (New York: Grove Press, 1963), p. 41, quoted by Liechty, 'Conflict and
     Corporate Identity' session 3, 8

408  Eric Gallagher, and Stanley Worrall, *Christians in Ulster 1968–1980*
     (Oxford: Oxford University Press, 1982), pp. 24–26

409  *The Confession of Faith* (Belfast: Graham and Heslip, 1933), p. 204

410  Karen Trew and Cate Cox, 'Dimensions of Social Identity in Northern
     Ireland', www.ccruni.gov.uk/research/qub/trew95.htm, accessed on
     24 July 2003

411  Trew and Cox's analysis investigates the 'Strength of attachment to the
     most popular identities' using five indices. I have quoted briefly from their
     results for 'Identity salience' (importance of that identity) and 'Cognitive
     commitment' (Degree of feeling rewarded)

412  Ibid., pp. 67–69

413  Richard Rose, *Governing Without Consensus: an Irish Perspective* (London: Faber
     and Faber, 1971), p. 208, quoted in Whyte, Interpreting Northern Ireland, p. 67

414  Edward Moxon-Browne, *Nation, Class and Creed in Northern Ireland*
     (Aldershot: Gower Publishing Company, 1983), p. 6, quoted in Whyte,
     Interpreting Northern Ireland, p. 68

415  David J. Smith, personal communication quoted in Whyte, I*nterpreting
     Northern Ireland*, p. 69

416  BBC Radio Ulster 'Talk Back', 19 August 2003

417  John Whyte, *Interpreting Northern Ireland* (Oxford: Oxford University Press,
     2001), pp. 67–71

418  Leonard, MA Thesis, pp. 22–26; Alliance Party, *Community Relations: Building a
     United Community* (Belfast: Alliance Party, 2003), pp. 9, 13–14

419  John Whyte, Ibid

420  Rupert Taylor, 'Consociation or Social Transformation' in John McGarry (ed.),
     *Northern Ireland and the Divided World*, pp. 41–46

421  Taylor, 'Consociation or Social Transformation', p. 41

422  'An Alliance Party Perspective upon the Belfast Agreement', *Fordham
     International Law Journal*, 22(4) (1999), pp. 1221–1249

423  T. Hadden, C. Irwin and F. Boal, 'Separation or Sharing? The People's Choice',
     *Fortnight* (December 1996), p. 356 Supplement; John Darby, *Northern Ireland:
     Managing Difference* (London: Minority Right Group, 1995), p. 5, quoted by
     Taylor, 'Consociation or Social Transformation', p. 43

424  John Whyte, 'Dynamics of Social and political Change in Northern Ireland' in
     D. Keogh and M.H. Haltzel (eds), *Northern Ireland and the Politics of Reconciliation*
     (Cambridge: Woodrow Wilson Center Press and Cambridge University Press,
     1993), quoted by Taylor, 'Consociation or Social Transformation', p. 43

425  A Gallagher, 'Dealing with Conflict: Schools in Northern Ireland',
     *Multicultural Teaching*, 13(3) (1994), p. 13, quoted by Taylor, 'Consociation or
     Social Transformation', p. 43

426  At the time of writing there are now sixty-two integrated schools

427  Andy Pollak, *A Citizen's Inquiry: The Opshal Report on Northern Ireland*
     (Dublin: the Lilliput Press, 1993)

428  Taylor, 'Consociation or Social Transformation', pp. 43–45

429  John McGarry, 'Northern Ireland, Civic Nationalism, and the Good Friday Agreement', in John McGarry, John (ed.), *Northern Ireland and the Divided World – Post-Agreement Northern Ireland in Comparative Perspective* (Oxford: Oxford University Press, 2001), pp. 109–136

430  This resembles John Paul Lederach's comment see footnote 64

431  McGarry, 'Civic Nationalism and the Agreement', in John McGarry (ed.), *Northern Ireland and the Divided World,* pp. 109–136

432  Seán Neeson, *Alliance News* (September-November 1998), pp. 4–5

433  Jack Smith, *Alliance News* (September 1972), p. 7; Allan Leonard, *The Alliance Party of Northern Ireland and Power Sharing in a Divided Society* (MA thesis: University College Dublin, 1999), p. 33

434  Paul Bew and Gordon Gillespie, p. 151

435  ibid., pp. 166–167

436  Edward Moxon-Browne, 'Queen's University Group Survey 1979', quoted in Denis Barritt, *Northern Ireland: A Problem to Every Solution* (London: Quaker Peace and Service, 1982), 132

437  John Whyte, *Interpreting Northern Ireland* (Oxford: Clarendon Press, 1990), Figure 10.1, p. 5

438  Brian R. Eggins, MPhil Dissertation, 2003, pp. 5–16

439  Frank Wright, *Northern Ireland: A Comparative Analysis* (Dublin: Gill and Macmillan, 1987), pp. 244 and 246

440  Bew and Gillespie, p. 197

441  Ibid. pp. 208 and 273

442  *The Concise Oxford English Dictionary* (Oxford: Clarendon Press, 1995), p. 1104.

443  Philip McGarry interviewed by Eggins, 20 June 2003

444  Alliance Party, 'Governing with Consent' (Belfast: Alliance Party, 1988)

445  Donald L. Horowitz, 'The Northern Ireland Agreement: Clear Consociational and Risky' in John McGarry, *Northern Ireland and the Divided World* (Oxford: Oxford University Press, 2001), p. 102

446  Philip McGarry, interviewed by Eggins, 20 June 2003

447  Fionnuala McKenna and Martin Melaugh, *The Northern Ireland Conflict Archive,* http://cain.ulst.ac.uk/issues/politics/election/ra1998.hm, accessed 30 May 2003

448  Fionnuala McKenna and Martin Melaugh, *The Northern Ireland Conflict Archive,* http://cain.ulst.ac.uk/issues/politics/election/re1999.htm, accessed on 30 May 2003

449  Fionnuala McKenna and Martin Melaugh, *The Northern Ireland Conflict Archive,* http://cain.ulst.ac.uk/issues/politics/election/rd2001.htm, accessed on 30 May 2003

450  Fionnuala McKenna and Martin Melaugh, *The Northern Ireland Conflict Archive,* http://cain.ulst.ac.uk/issues/politics/election/ra1998.htm, accessed on 30 May 2003

451  Remy Horton, 2002, d'Hondt PR calculator, www.compulink. co.uk/~broadway/pr95/, accessed on 16 July 2003. Sidney Elliott, 'The d'Hondt System Explained' (BBC News Online: Events: Northern Ireland: Focus, 28 November 1999),

http://news.bbc.co.uk/1/low/northern_ireland/accessed on 16 July 2003.

452   Bew and Gillespie, *A Chronology of the Troubles*, p. 332

453   McKenna and Melaugh, *Ibid.* http://cain.ulst.ac.uk/issues/politics/election/
rw1992.htm, accessed on 25 May 2003

454   Brendan O'Leary, 'The British-Irish Agreement' in John McGarry (ed.),
*Northern Ireland and the Divided World*, p. 74

455   Edward Moxon-Browne, *Nation, Class and Creed in Northern Ireland*
(Aldershot: Gower Publishing Company, 1983), p. 67

456   Wright, *Northern Ireland: A Comparative Analysis*, p. 246

457   Brian Eggins, MPhil Dissertation, 2003, pp. 5-16

458   Pauline Noblett, Secretary of Jordanstown Alliance Branch, at a branch
committee meeting in 1998

459   John Whyte, *Interpreting Northern Ireland* (Oxford: Clarendon Press, 1990),
pp. 21–22, 73

460   Allan Leonard, MA thesis, *The Alliance Party of Northern Ireland and Power
Sharing in a Divided Society*, (Dublin: University College Dublin, 1999), pp. 1,
22–26; Philip McGarry, *The President's Review* (Belfast: The Alliance Party,
1998), p. 21

461   Alliance Party, 'Submission to the International Body on Decommissioning'
(Belfast: Alliance Party Headquarters, December 1995), 3 quoted in Kirsten
E. Schulze, 'Northern Ireland and Lebanon' in John McGarry (ed.), *Northern
Ireland and the Divided World*, pp. 259–260

462   Wright, *Northern Ireland: A Comparative Analysis*, p. 242.

463   Bew and Gillespie, *A Chronology of the Troubles*, p. 136.

464   McKenna and Melaugh, *The Northern Ireland Conflict*, www.cain.ulst.ac.uk/
election/rw1974.http, accessed on 30 May 2003

465   Philip McGarry, interviewed by Eggins, 20 June 2003

466   Addie Morrow, interviewed by Eggins, 30 May 2003 and Seamus Close,
interviewed by Eggins, 24 June 2003

467   Leonard, Thesis, pp. 21–31

468   Alliance Party, *Review of Assembly Designation and Voting System*, (Belfast:
Alliance Party, November 2001), pp. 6–8

469   Oliver Napier 1977 quoted in Leonard, Thesis, p. 24

470   Addie Morrow, interviewed by Eggins, Belfast, 30 May 2003

471   Des Keenan, *Alliance News* (1977) quoted in Leonard, MA thesis, p. 25

472   Leonard, Thesis, p. 31

473   Ibid. p. 51

474   Donald Horowitz, 'The Agreement: Consociational, Risky' in John McGarry
(ed.), *Northern Ireland and the Divided World – Post-Agreement Northern Ireland
in Comparative Perspective* (Oxford: Oxford University Press, 2001), p. 9

475   Leonard, Thesis, pp. 21–31

476   Elliott and Flackes, *Northern Ireland Political Directory*, p. 1

477   Ed Moloney and Andy Pollock, *Paisley* (Swords, County Dublin: Poolbeg
Press Ltd, 1986), pp. 134–135

478  Eamon Maillie and David McKittrick, *Endgame in Ireland* (London: Hodder and Stoughton, 2001), p. 250 (one reference to Lord Alderdice)

479  John Whyte, *Interpreting Northern Ireland* (Oxford: Oxford University Press, 1990) (twelve references to Alliance)

480  McGarry, John (ed.), *Northern Ireland and the Divided World – Post-Agreement Northern Ireland in Comparative Perspective* (Oxford: Oxford University Press, 2001) (fifteen references to Alliance)

481  Wright, *Northern Ireland: A Comparative Analysis*, pp. 155, 237, 242–250

482  BBC TV, *Hearts and Minds*, 7.30 p.m., 29 May 2003

483  Bew and Gillespie, *A Chronology of the Troubles*, pp. 114, 116–117, 125

484  Alliance Party deputy leader Eileen Bell deposited a folder of about 115 press releases issued in 1999–2000 in the Linen Hall Library. Alliance Press Officer Stephen Alexander gave me a CD-ROM containing fifteen to twenty press releases per month with a total of 324 in 2001

485  For example in the *South Belfast News* (23 August 2003) Alliance Councillor and Assembly candidate, Geraldine Rice has three articles: one a 'Political Platform' about Planners (with a photograph), one about cars involved in robberies (with another photograph) and one about speeding. In addition Alliance Councillor Michael Long has a piece about the Robinson Leisure Centre (with a photograph)

486  Frank Wright, 'Reconciling the Histories of Protestant and Catholic in Northern Ireland' in Joe Liechty and Allan Falconer (eds), *Reconciling Memories* (Blackrock, Co Dublin: The Columba Press, 2nd Edition 1998), pp. 128–148

487  Joe Liechty 'History and Reconciliation', in Alan D. Falconer and Joe Liechty (eds), *Reconciling Memories* (Dublin: Columba Press, 2nd edition 1998), pp. 152–163

488  Rex Cathcart, *The Most Contrary Region: The BBC in Northern Ireland 1924–1984* (Belfast: Blackstaff, 1984), p. 263, quoted in John Whyte, *Interpreting Northern Ireland* (Oxford: Clarendon Press, 1990), p. 123

489  Eggins, MPhil Dissertation, 2003

490  Joe Liechty and Cecelia Clegg, *Moving Beyond Sectarianism – Religion, Conflict, and Reconciliation in Northern Ireland* (Dublin: Columba Press, 2001)

491  Yvonne Naylor, *Moving Beyond Sectarianism: A Resource for Young Adults* (Belfast: Irish School of Ecumenics, 2001); Craig Sands, *Moving Beyond Sectarianism: A Resource for Adult Education* (Belfast: Irish School of Ecumenics, 2001); Yvonne Naylor, *Who We Are: Dealing with Difference* (Belfast: Irish School of Ecumenics, 2003)

492  Lederach, *Building Peace*

493  Ibid., p. xvi

494  Alliance Party, *Principles*, p. 20

495  Ibid.

496  For example until 2001 Alliance had councillors representing Lagan Bank in South Belfast and Pottinger in East Belfast. Sinn Féin has gained seats in both areas displacing Alliance

497 For example, the party declined to participate in the *New Ireland Forum* in 1983, *Alliance News* (December 1983), p. 3

498 Phillip McGarry, interviewed by Eggins, 20 June 2003

499 Revd Timothy Kinahan, interviewed by Eggins, Belfast, 1 September 2003

500 Liechty and Clegg, *Moving Beyond Sectarianism*

501 John Paul Lederach, *Building Peace – Sustainable Reconciliation in Divided Societies* (Washington DC: United States Institute of Peace Press, 1997), p. 39

502 Peter Walker, 'There's No Peace Without People', *Fortnight*, 413 (April 2003), p. 2

503 Allan Leonard, MA thesis, pp. 26–29

504 Ibid., pp. 28–29

505 Ibid., pp. 26–29

506 Editor, *Newsletter* (7 September, 2001)

507 Sam McBride, Political Correspondent, *Belfast Newsletter, 26th May 2014 Newsletter Election Special*

508 Leonard, Thesis, pp. 55–56

509 Philip McGarry, interviewed by Eggins, Belfast, 20 June 2003

510 Seamus Close Party Conference speech, Alliance Party, 'Conference Papers' for 7 April 2000

511 Alliance Party, 'Review of Assembly Designation and Voting System', November 2001

512 Seamus Close Party Conference speech, Alliance Party, 'Conference Papers' for 7 April 2000

513 John McGarry, *Civic Nationalism and the Agreement*, p. 123

514 Ibid., p. 135; footnote 48

515 David Ford, speech to Alliance Party Council, June 2011

516 Brian Eggins, *Alliance News*, April/June 2009

517 Sam Nelson, *How to Build an Effective Campaign* (Alliance Party, 2014)

518 Alliance Party, *Alliance Policy Summaries*, June 2006

519 Naomi Long, *Westminster Report*, Alliance Party Executive Report, March 2014

520 www.naomilong.com

521 'Long gets major backing on political donations', *Alliance News*, October–December 2013, p. 23

522 Edited on Naomi's behalf by her Press Officer Scott Jamison, 25 July 2014

523 http://allianceparty.org/page/justice-1

524 Stephen Farry, 'DEL Update' *Alliance News*, July–October 2013, pp. 4, 5

525 http://allianceparty.org/page/employment-and-learning

526 NEETs are persons Not in Employment, Education or Training

# Bibliography

## BOOKS AND ARTICLES

Alliance Party: 'Statement of Principles upon which the Alliance Party was founded on April 21 1970' in *Constitution and Rules*, 1970, 20

Alliance Party: Alliance Party of Northern Ireland, 'Statement of Principles upon which the Alliance Party was founded on April 21, 1970' in *Alliance Party Constitution and Rules* (Belfast: Alliance Party of Northern Ireland, 1970, revised 1974 and 1995), 20

Alliance Party: 'Members Questionnaire: Council Report' (Belfast: Alliance Party, 1998)

Alliance Party, 'Submission to the International Body on Decommissioning' (Belfast: Alliance Party Headquarters, Dec 1995)

Alliance Party, 'A Review of the Assembly Designations and Voting Systems', November 2002

Alliance Party: 'The Alliance Party's Strategic Plan 2000–20002' (Alliance Party: June 1999)

Alliance Party: 'Building a United Community' (Alliance Party January 2003)

Alliance Party: 'Governing with Consent' (Belfast: Alliance Party, 1988)

Harry Barnes, MP, *Hansard*, 19 July 1991

Denis Barritt, *Northern Ireland: A Problem to Every Solution* (London: Quaker Peace and Service, 1982)

Samuel Burch and Gerry Reynolds (eds), *John Wesley: A Letter to a Roman Catholic* (Belfast: Cornerstone Community and Clonard Monastery, 1987)

Paul Bew and Gordon Gillespie, *Northern Ireland 1968–1999 – A Chronology of the Troubles*, (Dublin: Gill and McMillan, 1999)

Erwann Bodilis, MA thesis, *The Alliance Party of Northern Ireland 1970–1993: Twenty Years of Combat for Peace and Progress* (Universite de Bretagne Occidentale, 1994)

John D. Brewer with Gareth I. Higgins, *Anti-Catholicism in Northern Ireland, 1600-1998: The Mote and the Beam* (Basingstoke, Hants. Macmillan, 1998)

John D. Brewer, Gareth Higgins and Francis Teeney, *Religion, Civil Society and Peace in Northern Ireland*, (Oxford: Oxford University press, 2011)

Edward Moxon-Browne, *Nation, Class and Creed in Northern Ireland* (Aldershot: Gower Publishing Company, 1983)

S. Bruce, *Paisley* (Oxford: Oxford University Press, 2007)

Rex Cathcart, *The Most Contrary Region: The BBC in Northern Ireland 1924–1984* (Belfast: Blackstaff, 1984)

Liam Clarke, 'Devolved policing is best way out of mess: policing needs the long arm of Alliance', *Sunday Times*, 2008.

*The Confession of Faith* (Belfast: Graham and Heslip, 1933)

John Darby, *Northern Ireland: Managing Difference* (London: Minority Right Group, 1995)

W.M. Dewar, *Why Orangeism?* (Belfast: Grand Lodge of Ireland, 1959)

Marva Down, *Powers, Weakness and the Tabernacling of God* (Ill.: Eedrmanns Publishing Co. 2002)

Aaron Edwards, *A History of the Northern Ireland Labour Party: Democratic Socialism and Sectarianism* (Manchester; Manchester University Press, 2009)

B.R. Eggins, MPhil Thesis, *The Contribution of the Alliance Party to Reconciliation*, (University of Dublin, 2003)

Sidney Elliot and William D. Flackes, *Northern Ireland Political Directory, 1968–2000*, (Belfast: Blackstaff Press, 2001)

Evans and Duffy, G. Evans and M. Duffy, 'Beyond the Sectarian Divide: The Social Bases and Political Consequences of Nationalist and Unionist Party Competition in Northern Ireland', *British Journal of Political Science*, 27 (1997) 47–81

Jocelyn A. J. Evans and Jonathan Tonge, 'The Future of the radical centre in Northern Ireland after the Good Friday Agreement', *Political Studies*, 2003, Vol. 51, 26–50, A Survey of Alliance Party members, 2001

Stephen Farry and Seán Neeson, 'Beyond the "band-aid" approach. An Alliance Party Perspective upon the Belfast Agreement Fordham International', *Law Journal*, 22(4) 1999

David Ford, 'Party Leader's Speech to Conference 2003', *Alliance*, (March and April 2003)

David Ford, 'Alliance Says No?' *Alliance News*, July–August

H.W. Fowler and F.G. Fowler (eds), *The Concise Oxford Dictionary* (Oxford: The Clarendon Press, 1958)

A. Gallagher, 'Dealing with Conflict: Schools in Northern Ireland', *Multicultural Teaching*, 13(3), 1994

Eric Gallagher and Stanley Worrall, *Christians in Ulster 1968–1980* (Oxford: Oxford University Press, 1982),

Mary Gethins, *Catholics police officers in Northern Ireland – Voices out of silence* (Manchester: Manchester University Press, 2011)

Anthony J. Gettins, *A Presence that Disturbs* (Liguori, Missouri, Liguori Publications, 2002)

René Girard, *Violence and the Sacred* (Baltimore and London: 1981)

Marc Gopin, 'Alternative Global Futures in the Balance' in *Between Eden and Armageddon: The Future of World Religions, Violence and Peacemaking* (New York: Oxford University Press, 2000)

T. Hadden, C. Irwin and F. Boal, 'Separation or Sharing? The People's Choice',
     *Fortnight,* 356 (December 1996)

*The Holy Bible: New International Version* (London: Hodder and Stoughton 1988)

Alistair Horne, *Kissinger's Year: 1973* (Weidenfeld, 2009)

Donald L. Horowitz, 'The Northern Ireland Agreement: Clear Consociational and
     Risky' in John McGarry, *Northern Ireland and the Divided World* (Oxford: Oxford
     University Press, 2001)

John Hume, *John Hume: Personal Views: Politics, Peace and Reconciliation in Ireland*
     (Dublin: Town House and Country House, 1996)

IRA, 'IRA Statement of May 6', *Irish News* (7 May 2003), 6

D. Keogh and M.H. Haltzel (eds), *Northern Ireland and the Politics of Reconciliation*
     (Cambridge: Woodrow Wilson Center Press and Cambridge University Press, 1993)

J. Knight and N. Baxter-Moore, *Northern Ireland Elections of the Twenties* (The Arthur
     McDougal Fund, 1972),

Colin Knox and Padraic Quirk, '"Responsibility Sharing" in Northern Ireland Local
     Government', www.wikepedia.org/wiki/John_Larkin_(Northern_Ireland)

John Paul Lederach, *Building Peace – Sustainable Reconciliation in Divided Societies*
     (Washington DC: United States Institute of Peace Press, 1997)

Joe Liechty and Cecelia Clegg, *Moving Beyond Sectarianism* (Dublin: Columba Press, 2001),

Joe Liechty, 'History and Reconciliation: Frank Wright, Whitley Stokes, and the
     Vortex of Antagonism' in Alan D. Falconer and Joe Liechty, *Reconciling Memories*
     (Dublin: Columba Press, 2nd edition 1998)

Allan Leonard, MA thesis, *The Alliance Party of Northern Ireland and Power Sharing in
     a Divided Society* (Dublin: University College Dublin, 1999)

Naomi Long, '*Compromise will be necessary*', Special Feature article, *Alliance News,*
     October and December 2013

Denis Loretto, *Alliance, Liberals and the SDP: a personal memoir*

Eamon Maillie and David McKittrick, *Endgame in Ireland* (London: Hodder and
     Stoughton, 2001)

Martin McKenna and Fionnula Melaugh, *The Northern Ireland Conflict Archive*

Sam McBride, Political Correspondent, *Belfast Newsletter, 26th May 2014 Newsletter
     Election Special*

McGarry, John (ed.), *Northern Ireland and the Divided World – Post-Agreement Northern
     Ireland in Comparative Perspective,* (Oxford: Oxford University Press, 2001)

Philip McGarry, *The President's Review* (Alliance Party: December 1998)

J. McGarry and B. O'Leary, *The Northern Ireland Conflict: Consociational Engagements'*
     (Oxford, Oxford University Press, 2004)

Robert McGinty, 'Policing and the NI Peace Process' in John P Harrington (ed.)
     *Politics and Performance in NI* (Amhurst, Mass.: University of Massachusets Press,
     American Congress of Irish Studies, 1999)

John D'Arcy May, 'A Rationale for Reconciliation', *Uniting Church Studies,* 7 (1)
     (2001), 1–13

T.W Moody and F.X. Martin (eds) *The Course of Irish History* (Cork, The Mercier
     Press, 1967)

David Morgan, *The Fall of the House of Paisley* (Dublin, Gill and Macmillan, 2010)

Mo Mowlam, *Momentum: The Struggle for Peace, Politics and the People* (London: Hodder and Stoughton, 2002)

Yvonne Naylor, *Moving Beyond Sectarianism: A Resource for Young Adults* (Belfast: Irish School of Ecumenics, 2001)

Yvonne Naylor, *Who We Are: Dealing with Difference* (Belfast: Irish School of Ecumenics, 2003)

Sam Nelson, *How to Build an Effective Campaign* (Alliance Party, 2014)

New Ulster Movement, *NUM Annual Report 1970/1971*

New Ulster Movement, *The Reform of Stormont* (NUM Publication, June 1971)

New Ulster Movement, *The Way Forward* (NUM Publication, 1971)

New Ulster Movement, NUM Publication, *Commentary on the programme of reforms for Northern Ireland* (August 1971)

New Ulster Movement, *Violence in Northern Ireland* (NUM Publication, 1972)

New Ulster Movement, *Tribalism and Christianity* (NUM Publication, 1973)

New Ulster Movement, *Two Irelands or One* (NUM Publication, 1972)

Editor, *Newsletter* (7 September 2001)

Andy Pollock (ed.), '*A Citizens' Enquiry*', The Opsahl Report on Northern Ireland (Dublin: The Lilliput Press and Initiative '92, 1993)

Pope John Paul II, 'Address of Pope John Paul II at Drogheda, 29 September 1979' in *The Pope in Ireland – Addresses and Homilies* (Dublin: Veritas, 1979), 16–25

Fergus Pyle, *Irish Times*, 5 October 1987

Gillian Robinson, *Northern Ireland Social Attitudes Survey 1989–1996* (Belfast: CCRU, 1998)

Richard Rose, *Governing Without Consensus: An Irish Perspective* (London: Faber and Faber, 1971)

Constance Rynder, *Journal of Liberal History* 71, Summer 2011

Craig Sands, *Moving Beyond Sectarianism: A Resource for Adult Education* (Belfast: Irish School of Ecumenics, 2001)

F. Eugene Scott, *Western Journal of Communication*, 40(4), 1976 249–259

Kirsten E. Schulze, 'Northern Ireland and Lebanon' in McGarry (ed.), *Northern Ireland and the Divided World*

Secretary of State for Northern Ireland, *Northern Ireland Constitutional Proposals* (London: HMSO, 1973) Cmnd. 5259.

Northern Ireland Office, *Devolving Policing and Justice in Northern Ireland: A Discussion Paper* (Belfast: Northern Ireland Office, 2005)

*A Shared Future – a Consultation Paper on Improving Relations in Northern Ireland* (Community Relations Unit, OFMDFM, 2003)

Rupert Taylor, 'Consociation or Social Transformation' in John McGarry (ed.), *Northern Ireland and the Divided World*

Karen Trew and Cate Cox, 'Dimensions of Social Identity in Northern Ireland', http://cain.ulst.ac.uk/ccru/research/qub/trew95.htm

Peter Walker, 'There's No Peace Without People', *Fortnight*, 413 (April 2003)

Whitley Stokes, *Projects for Re-establishing the Internal Peace and Tranquillity of Ireland*

(Dublin, 1799)

*Ulster* (Harmondsworth, Middx. Sunday Times Insight Team, 1972)

John Whyte, *Interpreting Northern Ireland* (Oxford: Oxford University Press, 1990)

Wilhelm J. Verwoerd, 'Towards the Truth about the TRC: A Response to Key Moral Criticisms of the South African Truth and Reconciliation Commission', *Religion and Theology*, 6 (1999), 303–324.

Frank Wright, *N10orthern Ireland: A Comparative Analysis* (Dublin: Gill and McMillan, 1987)

Tony Wright and Matt Carter, *The People's Party: the history of the Labour Party*

## NEWSPAPERS

*Alliance News*

*Belfast Telegraph*

*Belfast Newsletter*

*Guardian*

*Irish Times*

*Observer*

*Sunday Times*

*Sunday World*

## WEBSITES

http://sluggerotoole.com/2014/04/06/the-11-new-district-councils/

www.absoluteastronomy.com

www.allianceparty.org

www.ark.ac.uk

www.bbc.co.uk

www.belfasttelegraph.co.uk

www.cain.ulst.ac.uk

www.davidford.org

www.electoral-reform.org.uk

www.nio.gov.uk/devolution_doc_pdf.pdf

www.naomilong.com

www.parliament.uk

www.wikipedia.org

## OTHER SOURCES

Alliance Party, Minutes of Council Meeting, June 1998

Alliance Party, Alliance Policy Summaries, June 2006

Alliance Party, 'For Everyone', February 2014.

Alliance Party, 'Briefing for Party Members on the Haass Talks and their outcome,' 2014

*The Agreement* (Belfast: The Governments of the United Kingdom and Northern Ireland of Ireland, 1998).

BBC, Radio Ulster 'Talk Back', 19 August 2003

BBC TV, *Hearts and Minds* 7.30 p.m., 29 May 2003

Rev Byron Bland, 'The Post-troubles Troubles: The Politics of Reconciliation in Northern Ireland', unpublished paper, 2001

Eileen Bell, MLA, Press Release, 13 November 2001

Eileen Bell, MLA, Press Release 24 September 2002

Eileen Bell, Interview, Stormont, 26 August 2003

Seamus Close, interview 24 June 2003

Seamus Close Party Conference speech, Alliance Party, 'Conference Papers' for 7 April 2000

www.community-relations.org.uk/fs/doc/CRC_Submission_to_CSI.pdf

David Ford, speech to Alliance Party Council, June 2011

David Ford, *The St Andrews Agreement*, nistandrewsbill161106

Revd Dr Norman Hamilton, Address to Newry District Inter-Church Forum Inaugural Meeting, Sean Holywood Arts Centre, Newry, 21 November 2010

Jim Hendron, *Personal Memoirs*, personal letter, 21 July 2009

Jim Hendron personal conversation May 2014

ITV, *A Truth Commission for Northern Ireland?* ITV 'Insight' programme, 11 April 2002.

Rev Timothy Kinahan, Interview, Belfast, 1 September 2003.

Joe Liechty, ISE Lecture, 'Theology and Dynamics of Reconciliation', session IV, 24 October 2001

Naomi Long, *Westminster Report*, Alliance Party Executive Report, March 2014

Philip McGarry, interview 20 June 2003

Martin McGuiness, Radio 5 interview reported in *Sunday Times*, 5 August 2001

Patricia Mallon, interview, 30 May 2003

John Manley, interview with Anna Lo MLA, *Irish News*, 20 March 2014

Addie Morrow, interview 30 May 2003

Sir Oliver Napier, speech at 40th Anniversary Dinner, Stormont Hotel, 4 June 2010

Sir Oliver Napier, interview with Sir Oliver Napier, 15 December 2004

Sir Oliver Napier, personal letter, 2009

Northern Ireland Information Service, Birthday Honours List 1999

Terence O'Neill, *Ulster at the Crossroads*, quoted in http://cain.ulst.co.uk/issues/politics/docs/uup/uup69.htm

St Andrews Agreement, *www.nio.gov.uk/st_andrews_agreement.pdf*

George Schöpflin, 'Civil Society, Ethnicity and the State: a threefold relationship', Paper delivered to Conference, 'Civil Society in Austria', Vienna, 20–21 June 1997

The Patten Report: Independent Commission on Policing for Northern Ireland, a New Beginning; Policing in Northern Ireland: the Report of the Independent Commission on Policing for Northern Ireland (Belfast: HMSO, 1999)

# Index